Growing Up with Language

Also by Naomi Baron

Language Acquisition and Historical Change

Speech, Writing, and Sign

Computer Languages: A Guide for the Perplexed

Pigeon-Birds and Rhyming Words:
The Role of Parents in Language Learning

Growing Up with Language ■ *How Children Learn to Talk*

■ Naomi S. Baron

Addison-Wesley Publishing
Company, Inc.

Reading, Massachusetts   Menlo Park, California   New York
Don Mills, Ontario   Wokingham, England   Amsterdam   Bonn
Sydney   Singapore   Tokyo   Madrid   San Juan
Paris   Seoul   Milan   Mexico City   Taipei

Chart 3 on page 42 is printed with permission from the American Physiological Society.

Library of Congress Cataloging-in-Publication Data

Baron, Naomi S.
   Growing up with language : how children learn to talk / Naomi S. Baron.
      p.   cm.
   Includes bibliographical references (p.) and index.
   ISBN 0-201-55080-6
   1. Language acquisition.   I. Title.
   P118.B278   1992
401′ .93—dc20   91-37652
                                                                                              CIP

Jacket design by Stephen Gleason
Text design by Barbara Werden

Set in 11-point Sabon by Shepard Poorman Communications Corporation, Indianapolis, IN
1 2 3 4 5 6 7 8 9-HD-95949392
First printing, April 1992

For Aneil,
who made the writing take so long
and without whom
this book could not have been

■ Contents

■ Preface

AUTHORS have personal odysseys shaping what their books are about and the covert agendas lingering beneath their surfaces. These are some highlights from my own journey.

Theory and Practice

My studies in human language began as an undergraduate at Brandeis University. At the time, Noam Chomsky was formulating his theory of transformational grammar down the river at MIT. Most of my teachers were devotees of Chomsky's work, and I commuted weekly to Cambridge to hear the master lecture. My first linguistics text was Chomsky's *Aspects of the Theory of Syntax*—hot off the press—which propounded an approach to language that was to dominate the field for more than a decade after its publication in 1965.

Chomsky's focus was on the abstract ways we put language pieces together to form sentences. In an attempt to define the grammatical abilities of a mythical Everyman, he dismissed most other aspects of human language. How individuals vary, what role the community plays in language development and use, how and why languages change: all of these vital questions were lopped off to fit Chomsky's procrustean bed. And like others of his time, Chomsky took speech as the exclusive object of study, dismissing written and signed language as irrelevant to linguistic theory.

My rebellion against this framework took shape during graduate training at Stanford University. There, a distinguished and diverse faculty encouraged the more daring—or foolhardy—among us to forge our own discipline. Over the next two decades, I probed individual and social causes that bring about language change. I tried to understand *why* children learn language, forsaking the study of grammatical *struc-ture* (which had assumed the dimensions of a minor religious cult) for analyses of language *function*. I began looking at how language is written and sometimes signed, using my research to rethink ideas about language development. Later I became interested in how technology affects the way we speak and write—from the printing press to the computer. Throughout, I kept wrestling with the gap between narrowly abstract theories of language and the context of real people communicating with each other.

Creating Language: Paint Chips, Violins, and Magic

Since the early 1980s, I have gradually drawn together the diverse strands of my research in an attempt to reconcile the gap between theory and practice in how language is learned. During this time, the study of language learning itself has evolved, with specialists increasingly acknowledging the unmistakable variety in language learning styles. Equally important, students of language acquisition have become interested in early mother-child "conversations" rather than focusing exclusively on the sounds emanating from children. These have been clear signs of progress but not enough.

Three lingering questions have continued to haunt me. The first concerns the role of parents (and, more broadly, families) in children's language odysseys: Can we predict the rate and style of individual children's language growth by understanding the familial ambiance into which babies are born? How much is the course of language acquisition determined by our species, how much by our idiosyncrasies, and how much by our personal and social histories?

My second question follows closely on the heels of the first: Can language be taught? All my training in normal first language acquisition had implied that children naturally flower into speakers, like dandelions after the spring rains. Yet my work with children afflicted with language disorders—childhood aphasics, the mentally retarded, children with cerebral palsy, deaf children—convinced me that overt language pedagogy has a critical role in normal language acquisition as well. But what? And how?

The third question has proved the most puzzling of all: How do children crack the language code? I could watch a range of children and their families as they grew up with language, and I had some ideas on how to gather information about language pedagogy. But how do you see into a child's mind?

As I pondered these questions, I slowly began to work out hunches, then theories, and finally the beginnings of answers. Ideas came from all quarters: careful observations and experiments, coupled with parent-child conversations overheard in airports and restaurants; the latest treatise on language acquisition, along with popular accounts that were sparse on theory but rich in common sense; hours of closeted reflection, supplemented by seemingly irrelevant encounters from daily life. These experiences, in turn, often became metaphors for the answers brewing within me.

An article on lead poisoning in children sparked my first serious inquiries into the effects of families on children's early language acquisition. Despite all the theoretical linguistic literature to the contrary, I refused to believe that the children described in this article—infants and toddlers left alone in public housing projects, pulling paint chips off the wall and ingesting them—would learn language the same way as middle-class age-mates. Quickly my interest expanded from availability of parental supervision to conversational opportunities, parental education, presence of siblings, and sexual stereotypes.

My ideas on overt language pedagogy—the next question—were shaped by two experiences as the parent of a young child. The first came when I happened upon a book describing the Suzuki method of teaching music to youngsters. In the first chapter, Shinichi Suzuki talked about children's amazing capacity to learn their native language. "The world's best educational method," he argued, "is found in the method of teaching the mother tongue." The underlying principles of language learning (according to Suzuki) include developing an ear for language and thorough mastery through practice, the same principles that became the heart of his method for early training on the violin.

But it was my second encounter that definitively brought the pedagogical message home. Like millions of other families around the world, my ideas about learning were indelibly changed by the revolution in children's television known as "Sesame Street."

GROWING UP WITH LANGUAGE

In a little more than twenty years, Joan Ganz Cooney, Jim Henson, and the staff at the Children's Television Workshop transformed the way we think about early childhood education: its methods, its audience, its possibilities. As the parent of a preschooler, I logged hundreds of hours watching Kermit the Frog, Count von Count, Grover, and Guy Smiley cavort across the stage of "Sesame Street," leading their viewers to learn abstract words, numbers, letters, and so much more.

As an educator, I was fascinated by the pedagogical techniques that the producers of "Sesame Street" created for drawing an amazingly diverse audience of little children (and their parents) into the learning adventure. As a student of literacy, I was intrigued by the extent to which the learning of speaking skills and of reading skills was intertwined. As a linguist rebelling against Chomsky's dogmas about the inevitability and uniformity of human language abilities, I was gratified by this commonsensical demonstration of how overt and repeated modeling indeed leads to language learning.

But what about the actual creation of language (my third question)? How do children do it? I was beginning to get a handle on the strategies children use to draw themselves into language communities. At the same time, I started to appreciate the need parents have to make this entrée swift and smooth and the extent to which parents give offspring the linguistic benefit of the doubt. (I refer to these learning strategies as **language orienteering** and to the communicative needs of children and parents as the **conversational imperative**.)

Was there an incisive way of talking about the wondrous process by which children learn language and the supportive (and self-interested) role parents play? Just before my son, Aneil, was born, I had become interested in the art of illusion as performed by magicians. In the process, I discovered an ideal metaphor for describing the interactive linguistic magic between children and parents.

Even the most astounding illusions generally have very simple explanations. Illusions succeed for two reasons: the attention of the audience is usually focused elsewhere, and the illusionist practices the trick until he or she perfects it. The audience sees only the polished result. Even when a trick fails, a savvy magician can manage to make the error look like part of the act.

The process of learning language is highly magical—in a very literal sense, though children are unwitting magicians. To the casual eye, the child's linguistic feats seem without reasonable explanation, and thus, many students of language acquisition have assumed that much of children's language learning is the predestined unfolding of innate structures. In reality, of course, children, like illusionists, work extremely hard to perfect their language skills. Like a sympathetic audience watching an amateur magician, parents of children learning to talk are understandably more interested in the end result than in dissecting the mechanisms behind it. Linguists, who have at least as strong a stake in unearthing the mechanisms, are often blindsided by the theoretical presuppositions through which they observe the acquisition process.

Not surprisingly, *Growing Up with Language* turns out to be two books in one. Primarily, it is a book written for parents and medical practitioners, educators and students on the hows and whys of language acquisition in children. But the book also embodies my personal answers to a collection of theoretical questions I have been living with over the years and with which I have finally made some headway.

Acknowledgments

In the course of writing this book, scores of people have lent a hand. My first—and most profound—debt is to my husband, Nikhil Bhattacharya. Although a philosopher's interest in language is somewhat different from mine, he has, as a philosopher of science, supported my skepticism about the research methodology of contemporary linguistics and as a philosopher of language tried to protect me from possible attacks by the shade of Ludwig Wittgenstein.

The next debt is to Charles Ferguson, my graduate adviser at Stanford. My thinking about how and why children learn language has been crucially shaped by a casual comment he made one day when I was confidently expounding (as only a first-year graduate student can do) on the mechanisms underlying language acquisition. I was talking about the process by which children learn to form plural nouns, and, following the Chomskian model in vogue at the time, I commented that children "internalize" such-and-such a rule in their heads. Ferguson looked at me for a long moment before replying:

"How do you know what is inside children's heads?"

How indeed. Since that conversation, I have tried to exercise caution before presuming to characterize the actual processes through which people create and understand language.

Hundreds of students have contributed to the constructive fray. In the courses I have taught at Brown University, Emory University, Southwestern University, and The American University, I have been especially grateful for the students who have refused to agree with me, driving me to rethink my own analyses and those forming the traditional canon. Dozens of toddlers and preschoolers I have encountered—children of friends and colleagues but especially children at The American University's Child Development Center—have made their way into the pages of this book through humorous examples and as living challenges to contemporary theories of acquisition.

A more definable number of colleagues, acquaintances, and institutions have contributed to the book's progress: reading the manuscript, suggesting (or locating) references, sharing examples of children's utterances, offering their expertise, lending personal support, and just being there. I extend my thanks (in alphabetical order) to the reference librarians at The American University's Bender Library, Betty T. Bennett, Felicia Eth, Bryan Fantie, Jane Isay, Laura Isensee, Martha Last, the Leavey Center at Georgetown University, Patti Mullens, Arthur Schildroth, Whitney Stewart, Theodore Turak, Rosana Velilla, Leslie Wharton, and Charles S. J. White. Early in the project, I was aided by a grant from the College of Arts and Sciences at The American University. During the final months, Amy Gash and Tiffany Cobb at Addison-Wesley were especially helpful in seeing the book through to publication.

Most of the time, I have listened to suggestions of friends and critics. Where I have not, the responsibility (and loss) are mine.

■ 1. Cracking the Code

The Journey into Language

IT WAS January 1991, and the evening news was filled with stories of the war in Iraq. Four-year-old Alex was glued to the television, entranced by the never-ending display of jets and bombing missions. With one toy airplane in each hand, he brought his own war zone to life as he narrated the events:

> "If the watcher plane sees a bad guy, it radio-shacks to the bomber plane, and the bomber plane blewns it up."

Like children everywhere, Alex was working to crack the language code.

This is a book about how children make sense of the incomprehensible linguistic babble into which they are born. Children gradually emerge as listeners and speakers and later as incipient readers and writers. Their own drive to decipher the linguistic world they are entering is matched by parents' need to integrate their progeny into family and community. This joint odyssey begins when children are born and is largely complete by the time they are age 5 or 6.

As with art, most adults do not know very much about how children learn language, but they nonetheless have strong suppositions about how the process works, when it is succeeding, and when things have gone awry. *Growing Up with Language* therefore begins by meeting readers on their own ground.

1

Tall Tales and Reality Checks: Beyond Boast and Concern

During the coffee break of a recent conference, I was chatting with a colleague about his 3-year-old. A mathematician by training, the proud father was bragging about his daughter's conceptual and linguistic abilities:

> "My daughter knows exactly how many days are left before her birthday. In fact, back when she was one, she used to go around saying, 'I'm one year old now, but I'm going on two.' "

My eyebrow shot up. That much vocabulary and grammar from an 18- or 20-month-old? My colleague began emending his story:

> "Of course, we coached her to say that."

A little more probing, and it came out that the utterance the little girl had actually imitated was

> "I'm one, going on two."

Tall tales arise from the limits of human memory along with an understandable yearning to cast our accomplishments (and those of our compatriots) in the best light. Exaggerations—describing "the one that got away" or the number of words a now-grown child knew at age 2—are sometimes made unwittingly but as often reflect a drive to distinguish ourselves and members of our families from the crowd.

Grains of truth generally emerge among layers of embellishment. My grandmother used to explain how as a toddler (age 1? age 2?—she was unclear) I would make my way around the local playground, pointing first at the swings, then the seesaw and the slide, demanding to ride on each. I'm told that I didn't "talk" yet but instead accompanied each point with an insistent grunt. At the other extreme, my in-laws report that my sister-in-law was "speaking in sentences" by age 10 months.

What can we make of such recollections? Probably little more than that I was slower to start using understandable speech than was my husband's sister. But how much slower? Did I understand more than I said? How long did it take for me to "catch up"? Just as stories of "the one that got away" are often vague on detail, precise dates and correctly remembered language utterances are hard to come by.

Both cases illustrate the need for reality checks—reality checks about norms and reality checks about differences.

A sequence of meetings I had many years ago with three young women has proved emblematic of the all-too-human fear of differences. I was associate dean at Brown University at the time, and these students had come, individually, to talk about their academic plans. All were first-semester sophomores.

The first woman stopped by a few days after the school year had begun. She was terribly worried that she had not yet identified an academic major. I was troubled by her anxieties; Brown did not require a declaration of major until April of the sophomore year, and the major would involve only around one-quarter of her overall course work anyway. Why was she concerned?

> "I've been talking with my roommates, and *they* all know exactly what *they* want to study."

The next week, another sophomore came by. Her problem had a familiar ring. She too felt pressured to find an academic niche because her closest friends were comfortably ensconced in majors and career paths. Later that week, the third student saw me, again fretting that she alone among her circle was without academic mooring.

I made it a practice, as time permitted, to send follow-up notes to students who had met with me seeking academic advice. As I began addressing envelopes to the folks I had seen over the past two weeks, it became clear that the three young women in question were roommates. I promptly summoned the three for a reality check to explain how individual uncertainties had led to the belief that everyone was "normal" but them. Had the roommates lied to one another? Not really, but they had strayed up to the very edge of academic folklore.

Comparable reality checks on children's development are invaluable for parents, even if the parents themselves are language specialists. I was bemused—and encouraged—to read the revelation by David Crystal, a renowned expert on child language acquisition and language disorders, that he was personally anxious when his 2-year-old son went through a brief phase of stuttering. Although Crystal has written convincingly that stuttering among toddlers and preschoolers (especially boys) is common and nearly always unproblematic, Crystal had difficulty maintaining objectivity when it came to his own child. (The issue of stuttering is visited at the end of Chapter 5.)

A central goal of this book is to help parents answer the single question that most preoccupies them about language development: "Is my child normal?" For parents who pass this hurdle, follow-up questions include "Is my child linguistically precocious?" or "What can I do to help my child get ahead linguistically?" *Growing Up with Language* addresses these two questions as well, but not in the spirit of "better baby" books designed to ensure a child acceptance into Harvard Law School. Rather, the book is designed to explain the sources of variation in normal language acquisition patterns and to illuminate how parents, as anchors in the language socialization process, can naturally enrich their children's understanding and use of language.

Language acquisition is a community process. Since communities are themselves shaped by social forces and practical realities, we need to consider how the complexion of contemporary living affects language acquisition.

Since the early 1960s, American families have undergone profound transformations affecting the ways we raise children. Today's parents are the first postimmigrant generation to be raising families in isolation from relatives. They are the first generation to grow up with television and the first in which the majority of women with children below the age of 6 are employed—up from 19 percent as recently as 1960. This is the first generation in which a sizable number of women have delayed motherhood into their late thirties or early forties and a generation in which middle-class mothers typically have completed college or beyond. Many children are being raised by single parents, and for the first time, a substantial proportion of men are assuming an active role in child rearing.

Assumptions we have traditionally made about how children learn language may need to be adjusted in light of the contemporary family environments out of which language grows. Does the age at which mothers give birth affect the kind of language they address to children? Do fathers who spend a lot of time with their offspring address young children differently from traditional hands-off fathers? How will the explosion of day care affect children's emerging language? Issues such as these undergird *Growing Up with Language*.

Variations on a Theme: Sarah, Ryan, and Alex

The first time I taught a course on language acquisition, I had among my students a number of parents, many of whom were at least ten years my senior. Fresh out of graduate school, I confidently explained (because I then still believed) that all children, regardless of who they are and what language community they are born into, essentially learn language the same way. One mother of three, sprawled out in the back row, cut me off mid-sentence:

"Come on. Anybody who's raised kids knows they're all different!"

Theory had run smack into practice.

She was, of course, right. While many essential commonalities can be identified, there is no single route that all children follow in the course of learning language. A realistic treatment of language theory and practice must take this diversity into account.

In writing this book, I have conjured up three imaginary children (each a montage of children I have known or heard about) through whose linguistic development we can sample how children crack the language code. This narrative technique borrows unabashedly from T. Berry Brazelton, who in his book *Infants and Mothers* introduced three prototypic types of babies: "average" (Louis), "quiet" (Laura), and "active" (Daniel). Each followed a "normal" yet markedly different path of early development.

As the mother of a newborn, I experienced the predictable range of anxieties over my baby's development. Brazelton's book proved invaluable in calming my fears. While Daniel might be far ahead of my son in the age at which he rolled over from back to front, my child was right on par with Louis and even ahead of Laura. In adopting the device of creating three distinct personae, I respond to the myriad of parents who have asked me over the years if their child's linguistic development is normal. Though overwhelmingly the answer is "yes," parents are most readily assured by seeing examples of other healthy children following their own youngster's developmental course.

Hence, Sara, Ryan, and Alex.

All three families live in or around a major East Coast metropolis. The families represent the social and economic spectrum of the American middle class, from divorced single mothers struggling to make ends meet, to thirtysomething two-parent families in which the wife stays home, to upper-middle-class families in which both parents have full-time professional careers.

Two major sectors of American society are noticeably missing. The first is families at the lowest end of the socioeconomic ladder. There is abundant evidence that children coming from the poorest households tend to be linguistically disadvantaged in comparison with middle-class children. Not surprisingly, the problems largely derive from inadequate education and nonsupportive parenting styles, not personal finances. A poor but closely knit working-class neighborhood has far more in common with a middle-class suburban enclave when it comes to language stimulation than with an equally impoverished neighborhood in which children are left to fend for themselves and receive little direct linguistic attention from adults. Teenage mothers who do not understand the importance of talking with a young infant or toddler are but one extreme of mothers in the broad middle-class cohort who do not recognize that leaving a child in front of a television set all day can stifle interpersonal and linguistic experiences. The model provided by parents who cannot afford books for their children or do not read themselves differs only in degree from that of middle-class parents who neglect to purchase books for their children and rely on television rather than the printed word for their own entertainment.

The second major slice of American society that is excluded is families in which the native language spoken at home is not English. Always a country of immigrants, the United States is now home to a burgeoning population of Hispanics, East Asians, and Eastern Europeans. The process by which their children become bilingual is itself the subject for another book. In Chapter 6 we will look at bilingualism but mostly in a context relevant to children growing up predominantly monolingual.

Who are Sara, Ryan, and Alex? Let's meet the children and their families.

Sara

Sara is the firstborn daughter of a middle-class couple in their thirties. Both were educated in small liberal arts colleges. Two years after her birth, Sara was joined by a baby brother, Michael. Sara is an outgoing child who talked fairly early, uttering her first word at age 9 months and beginning to combine words by the time she was 15 months. She does not hesitate to try things out—physically or linguistically.

Sara's father, an accountant, works full-time. Although devoted to his daughter, he leaves the majority of child rearing duties to his wife. He has no particular preconceptions about how children develop—physically, cognitively, or linguistically—and greets each of Sara's developmental milestones with spontaneous parental pride.

Outside of volunteer work with a community literacy project, Sara's mother generally stays at home, along with the Spanish-speaking housekeeper from Nicaragua. (Sara's mother studied a little Spanish in college, but her husband is strictly monolingual.) Following the pattern of her own mother, Sara's mother raised her daughter at home until she was 4, at which time Sara entered a nursery school program three days a week. Both Sara's mother and father had younger siblings, and they ultimately anticipate a family with three children.

As conscientious members of the middle class, Sara's parents are intent on providing their daughter with appropriate cognitive stimulation. The house is filled with "educational" toys. However, her mother and father have never explicitly talked about the language they use with their daughter, and both assume that teaching a child to read is the province of the elementary school.

Ryan

Ryan, born to parents in their mid-twenties, has an older sister, Cathy, who is four years his senior. A shy child, Ryan spoke his first identifiable word at 11 months and began combining words a few days before he turned 2. His parents, both of whom had several years of college at the state university, divorced when Ryan was 6 months old. At that time, Ryan entered full-time day care so that his mother could return to work as a hospital receptionist.

Ryan's mother has absorbed most of her ideas about child development from her own experiences as the second born of four children and from what she picks up from friends. Having spent much of her childhood caring for her younger brother and sister, she finds it natural for her own older daughter to assume this role with Ryan. Ryan's mother has no presuppositions about appropriate ages for language milestones, though she has heard that younger boys are often a little slower than girls. An art major in college before she dropped out to get married, Ryan's mother has no background to speak of in foreign languages, literature, or psychology.

When not at school, Ryan generally plays with his older sister or watches television. Most of Ryan's toys and books are hand-me-downs from Cathy. Pressured by the demands of a full-time job and of raising two children on her own, Ryan's mother finds little time to play alone with her son when there is no specific agenda. As a result, much of her language tends to be highly directive ("Finish your milk," "Get your shoes on, or we'll be late").

Alex

Alex was born prematurely—but healthy—to a couple in their forties. The only child of a lawyer (mother) and physician (father), Alex spends a lot of time with adults. As a toddler, Alex's comprehension far outstripped his production of language. (His parents used to joke that Alex might learn to read before starting to speak.) Although he spoke his first word at 12 months, Alex's earliest stable syntax did not appear until age 2½. Alex entered a half-day nursery program at age 2 and began full-time nursery school at age 3.

As people who have been in school much of their lives, Alex's parents have absorbed a lot of background—and preconceptions—about child development and the emergence of language. Besides the usual psychology courses in college, Alex's father did a pediatrics rotation while in medical school, and Alex's mother combed the technical literature on prematurity after her son was born. Alex's grandfather was a native speaker of German, and so Alex's father grew up bilingual; Alex's mother studied Latin for many years. A wordsmith by trade, Alex's mother is an avid reader and frequent punster.

Although both of Alex's parents work full-time, hours spent with their son are consciously filled with language. Alex's parents frequently discuss their son's linguistic progress. They debate what kinds of words and expressions to use with Alex, what books to buy for him, and how to enhance the boy's language skills.

In the coming chapters, we will come to know Sara, Ryan, and Alex (along with their families) more closely and will see how much family environment determines an individual child's course of language acquisition.

Language Components

What must Sara, Ryan, and Alex learn to become full-fledged members of a language community? Four essential language components. The smallest building blocks of language are **sounds** (that is, consonants and vowels, liquids and glides) that can be combined to make up words. Words individually have **meaning,** as do the phrases and sentences speakers construct using the rules of **grammar.** Speakers draw upon sounds, meaning, and grammar to construct **conversations** with each other.

Sound

The most noticeable part of human language is sounds (also called **phonology**). You overhear a conversation, and even if you cannot see the speakers or make out their words, from the sounds you can usually identify their age, sex, and sometimes even place of birth.

Our first impression of speakers depends heavily on their pronunciation. British linguist Gordon Wells reports that when he asked mothers what "features of speech they might attend to and correct" in their preschooler's language, the two most frequent answers were that children pronounce words correctly and that adults could hear distinctly what children were saying. In the United States, presidents with regionally identifiable accents—from JFK's Bostonian *idear* for *idea* to LBJ's Texan "mah fullow amerkins" or Jimmy Carter's Georgian pronunciation of *important* as *impowtent*—are often prejudged not on the basis of what they have to say but how they say it.

Sounds are carrying cases for meanings. Like canisters filled with helium, they are a means to some other end. However, as in the case of the gas and the canister, human language as we know it (with the exception of sign languages) would not be possible without sound.

Sounds are formed by manipulating the ways in which furnishings of the mouth (lips, tongue, teeth, specific landmarks on the roof of the mouth) and other denizens of the vocal tract (the pharynx, the epiglottis, the larynx—also known as the vocal cords) interact. There are three basic variables for distinguishing one sound from another:

1. The **place** in which the sounds are formed (e.g., *p* and *i* are produced in the front; *g* and *a* are made in the back);
2. The **manner** in which the sounds are formed (e.g., *p* is made by closing the lips together; *t* results from flicking the tongue off the bumpy area just above the back of the top teeth);
3. The **state of the vocal cords** (e.g., voiced sounds like *b* are formed by making the vocal cords vibrate; their voiceless counterparts, such as *p*, are made without such vibration. To feel the difference, place your fingers on your Adam's apple and try saying first *b* and then *p*).

Every language has its own complement of distinct sounds. American English has 35. A convenient way to look at them is by relative placement in the mouth. Think of the left-hand side of **Chart 1** as the lips and the right-hand side as the back of the mouth. Since letters in the alphabet do not uniquely correspond to sounds, the easiest way to get a handle on the spectrum of sounds is through sample words in which they occur.

The eleven vowels divide up fairly neatly by place of articulation: front, central, and back and high, middle, and low. If you try pronouncing just the two columns of vowels from the words in Chart 1, it sounds like two trombone glissandos. Although none of the vowels in American English is particularly difficult to pronounce, young language learners typically alight upon a handful of vowel sounds they initially use and expand their repertoires only gradually.

The 20 consonants can be clustered by place or manner of articulation, as well as by the state of the vocal cords. Some of these sounds are decidedly more difficult to pronounce than others (compare a simple *t* with the more complicated *th*). While there is some variation across children (e.g., Ryan found the *sh* of *shoe* easier than the *s* of *soup*), most children follow similar journeys, filling out their complement of consonants a little at a time.

CHART 1. The Sounds of American English						
VOWELS:						
beat				boot		
bit				could		
bait	but			boat		
bet				bought		
bat				bottom		
CONSONANTS:						
pat			tip		kid	
bat			dip		girl	
mom			not		sang	
	first	think	sip	ship		hat
	verse	that	zip	rouge		
				church		
				jerk		
LIQUIDS:						
rip			lip			
GLIDES:						
win			yes			

Besides the basic vowels and consonants, English has two liquid sounds, *r* and *l*, and two glide sounds, *y* (as in *yes*) and *w* (e.g., *work*). Young children often have a lot of trouble learning to pronounce these four sounds correctly. The problem is that liquids and glides aren't made by striking any one part of the mouth. The sounds *r*, *y*, and *w* don't strike at all, and the landing spot for *l* depends on the other sounds around it. Sara epitomized the problems of pronouncing liquids and glides whenever she launched into her favorite nursery rhyme:

"Mary Had a Yittle Yam."

In addition to these 35 distinct components that can be combined to form words, the English sound system includes a number of over-arching features that give language its melody: **pitch** or **intonation** (how high or low a sound is, determined by the rate at which the vocal cords vibrate), **stress** (putting emphasis on one or more syllables in a word or sentence), and **volume** (how loud an utterance is). These and other

11

sound features play roles in forming words into sentences and sentences into conversations. Children must learn that *black bird* is pronounced differently from *blackbird*, that women generally speak with a higher pitch than men, and that language users can manipulate features such as intonation, stress, and volume within a conversation.

Meaning

Meaning (also known as **semantics**) is the gas inside the sound canister. It is the subject matter of our words and sentences. Language lets us talk about objects in the real world (like the bee ready to sting the end of your nose), concepts (like the pain that will follow), things that do not exist but might (a cure for the common cold), or beings that never were (like unicorns, snarks, and the Piltdown Man).

Meaning exists at all levels of language. The tightness in my voice when I go for an IRS audit reveals my uneasiness, even if the words I use proclaim my innocence. Grammar is also a vessel of meaning. There is a vast difference between an *attorney general* and a *general attorney* or between the observation "This is an apple" and the question "Is this an apple?" In conversation, our choice of words and sentences conveys considerable information about ourselves, our attitudes toward the people with whom we speak, and our knowledge of the situation. If I address the president of the United States by his first name rather than "Mr. President," I signal that he and I are close personal friends (or that I am disrespectful).

Meanings arise through both convention and invention. As speakers of English, we know that the word *shirt* refers to a piece of clothing covering the upper torso, because that is the meaning other people around us attach to the word. At the same time, we commonly encounter objects or experiences we need to talk about but for which the community language fails us. The solution? We invent new words that fill the gap. When Ryan needed a way of referring to the blanket his mother used to roll up on the side of his bed to keep him from falling out in his sleep, he spontaneously came up with the term *holder-inner*. Such inventiveness is no different from what explorers do when they encounter new flora or fauna or scientists when they discover (or create) a new physical element.

The challenge of mastering meanings in a language comes because, like the nose of a submerged crocodile, a word reveals only a piece of its meaning each time it is used. How is a child to know that the same sound combination *bank* refers not only to the plastic pig into which she drops pennies but also to financial institutions, sides of rivers, and a spatial orientation of a plane in flight? We sometimes use the term *ice cream* to denote any frozen, flavored mixture ("Do you like ice cream?") and other times to point up a specific container of ice cream, which happens to be, say, chocolate ("Would you like some ice cream?"). In the process of learning what words mean, children naturally go through periods of confusion when their own internal meanings for words do not mesh with community definitions.

Grammar

If sound is the most obvious part of language and meaning is the least visible, grammar is the most mysterious. You cannot put your hands around grammar the way you can sound or even meaning. During their first four years, children learn fewer than three dozen distinct sounds. During the same period, a child may learn 1000 to 2000 words, but parents can still, in principle, write them all down. Sound and meaning are intuitively tractable (whatever the realities may be from a specialist's vantage point).

Grammar is a foreign domain. We do not have the categories at our fingertips. If asked to explain the difference between an independent and a dependent relative clause, most people change the subject. In the world of meaning, we can all physically point to referents for much of what we are talking about. With grammar, at best a handful of people feel they can "point to" a subjunctive or past perfect. Consequently, when we hear the half-baked sentences of young children (or foreigners), we know something is wrong and are able to correct it but often cannot articulate the problem.

Grammar operates at two levels: morphology and syntax. **Morphology** deals with combining the smallest units of meaning (**morphemes**) into words. The word *car* is a morpheme, since it cannot be decomposed into smaller units. The plural marker *-s* is also a morpheme, for the same reason. **Syntax** is the combination of words into phrases ("on my way"), clauses ("because the car broke down"), or sentences ("I'm now on my way, although because the car broke down, I'll be two hours late"). Children typically begin combining two words together (that is, using syntax) several months before they first actively combine two morphemes to form a single word. (Memorized plurals or past tenses obviously don't count.)

The appearance of even rudimentary syntax signals the crossing of a linguistic Rubicon because it makes the expression of complex meaning possible. Once Sara could only say

"Milk!"

leaving her parents to figure out whether she meant "The milk spilled on my shirt," "That's milk I'm drinking, all right," "You drink some milk with me," or "I want more milk." Even Sara's two-word utterances like

"Milk shirt"

"Drink milk"

or

"More milk"

constitute a giant (though still incomplete) step towards disambiguating meaning. Not surprisingly, when people ask, "Does your child talk yet?" they generally mean, "Does he put words together?"

Conversation

While sound, meaning, and grammar define the workings of language *in principle*, conversation is the realm of language *in practice*. The difference is as stark as the contrast between reading about how to do a swan dive versus actually springing off the high board. Every language has its own rules of praxis: for taking turns in a conversation, for answering the telephone, for properly opening and closing dialogues.

Underlying all of our conversational exchanges are conventions reflecting the speaker's age, sex, social status, and relation to the person being addressed. Every society has unwritten regulations about how men should speak with women, children with elders, and princes with paupers. A vital part of learning language is discovering what language style is appropriate to a given situation. By the time children are only age 3 or 4, they usually know to speak differently to an infant than to a peer, how to whisper, and when to be quiet.

The groundwork for conversational knowledge is laid long before children utter their first words. As children begin acquiring meaningful language, they harness a growing vocabulary and incipient grammar to lend clarity to conversational intent.

Forms of Language

The journey into language involves multiple strands of development. While all children have to master the four essential building blocks of language, they also need to learn to reflect on language itself (e.g., to be aware when two words mean the same thing or when a sentence is ambiguous; to recognize a pun or know how to find *le mot juste*). In addition, depending on the particular challenges presented to speakers in a linguistic community, language users may need to function in more than one language (that is, to become bilingual) or to create messages through some other medium besides speech—through sign language or, more commonly, through writing.

Language Awareness

Language awareness encompasses an array of abilities, some of which speakers demonstrate intuitively and others of which we articulate overtly. The gamut runs from recognizing you have made a mistake in your own speech, as when 4-year-old Ryan said,

"Which telephone are on you . . . are you on?"

to being able to explain what you did wrong. From playing rhyming games ("*big, fig, wig*") to composing rhymed verse. From understanding word plays created by others—

"Let's go to Baltimore, not Baltiless"

to coining your own verbal jokes. From knowing that two words are synonyms (e.g., *huge* and *gargantuan*) to explaining the subtle distinctions between them. And most important, from using language as an expressive tool to making language itself a topic of conversation—

15

"You just said something silly"

"Those two words don't mean the same thing"

"Babies say *nana* but I say *banana*"

or

"What do you call pumpkins in Japanese?"

All children develop some awareness of language, such as correcting their own mistakes or recognizing mistakes in the speech of others. The extent to which children hone sophisticated **metalinguistic** skills (that is, the ability to *talk about* language) and the age at which these abilities emerge are shaped by the language they hear modeled around them. Not surprisingly, children who rarely hear rhymes are unlikely to begin rhyming spontaneously, and children whose parents consistently call attention to differences in language style are prone to do the same. When parents tend to define new words they use, children commonly follow suit, as when 4-year-old Alex (who had many times witnessed his father dressed in fencing attire) volunteered this intentionally humorous definition of the art of fencing:

"You go up to a fence, and then you jump over it. That's fencing!"

Functioning in Two Languages

One special dimension of reflecting on language is noticing and being able to talk about variations in the ways people pronounce the same words or in the very words people use to refer to the same world of experience. What Bostonians call *tonic*, the rest of the country calls *soda*. When Americans say *yes*, Frenchmen say *oui*.

Children who grow up bilingual naturally learn early on that linguistic labels are no more than social conventions, and different societies follow different conventions. Yet even children growing up in monolingual households often find rich opportunities to reflect on the fact that neither pronunciations nor words are sacrosanct. Regional accents (*idea* versus *idear*) and word choices (*soda* versus *tonic*), not to mention encounters with other languages (from a visit abroad, the presence of a non–English speaking child at school, or teaching children to count to ten in Swahili) can also successfully lead children to talk *about* two languages and smooth the way for later functioning *in* two languages.

Sign and Script

Everything I have said about language so far—about sound, meaning, grammar, conversation, language awareness, bilingualism—has been cloaked in the mantle of spoken language. But speech is not the only medium through which people express themselves linguistically. Among children whose auditory systems prevent them from learning to speak naturally (or children whose parents are deaf), sign language is often the communication system acquired as a native language. In literate societies, language development includes not only mastering speech (or sign) but learning to read and write as well.

Why raise the issue of sign language in a book on normal language acquisition? Tens of thousands of children in the United States are deaf or profoundly hard of hearing, due to genetic inheritance, problems at birth, or childhood illness or trauma. The majority of these children are educated in special schools in which a system of manual communication is used to augment instruction in spoken and written English. Children whose parents are themselves deaf typically learn some version of American Sign Language as a native language, and deaf children of hearing parents frequently create their own signs for things, even if no sign language is modeled at home.

Children who sign rather than speak provide excellent reality checks on some notions we have about how children learn language. As we will see, studies of sign language acquisition by young deaf children help us rethink why normal children start speaking at the age they do— and not earlier. Familiarity with older signers enhances our understanding of how knowledge in one language domain (e.g., sign or speech) enables children to bootstrap their way to understanding in another (e.g., speech or writing).

Typical books on language acquisition conclude just before children begin reading and writing. Books on how children become literate generally have little to say about the acquisition of spoken language. In *Growing Up with Language*, we look at everything a child learns about language from birth to about age 5 or 6. Why? Because neither parents nor young children segregate speech from writing in the ways they use

17

language with each other. Early book reading is as much an avenue for learning new spoken vocabulary as an introduction to the formatting of written books (with covers, titles, beginnings, middles, and ends). "Sesame Street" skits teaching opposites like "in" and "out" are geared as much to explaining concepts as they are to fostering early decoding of written words. This book therefore outlines the foundations upon which more sophisticated literacy skills are later built.

Charting a Course

Parental interest and concern. Variations in learning styles. Language components. Forms of expression. How do we weave a mosaic from these strands to understand how and why children learn language?

Books on language acquisition generally adopt one of two approaches. The first is chronological—what normal developments can be expected during the first, second, third (etc.) years of life. The chronological tack provides a reassuring sense of natural progression. Unfortunately, normative histories can also generate anxiety, since many perfectly normal children do not achieve the same milestones at the same age (or even in the same order). In fact, thousands of children give short shrift to or even bypass some of these milestones altogether. While chronology makes for clear presentation, it also reduces variation to a homogenized and often unrepresentative norm.

The usual alternative to chronological development is presenting one component of language at a time: sounds, words, grammar, and perhaps conversation. This format is tailored for language acquisition specialists focusing on particular areas of language growth. Unfortunately, the component approach makes little sense to parents watching their children through time, particularly because so many strands of language are developing at once and influencing one another.

Growing Up with Language is written from the combined perspectives of a theoretician and a parent. As a language acquisition specialist, I have selected four conceptual themes through which we can understand how and why language emerges in children. As a parent, I have identified seven (sometimes overlapping) phases of language growth that mark major linguistic and conceptual milestones in joining a language community.

Each conceptual theme addresses a fundamental issue in language acquisition:

- Why do children learn language? (**Theme I: The Conversational Imperative**)

- Do all children learn language the same way? (**Theme II: The Phantom Norm**)

- How do children learn language? (**Theme III: Language Orienteering**)

- How do we measure language learning? (**Theme IV: Language Saturation**)

Theme I: The Conversational Imperative

Children learn to talk for much the same reason that adults chat with their dogs, strangers strike up conversations on long-distance trips, and foreigners persist in addressing one another in mutually unintelligible tongues. This motivation is the **conversational imperative**. By virtue of the conversational imperative, we tend to talk when in the presence of other sentient beings, regardless of whether we make ourselves understood. Our impetus for conversation may be a desire for social companionship, the practical need to convey information, or both.

The conversational imperative drives parents to speak even with babies who are too young to make articulate sounds. It also leads infants and toddlers to struggle to crack the code of human language.

Theme II: The Phantom Norm

The bulk of what is written about language acquisition leads us to assume that all children learn language the same way. However much we believe that every child is different and however often we acknowledge the impact of social forces on human development, even highly educated parents easily fall prey to declarations such as "Normal children begin combining words together at age such-and-such" or "All children learn the phrase 'Thank you' at age thus-and-so."

This **phantom norm** in which parents invest such credence is little more than the homogenized findings of a plethora of reports and studies. In truth, children vary enormously in their language learning paths,

19

although the variation is hardly random. By knowing where to look, we can identify distinct, predictable alternative routes.

Theme III: Language Orienteering

The processes by which children learn language are mysterious and confusing. Since we cannot see inside children's heads, we tend to concoct convenient (but untestable) hypotheses about how children learn. At one extreme, observers argue that children learn language through imitation. At the other, scholars postulate innate mechanisms that naturally lead children to "discover" the structure in language.

In *Growing Up with Language*, we look at children as sensible explorers who find themselves in an incomprehensible adult world. Driven by the conversational imperative (and aided by parents who are similarly motivated), infants, toddlers, and preschoolers develop ingenious, identifiable strategies for finding their way through the language maze. This **language orienteering** begins very early on but becomes most interesting once children begin to combine words.

Theme IV: Language Saturation

Measuring a person's linguistic knowledge is like counting trees in a forest. Much as the shorter trees are obstructed by their taller cousins, people do not use all the words or grammatical constructions they can understand. Continuing the analogy, in the forest, it is not always clear what counts as a tree. The sapling that just sprouted last spring hardly qualifies. But what about the one that took root the year before? Similarly with language learning. If 3-year-old Ryan sometimes says,

"Why the ball is rolling?"

and other times,

"Why is the ball rolling?"

what do we conclude about his understanding of word order in formulating questions? Or how do we count the number of words a child knows? Like the vanishing Cheshire Cat in *Alice in Wonderland*, children often learn words only to forget them a few weeks later, when the motivating context (such as the *sand* at the *beach*) is removed.

In measuring a child's knowledge of language, we naturally focus on the child. Yet language is quintessentially a social activity. We talk—and learn to talk—because we live with other people. What we actually know about language is often less important than what our fellow conversationalists think we understand. Measurement of linguistic knowledge relies as heavily on interlocutors' judgments as it does on speakers' emerging fluency.

A child learning language is like a sponge soaking up water. After a time, we assume that the sponge is **saturated**, though in fact, it can probably still hold more liquid. Speakers are saturated when accomplished members of the community do not notice anything unusual about the learner's usage. However, as with the sponge and water, speakers can invariably "soak up" more language.

These four themes—the conversational imperative, the phantom norm, language orienteering, and language saturation—provide the scaffolding upon which the chapters of this book are built. Each chapter focuses on a developmental phase of language growth:

- birth to first words (Chapter 2)
- first words to grammar (Chapter 3)
- grammatical development (Chapter 4)
- development in meaning, sound, and conversation (Chapter 5)
- language awareness (Chapter 6)
- literacy (Chapter 7)

The chapters themselves are roughly chronologically organized, although some of the issues raised (especially in Chapters 6 and 7) reach back to earlier phases of language learning.

Chapter 2 focuses on language development in infants, from birth to the time they articulate their first words. The chapter explores how the conversational imperative drives children's early attempts at communication, as well as motivating a style of adult speech known as baby talk. Combining these social dimensions with information on how biology shapes early language, the chapter concludes by tracing alternative paths to first words.

Toddlers amass a growing vocabulary that provides a foundation for the later transition from single words to grammar. With just a handful of sounds, words, and conversational techniques, children manage to express a wealth of ideas. This transition period is especially marked by vast differences among learners, and so Chapter 3 focuses on language variation and its sources.

Chapters 4 and 5 analyze the language strategies of preschoolers as they move from the earliest stages of grammar to becoming saturated speakers of the language. (By "preschoolers" I mean children between the ages of about 2 and 5. Linguistically, 2-year-olds form a natural continuum with 3-year-olds. Moreover, a growing number of children, especially by age 2½, are joining 3- and 4-year-olds in formal preschool programs.) Like explorers in an unknown land relying on a handful of tools for finding their way, preschoolers construct a range of strategies for negotiating the linguistic terrain. Chapter 4 centers on preschoolers' developments in grammar, while Chapter 5 follows preschoolers in their explorations of meaning, sound, and conversation.

Chapter 6 looks at how children learn to reflect on language, to function in two languages, and to develop facility with other language modalities. Chapter 7 draws together information from the early months of life to about age 5 or 6 on how children in a literate society such as the United States become acculturated in reading and writing. Following the Epilogue, the Notes provide recommendations for additional reading, information on contemporary research forums, précis on organizations devoted to special groups of language learners, and references to works cited in the chapters.

The chapters weave the stories of how three children and their parents worked together to create language. But what about the emergence of language among your own children or children you know? What guidelines can adults use to help foster and monitor the process?

The "Parenting" sections of bookstores and libraries are laden with suggestions on how to help children grow faster and smarter. This "better baby" literature includes an array of volumes specifically aimed at enhancing early language development. Some are written by psychologists, educators, or health professionals, while others are journalistic forays. A sampling of these books is described in the "General Reading" section at the beginning of the Notes.

How-to guidebooks can be helpful in confirming parents' intuitions about how to help a child develop linguistically. However, the analyses and recommendations in many of these books should be taken with hefty grains of salt. Although a number of the ideas are insightful, others confirm that a good proportion of the authors are innocent of serious acquaintance with the language acquisition process.

What can parents do to nurture language learning in children, and what problems should parents anticipate? The Ideas and Alerts section at the end of each chapter addresses these issues.

Finally, a few words about stylistic conventions. My solution to the absence of a neutral third-person-singular pronoun in English is to balance *he* and *she* when referring to children in the singular. I tend to speak of "parents" and sometimes specifically of "mothers" when talking about primary caregivers. Obviously, baby-sitters, relatives, and older siblings have important roles in child rearing, and increasingly fathers are major players as well. The choice of "mother" reflects the reality that in contemporary America, child care is largely the province of women. What is more, most studies of adult-child conversation have involved mothers, not fathers.

In citing examples from Sara's, Ryan's, and Alex's speech, I take license with conventional orthography for representing utterances that do not follow standard adult pronunciation rather than resorting to technical phonetic symbols. The one formal linguistic notation I sometimes use is for indicating a child's age: number of years, followed by a semicolon, followed by number of months (e.g., 2;6 refers to a child who is 2 years, 6 months old).

■ 2. The Roots of Language
From Birth to First Words

THREE-MONTH-OLD Ryan was lying on the bed while his mother changed his diaper. As she worked, she chattered about nothing in particular and happened to direct a playful *ph* sound at her son. Much to her delight, he gave her a *ph* in return. She escalated with a reply: *ph*. He rewarded her with the same. They continued for several rounds— she elated no longer to be addressing a brick wall and he delighted not to be packed off to his crib as soon as the new diaper was in place.

The first conversation was born.

Language learning emerges out of the language duet between adult and child that begins in the early months of life. Parent and child establish their own voices in the duet, with the roles evolving as the pair's needs and abilities change. Evolution on the child's side is strongly molded by her biology, the linguistic company she keeps, and her own unique personality.

Human language is profoundly a social enterprise. Even monologues involve talking with ourselves. We feel driven to talk with—even at— other people and to act as if we are being understood, even when common sense tells us we are not.

What drives us?

Imperatives and Duets

My favorite weekend writing haunt is the cavernous public eatery of a nearby university. Escaping my immediate surroundings, I sit for hours undisturbed and work.

GROWING UP WITH LANGUAGE

Over the months, I have developed a curious rapport with one of the cafeteria's employees whose job it is to straighten tables, vacuum floors, and herd patrons out at closing time. A self-possessed Korean-looking woman somewhere around age 50, she speaks no English, although she readily addresses American diners in her native tongue. How does she manage so forcefully to make us raise our feet so she can sweep underneath, bus our trays, and clear out on command? By virtue of the **conversational imperative**.

Because of the conversational imperative, when in the presence of another sentient being, people (at least in contemporary America) are inclined to talk. This inclination does not presuppose that the two conversational "partners" speak the same language or even that the listener speaks at all.

Consider three vignettes from the families into which Sara, Ryan, and Alex were born:

- Sara's family included Freya, a 5-year-old German shepherd. Each evening when Sara's mother lay out fresh food and water for Freya, she paused to "chat," encouraging the dog to eat, reminding her that next week would be bath time, and complaining about how much hair Freya shed about the house. Freya, of course, never replied.

- Ryan's mother, as we have already seen, tended to vocalize when changing her infant son's diaper. As the little boy lay making incomprehensible sounds, she naturally upheld both sides of the conversation:

  "So your diaper needed changing? Now that feels better, doesn't it? Are you hungry? Yes, I thought you were. Do you want to eat now or when Cathy does? Now? O.K."

- Like many other new parents, Alex's mother had set up a baby monitor in the room of her newborn son so she could respond to the child's every whimper. Religiously, she carried the receiver with her as she moved about the house. Whenever she heard cries coming over the airwaves, she would address the receiver:

  "Hold on, pal. I'll be right there. Don't cry, Alex!"

and then dash off on her rescue mission. The irony is that the monitor was a one-way device. None of her words of solace were transmitted back.

Why are we ruled by the conversational imperative? Because we attempt to make sense of our social interactions. We justify the anthropomorphic feelings we have for our dogs if we can talk with them. We handle the reality of one-sided conversation with a newborn by providing enough language for both of us.

The conversational imperative does more than feed delusions of being understood. As we raise young children, the conversational imperative leads to a self-fulfilling prophecy: the very act of talking to infants as if they understand us is the single most important thing we do to help children become full-fledged participants in a language community. The main reason children succeed in learning language is that they are born into social groups in which language is the medium of exchange. Infant cooing and babbling increase when adults verbalize back. Toddlers imbibe the sounds, words, and phrases they hear around them.

But mastering a native language is hardly child's play. The fact that every normal child moves from total incomprehension at birth to sophisticated speaking and understanding by about age 5 attests not only to the remarkable efforts children put into the process but also to the social and personal drives that lead children to figure out the system.

A profound force underlying language development in human beings is the fact that we have things to say to those around us. Children, who have so little control over their physical environment, feel this need from the start. Their lack of articulate expression both generates frustration and provides a superb motivation to master the language tools necessary to make themselves understood.

Children have a great deal they want to tell us. Much of it initially relates to creature comforts: hunger, pain, wetness, disorientation. Over time, as children learn that objects and activities have names, the drive to articulate comes (at least in part) from specific desires for milk, a ride in the car, another bedtime story. By the time children become 2 or 3 years old, their increasingly complex emotions need avenues of expression. A frequently heard admonition of nursery school teachers to their young charges is,

"Use your words!"

(in lieu of arms or tear ducts).

Children quickly realize that besides offering a means of expressing what is on their minds, language provides an immediate hook into a social relationship. Adults learn to make small talk with people they have never met before. Three- and 4-year-olds discover that by asking

"You know what?"

(regardless of whether they have anything to say) they can capture an older person's attention.

Even children who cannot decipher one another's sounds spontaneously initiate verbal exchange. I will never forget my first visit to a kindergarten classroom at the Rhode Island School for the Deaf. Anticipating silence, I was astonished to hear exuberant (though unintelligible) sounds spilling out into the halls. Speech is a natural accompaniment to human activity: babies squeal with delight, fans cheer at ball games, audiences boo down speakers. Only through long years of socialization do we learn to channel our vocalizations into articulate language (and to restrain ourselves when social decorum calls for quiet).

The emergence of conversation as a natural expression of human bonding is partly rooted in the desire to belong. Children learn a surprising amount of their language—and notions of appropriate conversation—by shadowing the language they hear around them.

Consider a scene from Ryan's household. Ryan's mother was hurrying one morning to get her children to school and herself to work on time. As she bolted out the front door, 4-year-old Ryan lingered on the top step, surveying the autumn scene:

"What a mess!"

he complained.

"We have to get all these leaves cleaned up!"

Why does a 4-year-old decide that fallen leaves are detritus rather than a source of beauty and enjoyment? Because two days earlier he had heard just this sentiment from his older sister, Cathy, who had been conscripted to rake the leaves from the front yard. The drive to be part of a social universe that is suffused with language is powerful indeed.

Given that children are motivated to talk—and parents (along with others in the local environs) to talk with them—how do the two sides team up to form a **language duet**? The first step is to divide up the conversational load. Occasionally the two play the melody in unison, but more often portions of the composition are parceled out. The players' roles are complementary though not always equal. One may render the melody and the other harmony. The melody line may shift back and forth, or the first player may dominate the piece, with the second entering only at selected intervals.

When the language duet is played by a young child and an adult, the conversational load undergoes dramatic changes over the first few years. From the time their children are born until they reach their second or third birthdays, parents bear major responsibility for initiating and maintaining conversations. This responsibility entails getting the child's attention, setting a topic (often by posing a question), encouraging a response, and trying to keep the give-and-take of comment (or question) and reply going.

Before a child has any recognizable words, the adult generally plays both lines in the duet (like Ryan's mother's "Are you hungry? Yes, I thought you were"). As children begin to find their own conversational voices—having something to say and knowing words to express their thoughts—the conversational burden becomes increasingly distributed.

Yet the dynamics of conversational load are also highly sensitive to the personalities of the players in the duet. Sara, for example, began to dominate "conversations" with her mother and father by the time she was a few weeks old. During the early months, Sara's own vocalizations led her parents to vocalize back. By the time she was 1½ years, Sara was padding about the house demanding names for the objects in her environment.

Alex began as the silent type. For nearly the first year, he almost never "spoke" unless spoken to. From ages 1 to 3, he was also comparatively quiet, especially in contrast with his parents, who offered running monologues and attempted (often unsuccessfully) to coax a linguistic response out of their son. Alex did not seriously begin to initiate conversations until almost age 3.

Ryan took the middle ground. As an infant, sometimes he would begin the conversational duet, and other times his mother or sister would. During the next few years, this balance continued (e.g., his mother often labeled objects, but Ryan also demanded names for things).

While Sara, Alex, and Ryan assumed different conversational leaderships roles, in each case, their parents accommodated harmoniously. What happens when parent and child are out of sync (e.g., both parent and child insist on being "leaders," or a loquacious child is teamed up with a taciturn mother)? Common sense tells us that such mismatches can get children off to a rocky start. For the good of all, conversationally dominating mothers will do well to adjust their own behaviors, since infants and toddlers, not yet capable of self-discipline, cannot do the accommodating. And mothers who don't naturally uphold their end of the conversational bargain may need to work actively to prevent frustration or potentially even linguistic delay in their children.

In the early stages of the language duet, both parents and children must do some accommodating. Driven by the conversational imperative, parents naturally suspend disbelief at their children's babbling (or even silence) and keep the conversational ball in motion. But children themselves also have a vital role in the suspension of disbelief when they listen intently to words and sentences that make no sense and keep working at the problem until they successfully decode adult mutterings.

Given this mutual commitment from parent and child to include the newcomer in the conversational community, how do parents aid young children in the induction process? In many societies of the world (including the United States), adults specially tailor the language they use in addressing children. Such tailoring is known as **baby talk**.

Baby Talk

Sara had started nursery school a few weeks earlier. As a curious 4-year-old, she immediately gravitated to the sand table, which housed a collection of socks (for filling) and molds of many shapes and colors.

Sara's mother, who had brought along 2-year-old Michael, turned for a moment to confer with her daughter's new teacher. From the corner of her eye, she saw Michael's cupped hand meet his lips. Having joined his big sister at the sand table, Michael was sampling its contents.

"That's very bad. You shouldn't eat that, Michael!"

his mother called out as she wrenched the little boy's hand away from his mouth.

"No eat! No eat!"

"No eat" is hardly standard English. Did Sara's mother misspeak herself in the confusion of the moment? Not at all. She was engaging in a deliberate form of **baby talk**.

Baby talk is a special language style many adults use in addressing infants and young children. The style may include speaking in a higher pitch than is normally used with other adults, repeating their own words, (e.g. "That's a duck, Sara. That's a duck"), asking a lot more questions, weeding out complex vocabulary, substituting special names for everyday things (such as *choo choo* for *train* or *kitty* instead of *cat*), using shorter sentences, or even simplifying grammar to the point of ungrammaticality (as in "No eat!").

Baby talk styles are found in most cultures around the globe, though many specific features differ from one society to the next. Adults often do not recognize they are addressing children in a special language style. When made aware, they are prone to disagree on whether the effects of baby talk are good, ill, or irrelevant.

The language style we call baby talk is really multiple linguistic threads joined by an attitude—an attitude that special language adaptations are appropriate when addressing young children. The threads are drawn from all four basic components of human language: sound, meaning, grammar, and conversation. While some forms of baby talk are obvious when you hear them (like calling a *train* a *choo choo*, or saying "No eat!" for "Don't eat that!"), others are more subtle and become clear only in retrospect (e.g., tending to ask more questions of children than of adults or consistently expanding upon what children have just said). Like the platters restaurant goers build for themselves at salad bars, the actual baby talk an adult uses is a highly individualized collection, drawn from a sizable array of possibilities.

What are the common forms of baby talk found in American society? **Chart 2** presents a spectrum of possibilities.

Why do parents (or adults more generally) slip into using baby talk with young children? When pressed, parents offer two explanations. The first is educational. By using baby talk, parents simplify the language, thereby making it easier to understand. For some forms of baby talk, this rationale makes obvious sense. It stands to reason that by slowing down the rate of speech, eliminating difficult words or grammar, and using a lot of repetition (both of their own speech and of their children's), parents assist in the learning process.

But what about other baby talk features, such as higher pitch, using plural pronouns in lieu of singulars, or echoing children's invented words? Do we really believe that these linguistic gymnastics promote faster language learning? Hardly. Instead, they serve a second function: to enhance social integration with children by expressing emotion (e.g., through heightened pitch), exercising control (repeating your own words to capture the child's attention), or simply working to keep the communication channel open by building upon a child's interests.

How does the social function of baby talk work? By the same conversational imperative that led Ryan's mother to "chat" with her 3-month-old or Alex's mother to talk back to her one-way baby monitor. The adult speaker herself, by the language she uses, reinforces her affinity with her interlocutor, regardless of the pedagogical usefulness of the language or even of the "listener's" capacity to respond. When Alex's father would ask of his son,

"Would you like some *ish* [= *water*]?"

his echoing of Alex's neologism strengthened their personal bond rather than providing a vocabulary lesson. (Alex had coined the word *ish* onomatopoetically after encountering a fountain. See Chapter 3.)

Choices and Consequences

From among the available baby talk threads a language community has to offer, adults make their own selections. Their choices heavily reflect the baby talk they have heard used by others, since especially first-time

CHART 2. Common Baby Talk Features

SOUND

higher pitch than is normal in language addressed to adults

greater range of frequencies (moving back and forth between high and low pitch)

louder volume

slower rate of speech

clearer enunciation

emphasis on one or two words in a sentence ("Is that your very own *apple juice*?")

special pronunciation of individual words ("My, what a *bi-i-i-g* boy you are!")

echoing child's incorrect pronunciation (*bozer* for *bulldozer*)

MEANING

substitutions (*choo choo* instead of *train*)

diminutives (*kitty* for *cat*)

semantically inappropriate words (calling an orangutan a *monkey*)

echoing child's invented words (using a child's onomatopoetic name of *ish* for *water*)

coining nonstandard words (labeling a pigeon a *pigeon-bird*)

GRAMMAR

grammatically simple utterances

shorter utterances

use of **nouns in lieu of pronouns** ("Daddy wants Alex to brush his teeth")

use of **plural pronouns in place of singular** ("Shall we brush our teeth now?")

intentional ungrammatical usage ("No eat!" for "Don't eat that!")

CONVERSATION

restricted topics (generally limited to the present, immediate past, or very near future)

provision of **both questions and answers** by adult ("Shall we change your diaper now? Yes? O.K.")

more **questions**, fewer declaratives

sentences naming objects ("That's a duck, Sara. That's a duck.")

repetition of own utterances ("Would you like some cheese? Would you like some cheese?")

repetitions, expansions, recastings of child's utterance (in response to Ryan's "All gone," his mother continues, "Yes, all gone" or "Your milk is all gone" or "Would you like some more?")

parents have little independent idea about what an appropriate way of speaking with a young child might be. But other variables enter the construction of a baby talk style as well. Chief among them are parental age, level of education, the amount of time spent with the child, and

33

the extent to which parents are aware of the kinds of language modulations they are using.

An additional factor is the child's age and level of linguistic sophistication. Some baby talk features (e.g., high pitch, large frequency modulations) are most common when addressing infants. Others (e.g., repetition, heightened grammaticality) are especially prevalent as toddlers begin using recognizable language. However, since so much of baby talk is unconscious, many parents do not eliminate an age-inappropriate baby talk feature (such as calling a bulldozer a *bozer*) until the child is articulate enough to ask the parent to call a halt ("Not *bozer*, Daddy. It's *bulldozer*").

To get an idea of the variety of baby talk practices in contemporary America, let's look at the families of Sara, Ryan, and Alex.

The baby talk style Sara's mother used most closely matches our intuitive assumptions about what baby talk sounds like. Recall that Sara's mother, who is college educated and in her thirties, stayed home full time until her daughter was 4. The style of language she uses in addressing Sara largely derives from the ways in which she has heard other mothers (including her own) addressing children.

What does such classical baby talk sound like? Phonologically, Sara's mother's speech is marked by very high pitch (the highest of the three mothers) coupled with clear enunciation, even to the point of over-enunciation. In choosing her words, Sara's mother frequently simplifies her vocabulary, substituting *tumtum* for *stomach*, *quack quack* for *duck*, and *doggie* for *dog*. (Simplification is often in the mind of the beholder.) At the same time, she is prone to use semantically inaccurate names that reduce the variety of words with which her small daughter must cope—calling an orangutan a *monkey* and the ocean a "big lake."

In her grammar, Sara's mother is also prototypic. Her sentences are far shorter and more grammatically simple than those she generally uses in addressing adults. As we have already seen, she does not hesitate to use intentionally ungrammatical sentences ("No eat!") when she believes her simplified language will be more readily understood.

Conversationally, Sara's mother restricts her topics of discussion, repeats many of her own utterances, asks many questions, and, especially when Sara was an infant and toddler, often provided the answers as well. Two of the most distinctive features of her conversational style are her frequent repetitions and expansions of Sara's words and sentences, plus her role as "language tour guide"—

"That's a duck, Sara. That's a duck."

This child-centered conversational style is facilitated by the fact that outside of caring for her children (clearly a full-time job in itself), Sara's mother has no other major calls on her time.

The contrast between the child-directed speech of Sara's mother and that of her father is stark. If you briefly overheard Sara's father conversing with Sara, you would be hard pressed to identify anything special. More extensive observation would reveal a few differences from normal adult discourse—clearer enunciation, a few diminutives like *kitty* and *doggie*, and generally shorter sentences about a more limited range of topics. Significantly absent are the prominent benchmarks of baby talk, such as heightened pitch, repeated naming of objects, and expansion of children's early grammatical attempts.

The kind of language Sara's father uses with his daughter reveals a good deal about his approach to fathering. A typical educated middle-class father, he is devoted to Sara yet spends very little time alone with her. When they are together, he treats her as (nearly) a linguistic equal, despite her still highly constrained command over the language. As a result, he tends to use more sophisticated vocabulary and syntax with Sara than does his wife, not through an attempt to lead his daughter to new linguistic heights but because he is unaware of any reason to make adaptations in his speech.

Listening to Ryan's mother, initially you might not notice differences between the way she and Sara's mother converse with their children. Both adapt their sound patterns (high pitch and wide frequency variation), both lace their speech with substitutions (*choo choo* for *train*) and diminutives (*piggy* for *pig*), and both make an occasional inappropriate word choice (*fish* for *whale*). In addition, their sentences are shorter, more grammatical, more filled with questions, and more restricted in topics than the conversation they use with adults. Both tend to use plural pronouns in lieu of singular ("Let's brush our teeth") and to repeat their own utterances. But two critical features are less common in the language Ryan's mother uses with her son—an absence that becomes apparent only when you observe her language with Ryan over an extended time.

The first difference is in the number of times the mothers spontaneously name objects. Until Sara was almost 3, her mother devoted considerable energies to pointing out objects and their names ("Do you see the duck, Sara? That's a duck. Can you say "*duck*"?). Ryan's mother engaged in much less unsolicited naming, in part because she always felt pressed for time and in part because it never occurred to her that such direct pedagogy was necessary.

The second discrepancy is in the amount of repetitions, expansions, or recastings of children's utterances. While Ryan's mother obviously did some massaging of Ryan's words (such as expanding Ryan's "All gone" to "Your milk is all gone"), she capitalized far less on her son's spontaneous language than Sara's mother did on her daughter's. Again, extensive use of these linguistic devices presupposes either the luxury of time to make small talk (which comes more easily when there is only one child to attend to and no rigid schedule to keep) or concerted effort on the part of the parent to use such conversational extenders.

Do age and education lead to special baby talk styles? Alex's mother was 40 when her son was born. As a lawyer (and avid reader), she was enormously sensitive to language and had clear notions about the best way to nurture her son's linguistic and cognitive growth. Alex's development was a frequent topic of conversation between husband and wife.

The language Alex's mother used with her son bore clear baby talk features, but you sometimes had to listen carefully to hear them. The two modifications she commonly made to her normal sound patterns were to put special emphasis on one or two words in a sentence (especially on a new or difficult word—"Shall we open the *en-ve-lope* together?") or to lend a special pronunciation to a word to mark it with affection ("Are you a *bi-i-i-g* boy?").

In her vocabulary, Alex's mother generally avoided substitutions (*choo choo*) and diminutives (*piggy*). On the contrary, she intentionally used relatively complex vocabulary ("Isn't that a *humongous* dish of ice cream?"). Occasionally she echoed her son's incorrect pronunciations (*bozer*) or invented words (*ish*) but was more likely to lapse into these words when relaxing with her husband ("While you're downstairs, would you get me a glass of *ish?*") than when addressing Alex. The one lexical baby talk feature to which she often gravitated was the use of a select number of nonstandard words carefully designed to teach class relationships—coining *pigeon-bird* (as a parallel to *black bird* or *blue bird*) and *salmon-fish* (on par with *bluefish* or *rock fish*).

In her grammar, Alex's mother followed the predictable trend of using shorter, more grammatically correct sentences. In a few instances, she veered into ungrammatical constructions but always with a purpose. When Alex was 2, he would often stretch out his arms and demand,

"Up!"

His mother's response,

"Do you want some more up?"

was, of course, ungrammatical, but it was also a direct attempt to build upon her son's linguistic usage. Alex's mother also tended to substitute nouns for pronouns whenever possible ("Does Alex want to get into the car now?") in the hope of teaching Alex more names of people and things.

Conversationally, Alex's mother focused intently on expanding her son's language. Like Sara's mother, she was an active language tour guide, naming objects everywhere she and her son went. Alex's mother repeated, expanded, and built upon nearly every utterance her son made. Since Alex's mother worked full time from the time the boy was 3 months old, leaving her diminished opportunities for the sort of conversational banter Sara often shared with her mother, Alex's mother consciously seized on any shared moments—talking while brushing teeth, talking while getting dressed, talking while shopping for groceries.

Like Sara's father, Alex's father was away from the house (and his child) much of the day. However, Alex's father actively shared the child rearing—and conversational—responsibilities with his wife. The effects of this social profile on the language Alex's father used with his son were profound. Feature for feature, the man's language more resembled classical baby talk than did the language used by Alex's mother. Although Alex's father did not indulge in a particularly high pitch, his frequencies undulated dramatically, and his rate of speech was slower than that of any of the three mothers. Equally prominent was his volume. When addressing his son, Alex's father orated as if to a crowd. Curiously, such heightened volume was also his instinctive response when conversing at international medical conferences with physicians who did not understand much English. Obviously turning up the volume (whether with children or adults) serves no practical purpose if the listener doesn't understand what you are saying. Yet since increasing the volume does help on other occasions (e.g., when addressing people who are hard of hearing), the attempt makes intuitive sense.

Alex's father frequently echoed the words of his son—repeating Alex's incorrect pronunciations (*bozer*), his invented words (*ish*), and, more generally, Alex's slowly emerging word combinations. Unlike Alex's mother, who more often expanded or recast Alex's words, his father was more likely to repeat his son literally.

Five parents. Five baby talk styles. What are the effects of these parents' linguistic choices?

Perhaps surprisingly, the primary benefactor of baby talk is often adults, not children. In the process of adjusting their language, parents acknowledge the importance of their child as a member of the conversation. Many of the most common forms of baby talk have little if any direct ramifications for language learning but prove ideal avenues for establishing social rapport. The list runs the gamut of language categories: in **sound**, special pronunciations and echoing of children's incorrect pronunciations; in **meaning**, the use of substitutions and diminutives, and echoing of children's invented words; in **grammar**, use of plural instead of singular pronouns and intentional ungrammatical usage (of the "No eat!" variety); and in **conversation**, repeating your own utterances and providing both questions and answers in a dialogue.

Does parental baby talk benefit children as well? While researchers continue to debate how to interpret their data, it seems clear that a number of baby talk features are likely to facilitate language learning.

In **sound,** the use of heightened pitch, large frequency modulations, and louder volume can all help capture a child's attention, and slower rate and clearer enunciation are obvious boons to anyone attempting to make sense of an unknown language. In the same vein, placing special emphasis on one word (as Alex's mother was prone to do) helps single out that word and make it easier to learn.

In **meaning,** the use of semantically inappropriate words (like *monkey* for *orangutan*) can prove conceptually beneficial for young children (generally below age 2) who are struggling to puzzle out categories of objects in the world. However, we should not forget that toddlers and preschoolers are veritable language sponges and can absorb a vast array of complex words. If a typical 3-year-old can learn the words *tyrannosaurus, diplodocus, brachiosaurus, apatosaurus, triceratops, stegosaurus,* and *pteranodon*—and correctly identify the dinosaurs that go with them—surely he can handle words (and concepts) like *orangutan* (versus *monkey*) and even *gargantuan, humongous,* and *huge* (alongside *big*).

Grammatically, it makes intuitive sense that simpler and shorter utterances from parents make it easier for children to crack the grammatical code. However, notions of simplicity and length are themselves relative. While no one would advocate the style of Henry James in addressing a 2-year-old, parents can also err on the side of oversimplification and neglect to provide their young children adequate grammatical models and challenges.

What about **conversational** features of baby talk? Restriction of topics can prove useful with very young children, but only up to a point. Filling one's conversation with ostension ("That's a duck, Sara. A duck.") is an excellent way of teaching children new words, as long as it is balanced with conversational give and take. Asking many questions provides multiple opportunities for children to enter the conversational stream, because most questions at this stage can be answered with a single word.

Perhaps the most demonstrable conversational benefit that parents can contribute to their children's linguistic development is the active use of repetitions, expansions, and recastings of children's own utterances. Simple repetitions confirm to the child that his language has been understood. Expansions provide an ideal medium for stretching a child's grammar to catch up with her linguistic intent (Child: "All gone." Adult: "Your milk is all gone"). And recastings are a natural way of teaching a child to integrate isolated utterances into conversation ("Yes, your milk is all gone, isn't it. Would you like some more?").

Can baby talk prove harmful? Hardly ever, even in the short run. Children continue to learn words and grammar from many sources (friends, teachers, other adults, books, television), even if parents persist in using limited vocabulary or grammar. In fact, it is often children, not parents, who demand an end to baby talk from parents.

The one instance I know of in which an aspect of baby talk temporarily can slow a child's normal linguistic growth is in the substitution of nouns for pronouns (e.g., Alex's mother's "Does Alex want to get into the car now?"). Pronouns are one of the trickiest grammatical constructions to learn because they have no obvious referent. The person I call *"you,"* you call *"I,"* and vice versa. On average, children begin using pronouns—albeit often incorrectly—by age 2½. Alex did not begin until almost 3, largely because his parents had consciously avoided using pronouns (especially first- and second-person pronouns) when addressing him. Once they became aware that they might be causing this grammatical delay, they promptly changed their speech, and Alex began picking up pronouns within a few weeks.

Early language is deeply rooted in the social community that nurtures young children. The conversational imperative motivates the early language duet, and baby talk provides a variable medium through which adults can structure conversation. But the social dimensions of language are not the only ingredients that determine the course of language development. Our biological makeup is an equally vital component, especially in the first few years of life.

Biological Gateways

Like any other living organism, a human child develops incrementally, with certain developmental milestones contingent on others. Infants cannot walk until their leg muscles have matured enough to hold them, and they cannot speak until their neurological, physiological, and gross motor development are sufficiently advanced.

The master gatekeeper in human development is the brain. The kinds of sounds an infant can make during his first year of life—cooing, then babbling, and finally recognizable words—are closely tied to maturation of the central nervous system.

A key neurological issue for language is **brain lateralization**. Human brains are "divided" into left and right hemispheres, with each hemisphere having specialized functions. Visual abilities are primarily centered in the right hemisphere and verbal abilities in the left. The degree of lateralization of these skills varies with age and sex, as well as with handedness (right versus left) and individual differences. Neurological studies indicate that brain lateralization (including lateralization of some language abilities) has probably begun by the time an infant is born. Over the next dozen years (but especially during the first five or six), the degree of lateralization increases, although the exact process by which (and the extent to which) it happens is still far from clear.

Since the greatest changes in lateralization seem to take place during the most intense period of language development, it seems logical that changes in lateralization help drive language learning. Unfortunately, current understanding of the human brain is not sufficient to prove (or discount) the theory. Some researchers believe that abilities in newborn infants to discriminate between sounds (abilities that depend upon lateralization) predict linguistic performance several years later, but such findings are as yet only suggestive.

Since we know that boys tend to lag somewhat behind girls developmentally, an obvious hypothesis is that brain lateralization proceeds more slowly in male children than in female. Ongoing research on children offers more contradictions than conclusions. Paradoxically, the clearest research findings indicate that *adult* men show a *greater* degree of lateralization for language-related processes than do women.

The emergence of language depends not only on neurological growth but on physical maturation (which, in turn, has neurological correlates). The very ability to speak presupposes changes in the vocal apparatus that begin taking place soon after birth. As **Chart 3** shows, vocal tract differences between newborns and adults involve not merely size but also relative placement of the component parts that enable us to speak.

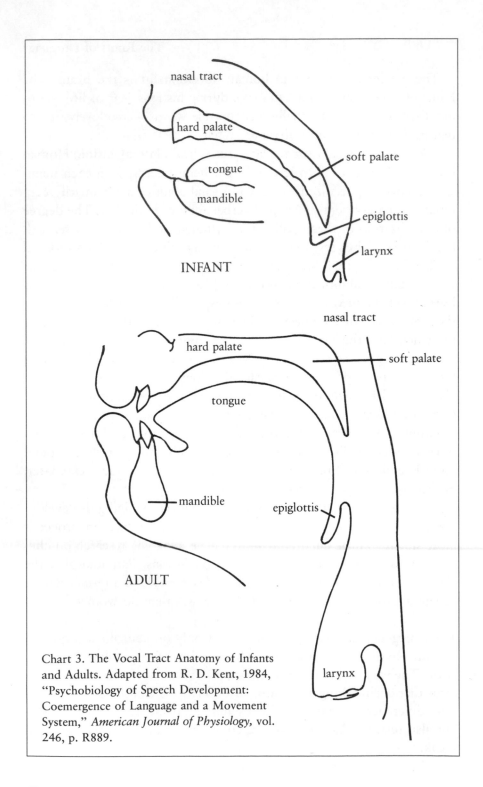

nasal tract

hard palate

soft palate

tongue

mandible

epiglottis

larynx

INFANT

nasal tract

hard palate

soft palate

tongue

mandible

epiglottis

ADULT

larynx

Chart 3. The Vocal Tract Anatomy of Infants and Adults. Adapted from R. D. Kent, 1984, "Psychobiology of Speech Development: Coemergence of Language and a Movement System," *American Journal of Physiology*, vol. 246, p. R889.

In newborns, the tongue is short and broad and is contained entirely within the oral cavity. (Only later does the rear third of the tongue descend into the neck.) The hard palate (the front part of the roof of the mouth) is also relatively short and wide, unlike the sharply arched palate in adults.

But the most critical difference for speech lies in the back of the vocal tract—in the larynx and the pharynx. The larynx ("voice box") in newborns is located just at the bottom of the oral cavity, and the pharynx (which will allow for the later production of differential sound frequencies) is not yet fully formed.

During the first year of life, the larynx descends, and a true pharynx is created. Why the anatomical shift? The early high positioning of the larynx permits human babies to breath through their noses and swallow (e.g., when sucking milk) at the same time—a highly useful combination. However, this original configuration (which approximates the vocal tract of nonhuman primates) makes it physically impossible to articulate the range of distinct sounds found in human languages. Experimental attempts in the 1940s and 1950s to teach spoken language to chimpanzees were physiologically doomed. Recognition in the 1960s of this biological roadblock led to the revised strategy of teaching chimps and gorillas linguistic signing systems, capitalizing on their natural manual dexterity.

The vocal tract continues to change up through puberty, when a child's characteristic high pitch gives way to the voice of adolescence. During this roughly twelve-year odyssey, many sound patterns are predictable from the size and shape of the vocal tract.

Infants, for example, typically go through a cooing and then an early babbling period between ages 3 and 9 months, when the sounds *k* and *g* are very common (hence, the adult words *coo* and *goo* in imitation of children's vocalizations). However, when babbling yields to articulate speech somewhere between 9 and 18 months, these *k* and *g* sounds are sometimes initially absent. What happens? The answer is anatomical. Infants, especially when lying flat on their backs, can easily produce *k* and *g* because the larynx is so high (up near the epiglottis and the soft palate). As the larynx begins to drop, producing these sounds requires more concerted effort.

Even up through age 5 or 6, children's vocal track configurations can hinder them from articulating individual sounds the way adults do. Many 2- and 3-year-olds have difficulty producing distinctions between *s* and *sh*, although they perceive the differences in the speech of others. At 2½, Sara still talked about her plastic *fis* (*fish*). At age 15 months, Ryan seemed highly sophisticated in his correct pronunciation of the word *shoe*—until you heard him ask for his *shoes* and *shocks* (*socks*). Not until over a year later did Ryan manage to pronounce a clearly recognizable *s*. Spectrograms of children's pronunciations of *s* and *sh* show that while the sounds are physically distinct, they are acoustically more like one another than the same sounds produced by adults. This greater similarity comes about because children's vocal tracts are smaller than adults', and the relative size of the glottal opening (between the vocal cords) in producing these sounds also differs from the opening in mature speakers.

What happens if a young child is temporarily hindered from vocalizing normally? A small number of children need to have an endotracheal tube inserted to facilitate breathing when the upper airway is obstructed. Recent studies of infants who had breathing tubes inserted before age 13 months (and who retained the tube for more than three months) suggest that the inability to vocalize normally as an infant or toddler can hinder language acquisition. Not only is the development of proper articulation delayed, but so is mastery of other expressive language skills. Moreover, these delays sometimes do not fully surface until children are 5 or 6 years old.

While it is obvious that the natural course of neurological and physiological development sets lower bounds on the language skills of growing children, is language acquisition also related to gross motor abilities such as moving arms and legs, sitting up, or walking? Linking language with motor development may help explain some common patterns in children's early vocalization. For example, most children pass through a period (generally between 6 and 10 months) in which their babbling consists of reduplicative syllables such as *dada*, *gaga*, or *baba*. Is it mere coincidence that reduplicative babbling generally appears around the same time that other repetitive rhythmic movements are becoming common? Researchers have suggested that reduplicative babbling may be an extension of the rhythmic movements of children's hands, arms, torsos, and legs that are so characteristic of children between the ages of 5 and 12 months.

The early language and gross motor development of Alex (who, recall, was born 6 weeks premature) lends support to the theory. Alex initially began to babble at 6 months, but compared with Sara and Ryan, he did very little babbling. He never babbled reduplicatively. And during the second half of his first year, Alex engaged in only perfunctory rhythmic movement. While 8-month-old Sara lay in her crib bicycling her legs, Alex only gave a few shoves against the crib bars. While Ryan gleefully banged both hands in unison on the dining table, Alex pounded a few times and quit.

Is gross motor development linked to subsequent language acquisition? Long-standing wisdom claims a correlation between the age at which a baby sits up, stands, or walks and emerging linguistic and intellectual abilities. A number of modern researchers have added corroborating evidence and have even argued for a relationship between early motor development and later reading skills; however, other studies have failed to reveal significant correlations between such gross motor abilities as rolling over, sitting, crawling, and walking, and toddler language skills (or general intellectual ability).

The issue of motor development raises a fundamental question about the difference between **language** and **speech**. We tend to use the terms interchangeably, although they hardly mean the same thing. Speech—the normal avenue for expressing language—is not the only option. Children suffering from cerebral palsy may develop sophisticated linguistic skills without gaining normal control over their vocal apparatus. And deaf children or hearing children of deaf parents often learn some form of signing as their native language.

In its earliest stages, the development of sign as a native language (e.g., American Sign Language, British Sign Language) proceeds at a different pace from the acquisition of spoken language. On average, while hearing children do not utter their first words until around 10 or 12 months, the first recognizable sign in children raised in signing households appears somewhere between 7 and 9 months. The ten-word landmark (again, on average) is reached at around 13 months in sign and 15 months in speech. And 50 words can generally be documented for signers at 18 months and for speakers at 19 or 20 months.

Why the discrepancies? Because of differing biological development in the visual and in the auditory cortex and because gaining motor control over the hands is easier than learning to manipulate the vocal apparatus. The visual motor region of the brain seems to mature before the speech area (Broca's area), and the visual cortex evolves more quickly than the auditory cortex. At the same time, parental input (and feedback) is simpler with sign than with speech. Parents have an easier time in modeling, manipulating, and deciphering children's physical hand movements than in influencing and making sense of children's primitive vocal attempts.

The biological fact that we are all humans ensures a high degree of commonality in the paths towards language saturation of children everywhere. Yet our biology also plays a fundamental role in distinguishing between individual children's language development. A vignette from Sara's early months illuminates what I mean:

- When she was 11 months old, Sara's paternal grandparents came to visit from Florida. Like any other proud relative, her grandmother marveled at the child's burgeoning vocabulary— already five recognizable words—and at her tentative but determined first steps. Knowingly, the grandmother mused, "All the Glovers are early talkers," referring to herself, her son, and now her grandchild.

Can we foretell a child's language development by knowing her gene pool? The value of these predictions would be enormous. If we knew that late talkers tend to beget late talkers, we would worry far less when an otherwise healthy 28-month-old hasn't yet uttered his first grammatical combination.

Anecdotes abound about genetic propensities to be early or late talkers. But is there concrete evidence?

Looking for a genetic basis for any developmental trait involves considerable detective work. In the case of long-studied diseases (such as hemophilia), sensory abnormalities (e.g., congenital deafness), or obvious physical characteristics (like hair color, general body structure, or dentition), the role of heredity is often easily established. More subtle characteristics such as the propensity to become overweight or to be shy are only now being tied to genetic explanations.

Attempts to find biological bases for cognitive skills (including language) are far more tenuous. Here, the complex balance between nature and nurture is mediated by seemingly countless variables—from maternal nutrition to fetal stress to the number of siblings at home. Although every child (and every home situation) is unique, several long-term studies have probed cognitive genetic legacies by studying twins (both those reared together and those reared apart) and adopted children. Since twins, for reasons we will explore in the next chapter, tend to follow their own special course of language learning, we will focus here on adoption studies.

The extensive Colorado Adoption Project probed genetic and environmental influences on children's individual development. Researchers were especially interested in comparing the cognitive abilities of adopted and nonadopted children with cognitive skills in their biological, adoptive, and nonadoptive parents. The data suggest that children's general intelligence correlates more clearly with biological parents than with adoptive parents and that correlations for verbal language skills become particularly clear by the time children are age 7.

Further evidence that biological parentage is a good predictor of language abilities comes from research on children who have developmental language problems. One study of second graders with difficulties in grammar, meaning, or conversational language use found that immediate members of these children's families were nine times more likely to have language problems than were the families of normal children. Another study, this one of children between ages 4 and 6 who had severe phonological problems, revealed that language disorders were common in their families as well. Still other researchers have shown that monozygotic (identical) twins are more likely than dizygotic (fraternal) twins to share problems in articulation, phonological skills, or stuttering.

Although these studies tell us little directly about early language acquisition patterns in normal children and normal families, their implications are highly suggestive. Earlier in this chapter, we saw that rates of neurological, physiological, and gross motor development can influence the rate of early language growth. We have just seen that family genetics play a significant role in the development of our physiology, personality, and cognitive abilities. The possibilities of connections are tantalizing.

When I teach courses on child language acquisition, I often pose an open-ended question on my final examination: "You have just been awarded $1 million to study any problem in language acquisition you wish. Outline your project." Many parents—myself included—would welcome this expenditure of funds on exploring whether genetic legacies influence the rate of early language development. What kind of evidence would we look for? For starters, we would ask such questions as,

> At what age did each parent begin to babble? use a first word? combine words together?
>
> Did either parent stutter as a child?
>
> Did either parent have difficulty in learning to read?

If we could control for environmental conditions (a daunting challenge), we might well find a biological explanation for at least part of the variation we see across children.

Getting to *Dada*

When does language acquisition begin? Yuppie cartoons show husbands intently reading to their pregnant wife's abdomen. Some medical practitioners have taken the image seriously. According to Dr. F. Rene Van de Carr, a California obstetrician, fetal learning can begin several months after conception, and so he founded Prenatal University to train parents-to-be how to get a head start on early pedagogy. Dr. Van de Carr suggests, for example, that mothers begin stroking their abdomens and saying, "Stroke, I'm stroking you," and that families make prenatal audiotapes (to be played daily with headphones on the broadened belly) to introduce Mom and Dad ahead of time, so they won't be strangers in the delivery room.

Can unborn babies really understand sounds from the outside world? Contemporary research shows that sometime between 24 and 28 weeks of gestation (during the sixth month of pregnancy), fetuses respond to sounds. The question is, What do they hear?

For years, reports have trickled in that unborn babies register differential responses to music heard in the womb. One audiological study notes, for example, that when mothers-to-be listened to Mozart or Vivaldi, the fetal heart rates of their babies became steadier and the level of kicking decreased. Other selected forms of music (from Beethoven to rock) generated more violent fetal kicking.

But what about fetal perception of human speech? A team of scientists in France has been studying the reception of actual human voices from the baby's vantage point. After inserting a small microphone into the uterus to pick up speech from the "outside" and recording what was received "inside," the researchers played the tape back to independent observers. Of the 3000 sounds recorded, the observers were able to recognize only 30 percent of them. However, when the recording of a nursery rhyme (received in the womb) was analyzed by special equipment, it became obvious that the intonation pattern on the tape was perfectly received in utero. While individual sounds are probably not perceived prenatally in any reliably distinct way, intonation patterns (what in Chapter 1 I called the overarching melody features) are.

These findings may account for some fascinating data on the auditory preferences of newborn infants. One group of psychologists has been studying how much fetuses have already learned about sounds by the time they are born. The researchers used a special nonnutritive sucking technique, where newborns easily learn to suck in one of two patterns on a nipple attached to a tape recorder to choose between two recorded voice messages. In one study, the first recording was of the baby's mother and the second of another woman's voice. The newborns' sucking preferences were to hear their own mothers' voices, suggesting familiarity from close contact over the months while in the womb.

A second experiment, again using the sucking choice technique, called upon mothers during their last 6½ weeks of pregnancy to read to their fetuses, twice a day, Dr. Seuss's rhyme-filled book *The Cat in the Hat*. Once the babies were born, experimenters offered them the opportunity to choose (through the appropriate sucking pattern) to hear their mothers read either *The Cat in the Hat* or another children's poem, *The King, the Mice, and the Cheese*, which has a different metric pattern. The newborns preferred *The Cat in the Hat*. Both of these studies suggest not only that infants can distinguish intonational differences before birth but also that they can remember what they heard before entering the outside world.

When do infants begin to distinguish between the several dozen distinct sounds in a language? While researchers have demonstrated that infants in the first few weeks of life can perceptually distinguish between basic speech sounds, it is not clear that these initial inborn skills carry over beyond age 6 or 7 months (much as newborns lose their initial ability to "walk" or infants lose their early facility in pronouncing *k* or *g*). It seems that children need to begin all over again by the time they start formulating recognizable words.

Most of what we know about young children's evolving linguistic abilities comes from the sounds they actually produce. What are the roots of articulate speech? Let's listen in.

Early Sounds

Ten-week-old Ryan was crying. What was the problem? Ryan's mother was not sure. Hunger? Ryan rejected the bottle outright. Wetness? A quick check ruled out that possibility. Too hot or cold? The room was a steady seventy degrees. Perhaps Ryan was lonely, and some holding or rocking would help. These moves only made matters worse. The crying continued and, in desperation, his mother started her blind round of possible remedies over again.

In nearly all babies, the meanings of one or two cries (e.g., of intense pain) are easy to identify. But what about the rest of the loud vocalizations that characterize infancy? Many parents claim they can discern distinctive cries when their babies are hungry or uncomfortable or want attention, though other parents believe no such differences exist in infants' vocalizations. Over a century ago, Charles Darwin claimed that babies cry differently when they are hungry than when they are in pain, but more recent studies have failed to garner conclusive evidence that infant cries are perceptually distinguishable or even that they are phonetically distinct.

Why do numbers of parents maintain they can detect different meanings in their infants' cries? Context is one explanation. The fact that a baby has just fallen, has been left alone too long, or is past her regular feeding time leads the listener to read meaning into the child's vocalization. Such inferences often transcend the acoustic information given. (In fact, we have no independent evidence that babies themselves are conscious of the source of their unhappiness, much as adults sometimes become grumpy when they are hungry but don't recognize why they are in ill humor.) Another possibility is that the experiments to date are flawed in design. Most studies have kept the length and intensity of crying constant and studied only qualitative differences in cries. Some researchers have suggested that the real differences lie in length of crying and in growing intensity over time, variables that have received very little attention. And there is always the possibility that some children really do vary their cries while others do not.

The first discernible noises that genuinely sound language-like typically appear around age 2 to 4 months. From deep in the back of the throat emanates a sequence sounding like *ku* or *gu*. As we have already seen, **cooing** is a physiological, not a linguistic, development, since the ability to coo disappears with normal maturation of the vocal tract.

Somewhere between 4 and 8 months, most children begin playing with sounds in patterns we call **babbling**. Babbling means what it intuitively seems to: making language-like sounds that have no identifiable meaning.

What kinds of sounds do children babble? Babies have been known to utter sounds not only unknown in the language of the community around them but even unknown in any language on record. It used to be said that children babble all the sounds possible in human language, but that claim is clearly wrong. Moreover, some children are prolific babblers, and others are not.

Common early babbling sounds include single vowels, consonants that stop the flow of air in the mouth (e.g., *p, b, t, d*), nasals (*m, n*), and consonant-vowel combinations. By age 6 months to a year, most children babble extended sequences of sounds, often repeating (or **reduplicating**) the same syllable (e.g., *papapa*). However, as we saw with Alex (who had no two-syllable utterances until well after his second birthday), reduplicative babbling is not universal.

If babbled sounds have no meaning, why do infants and toddlers babble? Largely for the same reasons they crawl and turn over and throw things out of their crib: to exercise their bodies and explore the world. Listen to—and watch—a 6- or 7-month-old babbling. His mouth has the plasticity of an accordion: opening and closing, narrowing and widening. Sound wells up inside from the throat, and then the articulators go to work. The lips happen to clamp shut, and you hear a *p*. The tongue gets stuck in the middle, and a *t* comes out. The velum (at the back end of the soft palate) flips down, and you get an *n*. To say that the child "intends" to babble one sound or another is to forget that sound-making at this stage is overwhelmingly a form of play.

A second function of babbling is to make social contact. If you don't know the words, you can at least go through the motions. Some 8- or 9-month-old babblers are already accomplished conversationalists. They know when it's their time to "speak" and when to be quiet. In the later stages of babbling, many children incorporate a number of intonation features from the surrounding language community, making their vocalizations sound deceptively speech-like.

As adults, we vary a good deal in when we tend to talk. Some of us prattle on when driving with a companion, while other relish the silence. Babies also differ in when they like to babble. Outgoing babies like Sara, for whom babbling is primarily a vehicle for social interaction, typically are at peak form when in "conversation" with adults. Other infants, like Alex, are most circumscribed in their choice of babbling venues. For nearly six months, Alex's two exclusive times for babbling were on the changing table (when he was literally face-to-face with his mother or father) and when sitting in his high chair with his mouth full of food.

Is there any linguistic future in babbling? The answer depends in part on a child's babbling style. Not all children babble the same amount, the same number of sounds, or for the same number of months. Some children, like Sara, cease babbling around the time they utter their first word (typically around 12 months), while others (such as Ryan) continue babbling for at least another year, by which time they may have spoken vocabularies of several dozen words. Still other children, including Alex, progress in stages. Alex had babbled desultorily from about age 6 to 12 months. He then switched his attention to words for the next half-year, only to launch a babbling renaissance at 18 months, which would continue for nearly a year.

For children who cease babbling before the community reinforces particular sounds the children are producing, we hardly expect to find much continuity between babbling and speech. However, for children whose babbling elides into speech or continues alongside words for some months, there is growing evidence that the sounds of late babbling become the sounds of early speech.

First Words

> Someone was pumping water. Annie placed Helen's hands under the spout and "as the cool stream gushed over one hand, she spelled into the other the word *water*, first slowly, then rapidly. I stood still, my whole attention fixed upon the motions of her fingers. Suddenly I felt a misty consciousness as of something forgotten—a thrill of returning thought; and somehow the mystery of language was revealed to me. I knew then that W-A-T-E-R meant the wonderful cool something that was flowing over my hand. . . . I left the well-house eager to learn. Everything had a name, and each name gave birth to a new thought. As we returned to the house every object which I touched seemed to quiver with life."

Until she was 19 months old, Helen Keller had been a normally developing, bright child, who was already speaking some words, including *wah-wah* for "water." Then a high fever (of unknown cause) rendered her deaf and blind, and she gradually stopped uttering even the words she had once known. Five years later, under the guidance of Annie Sullivan, Helen Keller experienced an ephiphany that day at the well: words have meaning.

It is tempting to assume that all people undergo an *aha* experience about the time they begin to talk. Among children and adults who do not learn language at the usual time due to physical disabilities (such as Helen Keller or deaf adults who don't learn spoken or signed language as children), such *aha* experiences have sometimes been reported. Yet for normally developing children, the transition to meaning is usually more like focusing the lens of a camera to bring an already present object into sharp focus.

By the time they begin using recognizable words, children with normal hearing have been barraged with language by parents and other caretakers (including television) for thousands of hours. In the average household, a few dozen labels for objects and actions (including such words as *mommy, daddy, milk, no,* and *up*) have especially high frequencies in the language adults emphasize to very young children. Typically children show signs of understanding dozens of words (e.g., by pointing to a picture in a book or selecting an item from a high chair tray) months or, in some cases, years before speaking the words themselves. However, given the extraordinary problem of assessing infants' language comprehension, we can only say with certainty that most children understand some words between ages 6 months and a year.

Where do children's first spoken words come from? A combination of sounds and meanings.

The sound component may originate from a number of sources. Sounds occurring in first words often echo words frequently used in children's presence. The first word of one of my colleague's children was *turtle*, pronounced (so I am told) with all the requisite consonants and vowels. The family had a music box in the shape of a turtle, which the boy often played with and which his mother often referred to by name.

More commonly, the source is sounds children are babbling about the time they utter their first word. Though not all children have the same favorite babble sounds, many heavily use *duh* (or *da, dada,* or *duhduh*) in the later months of babbling. Why the preference for *duh*? Because it is so easy to say. Try it out, starting with your mouth in repose and feeling where your tongue is. Now push your tongue off the roof of your mouth like a diver off a springboard, let your vocal cords vibrate, and open wide. The result: *duh*.

But what does *duh* mean? And how does it get its meaning?

A common source of early word meaning is unintentional Skinnerian shaping. In behavioral psychology, animals are reinforced for emitting behaviors that the experimenter wants to establish. Typically the animal does something accidentally (like pressing a lever at the end of its cage). Immediately the action is rewarded (e.g., a food pellet drops out of a hopper). The animal learns to associate that action with a reward.

Children on the verge of uttering a first word are generally active babblers. By the conversational imperative, such babbling primes parents to find meaning in children's vocalizations. Upon hearing

"*Duhduh*"

when Sara's father leaned down to give his daughter a kiss, the elated family reinforced Sara's behavior, proclaiming,

"Yes, that's daddy! Did you hear, everyone? Sara just said *daddy!*"

and conferring many rounds of kisses on Sara.

Perhaps Sara really did say *daddy* on her own. Yet she may also have been emitting a meaningless babble of *duhduh*, much like a rat tripping over a lever. That babble then acquired meaning through parental rein-forcement.

How often is teaching rather than independent innovation the source of a child's first word? We do not know. Obviously we cannot ask the child. Even watching the phenomenon unfold before your eyes, you would often be hard pressed to know for sure who originated the meaning.

In some cases, children clearly select their own early words. A child fixated on boats may well have *buh* as a first identifiable word. Children have been known to light upon *no*—hardly a word that parents inten-tionally reinforce. The first word of Ryan, who had been in full-time day care since age 6 months, was *mine*, learned from the constant proc-lamations of competitive (and vocal) 2-year-olds at his center.

Yet other times, children take sounds they readily babble and pair them with meanings in which they are interested. Alex's first word was *duh*, but it didn't mean "daddy." When he was 12 months old, Alex's mother had taken him for an afternoon in the local park. Sitting in his stroller, Alex spied a dog. He had seen dogs before, in both picture books and real life but had never shown much interest in them. This occasion was different. With finger outstretched, Alex threw back his head and exclaimed,

"*Duh!*"

The first word was born.

A few days later, mother and son were back in the park, the destina-tion being a pond that served as home to a dozen ducks. On earlier walks, they had stopped to feed the ducks, but Alex generally hoarded the bread for himself. This time, when his mother asked,

"How about feeding the ducks, Alex?"

his response was a gleeful

"*Duh.*"

A second word was born. What about *duh* for "daddy"? That move took another three months.

The task of identifying children's first words is often fraught with problems. For all our desire to read meaning into babble, we may over-look meaningful utterances we do not understand. While Alex's *duh* conveniently bore phonological resemblance to *dog* and *duck* and was uttered in their immediate presence, Ryan's mother was hardly expecting *muh* (= *mine*) as a first word and failed to notice it until several weeks after its first appearance.

We also need to keep in mind that when children begin using words to refer to objects and events in the real world, their meaning for a word is probably not the same as ours. By the time we become adults, we have built up complex definitional networks, based on a wealth of experiences of using words in varied contexts and years of schooling during which we are taught to define words in isolation. Children's introductions to the world of meaning typically involve isolated words used in highly specific situations. A child's use of the word *daddy* may refer to all men, not exclusively his progenitor. *Mommy* might mean "Give me comfort" and not refer to people at all. In hearing children's early words, adults have no clear way of figuring out what their child's initial words really mean. During the second year of life, children's word meanings may be equally idiosyncratic, but it gradually becomes easier to puzzle out what children intend when they talk.

■ IDEAS AND ALERTS

How Can I Help?

Be an active conversational partner.

Initiate conversation with your infant, especially if he or she tends to be a quiet child. One-sided conversations may at first seem unnatural, especially to first-time parents (or parents who have never had pets). In short order, though, you will come to feel at ease.

If your infant has other siblings close in age or is in a day-long child care program, take special care to ensure your baby gets adequate language stimulation from adults. The more you talk with your infant individually, the better off both of you will be.

Talk as if your infant understands what you are saying.

When I was in the tenth grade, my biology teacher stunned his students by referring to us as "Miss Schafer" or "Mr. Schreiber"—not as "Ellen" or "Jerry." His strategy of treating us like adults induced us to think like adults and talk like budding biologists. In the same way, parents can generate self-fulfilling prophecies by addressing their young children as if they understand what is being said. While the process may take four or five years, children gradually rise to match the language model presented to them.

For parents whose children have encountered an early biological setback (such as prematurity, hearing impairment, blindness, or a tracheotomy curtailing normal vocalization), presenting an active and rigorous language model becomes especially important. All too often parents talk down to—or do not talk at all to—such children, with the expected unfortunate results.

Use a language style with which you are comfortable.

Don't worry about how you sound to other adults when you talk with your child. Whatever baby talk style makes you comfortable will best help you and your child establish conversational rapport. Your affect, not your content, is more important at this stage.

Avoid excessive use of pacifiers.

While pacifiers can be very helpful in calming infants, their use should be monitored. It stands to reason that children whose gums are clamped around a pacifier cannot freely vocalize. Excessive use of pacifiers can be especially problematic as children become toddlers and active users of intelligible language. I have seen toddlers need to remove their own pacifiers when they wish to speak, hardly a condition encouraging language learning.

Should I Be Concerned?

How long will it take my premature child to catch up linguistically?

Each year, nearly 10 percent of all babies born in the United States are premature (at least three weeks early). Premature babies who have no other physical problems (e.g., retardation, blindness, low birth weight for the gestation period) are often slower to mature (including linguistically) than normal-term babies. Although experts differ in their prognoses, one of the most thorough studies suggests that by age 4, most premature children have caught up linguistically. (Compare this finding with premature babies at 9 months: While fewer than 10 percent of the preemies in one study had any recognizable words, 80 percent of the control group spoke between one and three words.) Some of the delay may be neurological, but in other cases, the main issue is that the vocal apparatus needs time to mature.

What can parents do to help? Interact with premature babies no differently than you would with term babies. Parents who persist in talking with their babies—even when the babies show little response and initiate very little vocalization on their own—will eventually reap the benefits of these linguistic efforts.

What if my baby doesn't vocalize spontaneously or in response to my conversational initiatives?

In children less than a year old, it is sometimes extremely difficult to figure out why they do little vocalizing. Even infants who are subsequently diagnosed as deaf or profoundly hard of hearing typically vocalize and coo normally up to around age 4 to 6 months. (Problems with hearing-impaired children often first become evident around age 6 months, when their babbling takes an abnormal phonological path.)

Prematurity or physical disability at birth can also restrict early vocalization. Premature babies are often quieter than infants born at term and less likely to vocalize or to respond to speech from others. Babies with physical problems (e.g., in breathing, in controlling the muscles that produce speech) may need professional intervention to facilitate normal development.

Finally, some babies are simply quieter than others. As with premature infants, the best strategy is for adults to continue upholding both sides of the conversation without overwhelming the baby with constant stimulation.

Can ear infections affect language development?

Young children are highly susceptible to otitis media, an inflammation of the middle ear, with effusion (that is, a collection of fluid). In acute otitis media, the middle ear becomes infected. In secretory otitis media, fluid accumulates in the middle ear, without accompanying infection. By the time children are 3 years old, about one-third have had at least three episodes of acute otitis media. More than two-thirds have experienced at least one middle ear infection.

Otitis media can affect children's hearing. During an episode of inflammation, children have some degree of hearing loss, although normal hearing generally returns. If children have recurrent ear problems, hearing can be affected over an extended period. Since otitis media (with accompanying hearing loss) is especially common during the second six months of life, a critical time for babies making the transition from random babbling to echoing sounds heard in the community, otitis media can potentially hamper language acquisition.

Research indicates that persistent ear problems (and temporary hearing loss) can affect language development in children as young as 1 year and perhaps up through the early school years. One study showed that 1-year-olds with a history of otitis media had lower expressive language scores than babies who were free of otitis media. The data suggest that children who suffer from otitis media over extended periods of time are prone to have lower language scores in the second and third years of life as well. There may even be a relationship between the number of days below age 3 that a child has otitis media and subsequent phonological problems among 7- or 8-year-olds.

Since otitis media (and the accompanying temporary partial hearing loss) are so common, parents should not rush their children into invasive medical procedures (such as draining the ear). However, prompt attention to occurrences of otitis media (often signaled by infants and toddlers pulling at their ears) can help stem the fluid buildup or infection. In the case of recurrent ear problems, it can also help prevent prolonged hearing loss and possible language delay.

What if my child doesn't have any recognizable words by age 14 or 15 months?

Every expert has a different age by which parents should become concerned if their child has not begun using recognizable words. Some suggest professional evaluation if a child is not producing words by 14 or 15 months, though more often, 18 months is taken as the far end of normal development.

What might be wrong? In many instances, nothing. As we will see in the next chapter, timing for language development in normal children is highly variable. At other times, the problem is real. The difficulty is in knowing when. After eliminating identifiable causes for a late linguistic start (e.g., prematurity, hearing problems, physical impairment, retardation, childhood autism), parents may be left with the unsettling conclusion that their child has a "language delay" of unknown etiology. Such language delays are more clearly diagnosed during the latter part of the second year of life or the beginning of the third, when most children begin combining words together. Therefore, we will wait until the end of Chapters 3 and 4 to talk about causes of and reponses to language delay.

■ 3. Language on a Shoestring
From First Words to Grammar

LIKE A NUMBER of other families attempting to lend sanity to child rearing, Sara's parents engaged a part-time housekeeper when their daughter was 12 months old. The family opted to hire a recent émigré from Nicaragua. The only hitch was that the woman spoke no English, and Sara's mother had only a smattering of Spanish.

There was no time for language lessons on either side. The housekeeper (a hard-working woman with a grammar school education) stuck to her native tongue, so Sara's mother did most of the accommodating. Relying upon whatever Spanish she could remember—a few hundred words, the present tense, and some hazy traces of once-memorized dialogs about catching a train in Madrid—she gamely struggled to explain which laundry should not go into the dryer and what time to put Sara down for her nap.

The result would hardly earn a passing grade in first-year Spanish. Sara's mother's pronunciation was highly Anglicized, the grammar was more English than Spanish, and her vocabulary was laced with descriptive phrases (e.g., *cama pequeña* [literally "bed little"] instead of the appropriate Spanish *cuna* for "crib"). Yet given their mutual desire to communicate, coupled with concrete topics of discourse (like laundry and naps), Sara's mother managed on a linguistic shoestring.

As children move from first words to grammar (usually during the latter part of their second year), they also function on a linguistic shoestring. With a dozen or so distinct sounds, an active vocabulary of anywhere from a handful to over a hundred words, and, in some cases, a little rudimentary syntax, they, like Sara's mother, begin piecing together utterances to make themselves understood.

The stage from first words to grammar is filled with immense variation. Some children cease babbling entirely, while others continue for another year or more. Spoken vocabulary may keep pace with comprehension, though for many toddlers, the gulf is vast. The "normal" spectrum for grammar ranges from no productive combinations until after age 2 years to initial combinations as early as 14 or 15 months. Yet regardless of their specific path towards grammar, children are masters of invention in their use of sound, meaning, and conversation.

The Phantom Norm

A number of years ago, I was studying a group of 1- to 3-year-old children, exploring how they learned to pronounce sound clusters like the *pl-* of *plane* or the *tr-* of *train*. The toddlers were brought each week to an empty classroom in a local nursery school, where we played informally and I recorded our conversations.

One afternoon, the mother of an articulate but shy 1½-year-old I had been working with cornered me after I completed the session with her daughter:

> "Is Alissa smart? I mean, is she *really* smart? We're planning to put her in a preschool for gifted children, and I've got to know if she's better at language than the rest of the kids here."

What could I say? Carefully I tried to explain I was only looking at a tiny segment of language development—pronunciation of a few sound combinations—but the mother refused to let go:

> "Then will you give Alissa a full set of tests—you know, there must be some tests—and write a letter I can use to prove how precocious my daughter is? 'Cause if we don't start developing her abilities now, she'll never get the right breaks in life."

Over the years, my reaction to this one pushy mother mellowed into recognition that parents naturally are concerned with assessing their offspring's development. The first hurdle for parents is to assure themselves that their son's or daughter's language development is normal.

Almost without exception, parents want to know what the average age is for children to reach such language milestones as the first word, the first 50 words, and the first syntactic combination.

But do averages make sense in the world of language learning?

As a teenager, I remember being fascinated by the statistic that American families averaged 2.3 children (plus the proverbial dog). I often tried conjuring up three-tenths of a child. Demographers' drawings of two large outline figures, coupled with two smaller shadows—plus another sliver—only fed my imagination.

As an average, the number 2.3 represented everyone by representing no one. In much the same way, the literature on child language acquisition—written by psychologists, linguists, pediatricians, speech and hearing specialists, journalists—describes average development. The problem is that while no one believes that any real family has 2.3 children, parents readily conclude that their child is at risk (or is wildly precocious) if his language deviates from the age milestones listed in a popular article or parenting book.

Parental anxiety about language development is understandably intense, especially during a child's first two or three years. Diagnostically, parents worry that failure to attain linguistic milestones "on schedule" may indicate physical or psychological maladies. Pragmatically, parents eagerly await active participation from their offspring to enhance parent-child communication. Parents seek linguistic partnership not only because of pressures from the conversational imperative but also to alleviate the frustrations of not understanding what their infant or toddler is trying to express.

As a result, parents persistently request specific ages for linguistic milestones against which to measure their child's progress. The surest cure for a fixation with precise ages for milestones is to read a cross-section of the literature and find that specialists themselves hardly agree on the average age at which early language developments take place. A review of a variety of highly credible sources—respected psychologists, pediatricians, linguists, and child development experts—leaves us with the distinct impression that a normative approach to exact language milestones can be confusing, anxiety producing, and of limited practical use.

What do the experts say? Depending upon whom you read, normal children produce their first words at age 7, 10, or 17 months; say 50 words by age 18, 24, or 26 months; and create their first word combination by age 16 months, 24 months, or as late as 30 months. Taken together, the experts offer a broad ballpark estimate on the stages and ages of normal language development. But to make sense of where in the spectrum a particular child falls—to decide whether to be concerned—parents need to understand how and why children differ in their language acquisition paths. (A comparative analysis of language milestones reported by a variety of specialists appears at the beginning of the Notes for this chapter.)

Sources of Variation

The way children learn language and the speed of that learning reflect an intertwining of biological givens, social dimensions, personality and belief structures, and perhaps intelligence.

Gender and Self-Fulfilling Prophecies

Ryan was born in late October. The summer before his fifth birthday, his mother began making plans to enroll him in the local kindergarten that fall. Handing her application to the school assistant principal, Ryan's mother met with an unanticipated response:

"I'd like to meet Ryan before placing him,"

the administrator began,

"but I suspect he'll join the pre-K class rather than enter kindergarten."

Bewildered at the prospect of her son being held back a year so early in life, Ryan's mother retorted,

"I was born in November, and I was never grouped with children younger than me!"

The assistant principal smiled knowingly:

"But Ryan's a boy."

At least up through adolescence, boys tend to lag behind girls developmentally. Differences are evident from the start. Pregnancies are more subject to spontaneous abortion or stillbirth with males than with females. Females mature faster in the uterus and have consistently higher Apgar scores at birth. (The ten-point Apgar test measures color, heart rate, muscle tone, reflex irritability, and respiratory effort one minute and five minutes after birth.) Boys are more prone to cerebral palsy, autism, and learning disorders. Boys vocalize less as infants and trail several weeks behind girls in uttering first words and in reaching a 50-word vocabulary. Over the next four or five years, the number of boys with developmental language problems is likely to be at least double that of girls. And social development in boys typically lags behind that of same-aged girls.

Why these differences? Some of the variation stems from sex-linked disparities in biological maturation, but social factors are equally critical.

The first trip Alex's mother made to purchase baby clothes occurred under strained circumstances. Since her son was born more than a month before she planned to buy his layette, she found herself with a week-old baby still clad in hospital-issue T-shirts. Reaching the store a few minutes before closing, she hurriedly asked where to find clothes for newborns.

"Boy or girl?"

the woman behind the counter asked with measured tone.

Boy or girl? Alex's mother was shopping for a tiny creature more resembling Yoda from *The Empire Strikes Back* than the cherubs on a diaper box. Newborns do have some ability to distinguish colors, but there is no evidence for sex-linked preference. Yet positioned to the right were serried ranks of pink kimonos and smocks, and to the left, their blue counterparts.

Gender stereotypes such as these pervade the American fabric. Do parents also speak differently to male infants and toddlers than to females?

Many researchers have reported that American mothers talk more with their daughters than with their sons. One study revealed that mothers were more likely to imitate the vocalizations of infant daughters than of infant sons. Another found evidence that mothers vocalized more to 1-year-old daughters than to 1-year-old sons. And a third noted that mothers talked more to 2-year-old daughters than to 2-year-old sons.

When mothers converse with their children, what do they talk about?

One expert on children's language development reports that American parents tend to use more words about feelings and emotions when they read to toddler girls than in reading to same-aged boys. Not surprisingly, by age 2, girls have the edge over boys in vocabulary conveying emotions or feelings. Two researchers studying the speech of upper-middle-class mothers to their 2-year-old boys and girls report that mothers with daughters were more likely to ask questions, repeat their children's utterances, and use long sentences themselves than mothers with sons. At the same time, the mothers of boys are more prone to use imperatives than mothers of girls. Parental baby talk features such as questions, repetitions, and expansions of children's utterances help promote conversation and facilitate children's language learning. The differential implications for development in boys versus girls are obvious.

In marked contrast, a study done in Greece concluded that young boys, not girls, seemed to have the linguistic advantage. Unlike their American counterparts, the infant males in this study vocalized more than the females. Why? Their adult caretakers (the children were orphans) vocalized more to the boys than to the girls—a reflection of Greek attitudes about the relative importance of male offspring.

How do children respond to language addressed to them? Studies have repeatedly shown that the amount that parents converse with children directly correlates (under normal circumstances) with children's early language acquisition. Differing patterns of conversation with boys versus girls can directly affect the rate at which males and females learn to speak, not to mention the kinds of language they begin using. Unwitting assumptions we make early in children's lives about how we should talk with them can generate self-fulfilling prophecies about linguistic growth.

Acquisition in Context

Gender is but one strand in the familial web in which a child is reared. Many other social dimensions shape the direction and timing of a child's language acquisition, including parents' educational accomplishments, levels of tension in the household, attitudes towards discipline, the amount that adults in the house read, and policies on watching television.

But probably the single most important household variable is the company the child keeps. Is she an only child? a twin? a younger sibling? How much direct language (and of what kind) do adults direct to the child, and to what extent is language modeled by age-mates? Depending on the number of players in the conversation—a duet, a trio, or even a quartet—young children generally adopt a language learning strategy that reflects their family circumstances.

As they start using identifiable words, children tend to cluster into two strategy groups. I'll describe the pure types, understanding that many children fall somewhere in between.

The first group (exemplified by Sara) begins using first words fairly early—often by 9 or 10 months. Their first 50 words or so are generally names referring to physical objects (including people) in the immediate surroundings. This early language style has been dubbed **referential** by psychologist Katherine Nelson.

Referential children are likely to have clearly articulated language. (Parents can generally understand what these toddlers are saying.) By the time referential children reach age 1½, they typically go through a rapid vocabulary spurt. As they begin using grammar, referential children are more likely to venture forth with their own word combinations than echo language they have heard from parents or older siblings.

Children in the second group (of which Ryan is a good example) are likely to be a little slower in beginning to talk, with first words often not appearing until age 12 to 14 months. The early meaningful utterances are more diverse, including phrases along with single words, and focusing on social interaction as well as on objects. Children following this **expressive** style are likely to have among their first few dozen utterances words (and phrases) like *please, thank you,* or *jump up.* They are also prone to acquire new vocabulary more gradually than their referential counterparts, sidestepping a marked vocabulary spurt.

One difficulty in studying the language of expressive children is that their pronunciation is not always clear, making it a challenge for parents to distinguish meaningful words or phrases from babbling. Expressive children are also more likely to echo the conversation of adults as they make their way to productive control over grammar.

What do referential and expressive styles have to do with family context? The early language style children adopt closely reflects the language they hear from adults. Referential parents tend to raise children with early referential language learning styles, and expressive parents are likely to rear expressive children. Referential mothers talk a great deal about objects in the environment and ask a lot of questions, and expressive mothers are more prone to use language geared to social activity or conversational formulas.

But what shapes parents' language styles? In middle-class America, a major determining factor is the number of children in the household. Referential children tend to be firstborn progeny, while expressive children are more likely to be younger siblings or twins. The same parents are prone to address their firstborn in a referential style (with predictable results) and to speak to their secondborn in a more expressive style (again, with the expected outcome).

Why? Because of the practical question of time. Time is always scarce in raising children. It is especially scarce when raising twins.

Suppose you have 180 minutes a day (the equivalent of three hours of nonstop talk) to converse one-on-one with your 4-month-old. Having twins immediately halves the talk time. Since the less language adults address to a child, the slower that child's early language development tends to be, it is hardly surprising that twins, on average, are slower to begin talking.

Are twins actually language delayed (a condition often requiring intervention from a specialist), or are they following a reasonable path of language acquisition, given their circumstances? Keeping track of and attending to the needs of two small children at once generates a complex set of conversational patterns, including parents speaking to both children simultaneously, parents speaking to one child but the other child listening, and both children speaking at once. Parents are hard pressed to spend time individually with each child in labeling objects or asking questions and awaiting answers. The result is a parental language style that is more social than referential, more controlling than open-ended. Twins are more prone to develop an expressive approach to language learning, which tends to be slower than the referential approach typical of firstborn children, who benefit from parents' undivided linguistic attention.

Some fascinating language patterns emerge from the unique conversational montage in families with twins. Young twins often function as a linguistic team, with one child answering the first part of an adult's question and the other supplying the rest. Twins compete for airtime with each other. They are exceptionally quick in responding to conversational openings. And while the amount of language spoken by twins is generally less than that of only children, the words twins do utter come out at a faster clip.

The twin situation—and the expressive language it engenders among parents and children—is hardly unique. A mother with a 4-year-old and an infant is caught in a similar linguistic bind. With two young children (even separated by several years), parents cannot engage in the same amount of individual conversation as with one. Adults must make compromises, and the younger child usually ends up with the shorter straw.

What is different about the language mothers address to their younger child when alone with her than when caring for an older child at the same time? One researcher showed that in households with a preschooler and a 1-year-old, mothers directed less "naming" language ("That's a duck, Sara") to the 1-year-old when the older child was present than when the mother and the younger child were alone as a dyad. Another study reported a similar discrepancy when mothers were reading stories to children. In one part of the experiment, mothers read stories only to their 2-year-olds, while in the second setting, both their 2-year-olds and their 4-year-olds were present. When both children heard the story together, the younger child regularly lost out in the conversational exchange. If the mother asked questions about the story, the older child responded to more than half the mother's queries before the younger child had a chance to speak up. In fact, the younger children's linguistic participation during these triadic reading sessions dropped to half the level of when mothers read to the younger children alone.

Studies of language development among young children in extended day care and nursery programs are still in their infancy; however, research thus far supports common sense. In settings with a small ratio of children to staff, children's language learning progresses well. In programs with more children per staff member, adult caregivers direct less language to the children, with the expected results of comparatively slower language growth.

Parents who leave their young children in full-time day care programs also contribute to the linguistic mix. One study of children in a middle-class nursery school found that parents with children in the program spent more time just in the evenings and weekends talking with their sons and daughters than did a control group of families whose young children were home all day, every day. We cannot assume that having a child (even an only child) at home with a parent will ensure that the adult is spending a lot of time in conversation with her child. And we also cannot presuppose that two children in the same all-day nursery program receive comparable amounts of linguistic attention at home.

Do children raised with other children—twins, younger siblings, children in formal day care programs or neighborhood play groups—ever have the linguistic edge over only children? The availability of a playmate who has ample time to "talk" often provides these infants and toddlers an advantage in early conversational skills. Since children left to themselves typically play *and talk*, what siblings or playmates may miss out on in vocabulary and grammar models is often balanced by rich experience in conversation with peers.

Personality and Presupposition

Beyond biology, beyond the family constellation, lie individuals. Each child has his own personality, and each parent has presuppositions about children and child rearing. How do these unique characteristics affect the course of language learning?

Individuality manifests itself in diverse ways during the first two years of life. A socially outgoing infant tends to vocalize more than a quiet child. A risk-taking toddler who plows ahead on stairs (only to stumble and pick herself up again) is more likely to attempt a word she can't quite pronounce than a more cautious youngster who takes one stair at a time—and leaves the word unsaid. An independent-minded 18- or 20-month old is less likely to imitate words and phrases spoken by others than a more socially directed child, who may shadow the words (and actions) of parent and peer alike. Children who are patient tend to practice new words and phrases and to take correction from adults; impulsive children do not.

The unique personalities of Sara, Ryan, and Alex emerging during their first few years created three very different paths to learning language. An outgoing, independent risk taker, Sara treated language like the rest of her toys: a challenge, a source of pleasure, but rarely a hurdle to overcome. Sara never hesitated to vocalize (she was a prolific babbler, especially when people were around) and later try out new words. As she edged toward syntax, she rarely spontaneously imitated anyone else's language and resisted correction from others.

Ryan was as cautious as Sara was flamboyant. Though he vocalized and babbled as an infant, Ryan often did so in isolation (in his crib at the day care center or at home). A happy but shy child, Ryan spent many hours shadowing his sister, Cathy, four years his senior. His major source of new words and phrases was imitation of Cathy's language.

Alex's personality was harder to peg. At first a very quiet and cautious baby, he gradually became more outgoing and more of a risk taker. When he first learned to climb stairs, Alex took great care with every step. Alex also chose silence rather than risk mispronouncing a sound or syllable. A turning point came at age 2;6, when Alex began using two-syllable (and two-word) utterances. Now he initiated conversations, tried out new words (often getting them wrong), and finally became a danger on the stairs. Yet strands of the earlier social caution remained. Until he was nearly 4 years old, Alex parroted much of the language (and actions) of parents and playmates. Such imitation eventually proved a boon to language, as Alex shot ahead of his age-mates in vocabulary and grammatical sophistication.

What about Sara, Ryan, and Alex's parents? How did their own presuppositions about children (and children's language) contribute to the acquisition story? Parents approach child rearing with a host of preconceptions about when children learn to talk, whether children understand more than they can say, the best age for learning to read. We also come with assumptions about our responsibilities as parents: Do parents play a major role in children's language development? Is baby talk helpful or an impediment? These attitudes toward language are often unconscious, emerging only as we watch ourselves raise our children.

Sara's parents represent the attitudes of the majority of educated, solidly middle-class families. In their eyes, children essentially learn language on their own, though a nurturing environment at home is essential. They assume parents should respond to their child's lead, in both language and developmental activities more generally.

Ryan's mother typifies the bulk of middle America that does not give language learning much thought, except when something goes awry. Like spring flowers, language grows in its own good time, given the barest of nurturing ingredients. Less anxious than more upwardly mobile parents such as Sara's about the precise age at which her son would pass various linguistic milestones, Ryan's mother was also less conscientious in using open-ended (rather than directive) language with her children. She made no special efforts to offset the conditions that led Ryan to develop an expressive language learning strategy (being a male second-born child of a single working parent).

What about Alex's parents—the most highly educated of the lot? While inexperienced in child rearing (neither had younger siblings), they assumed that the more you surround your child with language, the more the child stands to benefit. If anything, Alex's parents went overboard, rarely letting up in their constant language stream during Alex's first two years. When Alex finally began initiating conversation shortly after age 2½, his parents consciously had to stifle their entrenched habits of posing and then answering their own questions.

Gender, social context, and personality all contribute to the mix determining when and how an individual child begins using language. Is intelligence also a factor?

Do Bright Kids Talk Early?

For most of this century, observers of young children have hinted that early language development is a key sign of intelligence. Contemporary research has tended to confirm these assumptions. A group at Johns Hopkins University in Baltimore, for example, reports correlations between IQ at age 1 and the speed with which children pass a variety of linguistic milestones during the first two years of life, as well as between IQ at age 3 and rate of early vocabulary development.

Yet however intuitively appealing the connection between language and IQ, we must resist hasty conclusions. The number of confounding variables in language studies (not to mention IQ studies) is immense: sex, physical maturation, birth order, personality, parenting style, reliability of the testing procedure. Not surprisingly, additional investigations question the solidity of these intuitively obvious correlations between language and IQ.

The group at Johns Hopkins explored whether developmental milestones (age of walking, age of speaking two-word sentences) correlated with standardized IQ tests and if either measure predicted subsequent intellectual giftedness at age 7. The fragility of their results indicates how carefully studies such as these must be interpreted. When taken as a *group*, the children later diagnosed as "gifted" were found to have walked almost a month earlier and to have used two-word sentences more than eight weeks earlier than their "nongifted" counterparts. Similarly, the group scores for early intelligence tests correlated with a later assessment of giftedness. However, when the gross motor, language, and early IQ scores were examined for *individual* children, they were no longer reliable predictors of later intelligence.

Can the addition of other variables help sort out whether early language development is a sign of subsequent high IQ? One intriguing possibility comes from the work of Nancy Bayley, developer of the Bayley Scales of Infant Development (see the Notes for this chapter). Bayley has never claimed that her tests predict intelligence in later childhood or beyond. However, she and her colleagues reported an intriguing finding a number of years ago. While the language test items from Bayley's infant assessments showed no correlation with adult intelligence among *males*, a correlation did appear between infant language scales and adult IQ among *females*. Since linguistically, little boys tend to be late bloomers, Bayley's findings suggest that sex issues may well confound the entire language-IQ discussion.

If linguistic development might predict later IQ, do early IQ scores tell us anything about later language? One investigator found that IQ tests administered to babies from 4 to 18 months old correlated with a developmental language test given at age 2. Such findings may offer a prospective window on which infants are likely to have linguistic (or cognitive) difficulties in the future.

However, we must temper such predictions with appropriate auxiliary information. In Bayley's study, the level of social and linguistic stimulation in the home typically overrode early IQ as a predictor of language at age 2. Infants whose early IQ scores were low tended to be linguistically normal at age 2 if their families provided a nurturing social and cognitive environment. Infants with initially normal IQ scores often showed developmental problems at age 2 when their families offered less appropriate stimulation. Such reports lend encouragement to middle- and upper-middle-class families whose children seem off to a slow developmental start but raise serious concern for children from socially impoverished backgrounds.

Another vital piece of auxiliary information is what language abilities are being measured: speaking or understanding. Does a toddler's **production** of language (the easier skill to measure) accurately reflect his **comprehension?** In many cases, the answer is no—just as among adults.

School teachers often distinguish between active and passive vocabularies—words we use ourselves in speaking or writing versus the much larger vocabulary we understand (or can puzzle out from context). The potential disparity between language produced and language comprehended can be especially stark when second languages are involved. Children whose parents are not native speakers of the surrounding community language often grow up understanding the language of their parents but not speaking it fluently. Among adults learning second languages in school, many can formulate sentences (such as requesting directions to the train station) but not comprehend the spoken response.

Young children just making their way in language vary enormously in their ratios of comprehension to production. Typically children understand the meanings of some words (how many is very difficult to test) before they utter their own first word. When functioning on a linguistic shoestring, the discrepancy between comprehension and production can be immense, with a child spontaneously uttering, say, a dozen words, but clearly understanding the meaning of several hundred (as measured, for example, by identifications in a picture dictionary). Such passive vocabulary provides an immediate source of future spoken words.

Yet not all children follow this pattern. In many instances, comprehension and production keep reasonable pace with one another from the start. (That pace may be rapid or laconic.) A third possibility is for children to use words they do not understand or that they understand only partially. Many children as young as 18 to 20 months know the names of half a dozen colors but have not figured out which color goes with which name. The same is true for the directions "right" and "left"—a problem some people retain through adulthood.

Why this variation? Biologically, genetics (including sex and perhaps family propensity) or prematurity can delay the onset of articulate speech. Socially, children who receive less individual linguistic attention from adults are likely to be slower talkers, although we know little about their relative comprehension of language. Children with shy personalities are often slow to verbalize, though their level of understanding may be high.

Do bright children talk early? Albert Einstein did not. Einstein himself reported in a letter written in 1954 that

> my parents were worried because I started to talk comparatively late, and they consulted the doctor because of it. I cannot tell how old I was at the time, but certainly not younger than three.

Early speech may be a sign of intellectual potential, though slower vocal development often says little about IQ. Since a rich conversational environment provides a gateway to language as well as to cognitive growth, the language parents address to a child is almost certain to bear fruit, immediately or in the future.

Children approach language learning through diverse paths. Where do these paths lead in the odyssey from first words to grammar?

Juice Crayons: Language on a Shoestring

By the time she was 20 months old, Sara had learned to name 10 colors: red, blue, green, yellow, white, black, pink, purple, brown, and orange. Although she had problems with the initial *or-* in *orange*, Sara managed to pronounce a word approximating *o-enge*, used to label both the color and the fruit.

About the same time, Sara's mother began attempting to expand her daughter's gastronomic horizons. Sara had always been a good milk drinker, but she eschewed juice. Sara's mother tried a new tack: squeezing fresh orange juice. The two developed a morning ritual in which Sara selected two oranges, and her mother sliced and squeezed them. The novelty worked; Sara started drinking orange juice, and in conversation, *orange* became closely linked with *juice*.

Within a few days, another transformation occurred. Sara began replacing her early word for "orange" (*o-enge*) with the word *juice* (properly pronounced). Florida oranges were *juice*, the color of Sara's beach ball was *juice*, and so were her orange paints and crayons. Like all other children working through this early phase of articulate speech, Sara was managing on a linguistic shoestring to get her meaning across.

How do children evolve individual strategies for making do with limited resources in sound, meaning, conversation, and grammar?

Strategies with Sounds: Substitutions, Silence, and End Runs

Once children start using distinct sounds (and sound combinations) to label objects and events, they have begun the long road to language saturation. But where do the sounds themselves come from? In the early stages of recognizable spoken language, they are heavily drawn from the repertoire that typically emerges during later babbling. And so the familiar sounds of *p*, *b*, *t*, *d*, *k*, *g*, *m*, *n*, *a*, *i*, and *u* commonly show up in the first few dozen recognizable words. (These are also sounds that are especially frequent in adult words and are easy to pronounce.) The reduplicative structure common in later babbling typically carries over into first words as well (e.g., *dada* = "daddy," *mama* = "mommy," *gaga* = "doggie").

In many children, babbling continues even after several dozen identifiable words have emerged. Such babbling helps to fill the conversational void. Knowing 25 or 50 words hardly makes for a fluent conversationalist. Like adults who resort to repetition ("Would you like some milk? Would you like some milk?") because there is so little to talk about with infants and toddlers, 15- or 20-month-olds sometimes lapse into babbling when they have nothing specific to say—or that they know *how* to say. As children grow older, babbling can also serve as an attention getter. By age 2, Ryan had ceased to babble under normal circumstances; however, when he wished to curtail his mother's conversation with another adult, Ryan's reversion to babbling provided an expanded language base from which to enter the conversational stream.

What sounds do 1-year-olds avoid? The sounds that are infrequent in adult speech (e.g., the *zh* sound of *rouge*) or are difficult to pronounce (e.g., the *sh* of *shoe*). Common sense suggests that toddlers master the *s* of *soup* before properly handling the more complex *sh* of *shoes*. But what seems easier to an adult does not always match an individual child's developmental progression. Ryan could pronounce a very adult-like *shoe* by 15 months, but *soup* came out *shoup* until he was more than 2;6. This tendency to palatalize his consonants (that is, to bring the tongue farther back along the palate on the roof of the mouth) surfaced in other sounds as well. Ryan acquired the *j* of *juice* by 14 months (which is relatively early) but also tended to call a "truck" a *chruck*.

What makes a sound difficult to pronounce? Sometimes the awkwardness of getting the articulators in the right place (e.g., the *j* in *juice*) and sometimes the lack of a clear point of articulation (compare the clarity of bringing two lips together for *p* with the ambiguity of curling the tongue for the *y* in *yes*). Sounds can also be problematic because of their proximity to other sounds. Children may struggle in handling repeated syllables (e.g., *clop-clop*) or multiple syllables with differing phonological shapes (e.g., *heehaw*).

Several strategies for coping with the phonological complexity of adult words are especially common among children. The simplest is to lop off one or more syllables, typically those that are unstressed or that contain difficult sounds. Ryan said *pump* for *pumpkin* and *Nee* for *Whitney*. Another obvious tack is to replace difficult sounds with simpler ones or substitute reduplications for diverse syllables—hence, Sara's *Doan* for *Joan* and *wawa* for *water*.

Alex, who was limited to monosyllables throughout his second year, worked out a handy system for coping with multisyllabic words: combine the initial consonant with the final vowel. And so *tomato* became *toe*, *honey* was *he*, and *monkey* came out *me*. For words beginning with a vowel, Alex reversed the order of sounds, rendering *egg*, for example, as *gi*.

One result of the phonological gymnastics through which 1-year-olds go to make pronunciation manageable is homonyms. Fifteen-month-old Ryan used *buh* to refer to half a dozen things: "bottle," "banana," "brush," "book," "bulldozer," and "bowl." Ryan and his mother spent many a tearful exchange as Ryan plaintively proclaimed

"Buh!"

and his mother struggled to figure out what he wanted. Like the sages in Jonathan Swift's Academy of Lagado (who carried the objects they wished to talk about in sacks on their backs), she would produce first a banana, then a toy bulldozer, next a book, until she happened upon the particular *buh* Ryan had in mind. Those who assume that context will always disambiguate homonyms have not raised young children.

While substitutions and omissions sometimes provide viable strategies for conveying meaning through a limited number of sounds, another response is word avoidance. Take the simple words *yes* and *no*. While conceptually they function as a pair, young children typically learn to say *no* before mastering *yes*. Part of the reason is contextual. Children under age 2 or 3 are more likely to hear *no* than *yes*, given the sheer number of hazards from which adults must protect the young. The other reason has to do with sounds. Children learn to control the *y* of *yes* long after they have mastered the *n* of *no*.

Linguistic risk takers like Sara generally attempt any word they encounter for which they have a need. More reserved children such as Ryan and Alex commonly maintain a hands-off policy for words they cannot pronounce properly, no matter how useful those words might prove. Ryan's strategy was to avoid problematic words altogether (e.g., *yes*, *school*) until he felt sufficiently confident to make a reasonable stab. Alex's solution was to devise some idiosyncratic linguistic end runs.

From the time he was a year old, Alex had a consuming passion for airplanes. His family lived near the flight path of a major airport, and Alex's greatest joy was to stand on the back porch and watch planes make their approach. Unfortunately, the initial *pl-* cluster in the word *plane* proved too much to tackle, and for months Alex relied on a grunting noise to call attention to a plane overhead. One day (Alex was 1;10 at the time), the family was at the airport to pick up a friend. Alex's father pointed out a jumbo jet that had just taken off and said,

"Look at that plane go! See it go!"

Alex squealed back,

"Go? Go!"

For the next year, Alex's word for "airplane" was *go*.

Alex adopted a similar end-run strategy in finding a name for "water." Like the *y* in *yes*, the *w* in *water* proves difficult for many toddlers. Up until age 17 months, Alex had no word for "water." One afternoon while visiting a shopping mall, he hit upon a suitable substitute. The cavernous mall (one of the largest in the country) was dominated in one cul de sac by a fountain built in the shape of a mammouth water faucet. The noise of the falling water generated a spontaneous imitation from Alex:

"Ish!"

For nearly two years, "water" was known as *ish*.

Worlds of Meaning: Topics and Boundaries

What do toddlers talk about? The people, objects, and events that fill their lives. Since labels such as *mommy* and *milk* have obvious referents (while *practice* and *perhaps* do not), it is hardly surprising that most of children's early words are names for things. Perceptually, things that change (mommies leave the room, milk bottles become empty) are more noticeable than things that do not (e.g., mirrors, stairs). Accordingly, children's early vocabularies favor words referring to things in their environment that could be otherwise (Mommy back in the room, the milk bottle refilled).

Other factors influence the early vocabulary mix as well. Certain adjectives (such as *more*) and location words (e.g., *up* and *down*), not to mention verbs of change (e.g., *stop*, *empty*, *push*), prove highly useful in the lives of young children. Another variable is the information media to which toddlers are exposed. Today many children between ages 1 and 2 can count to ten and identify a host of shapes (circles, squares, triangles, and even hexagons) thanks to hours of watching "Sesame Street" and reading books with adults. A generation ago, children from similar sociocultural backgrounds did not have these words and concepts under control for another year or more.

Early vocabulary is also shaped by the sounds involved (e.g., the *y* of *yes*, the *sch-* of *school*) and individual interest. Even important parts of children's daily routines may go unlabeled until the child finds them worthy of naming. Ryan, for example, did not attempt a word for "diaper" until he was 22 months and his mother began active toilet training.

What do children's words *mean*? When we speak of children "learning words," we naturally assume (by the conversational imperative) that children *intend* the same meanings for words as we do. Only when a child's usage is at odds with adult expectations do we begin to recognize that as new members of the linguistic culture, children are still groping to understand the meanings behind labels.

Here are some examples of semantic independence in toddlers:

- Alex, at age 17 months, hit upon the word *ish* as a tractable name for "water," thereby avoiding the problematic *w*. Within a few weeks, Alex had overgeneralized *ish* as his name for anything associated with water: bathroom faucets, fire hydrants, lawn sprinkers, even hoses.

  Did Alex believe the single word *ish* correctly named each of these items? When he labeled a hose coiled (and dry) on a front lawn as *ish*, was Alex referring to the hose itself or to the fact that it could contain *ish*? When a child has a maximum sentence length of one word, it is impossible to know for certain. Experience suggests that children who overgeneralize are often cognitively quite sophisticated, lacking only the linguistic wherewithal to encode distinct meanings. Alex's reliance upon *ish* as a substitute for *hose* or *faucet* is no different from Sara's mother calling a crib a *cama pequeña* because she could not remember the correct Spanish word *cuna*.

- Like many other children, Ryan loved chocolate ice cream. He tolerated other flavors, but chocolate was his clear favorite. By age 18 months, he knew the term *ice cream* and used it often. However, until he was nearly 2½, Ryan interpreted the term as referring only to chocolate ice cream. Then he learned the word *chocolate*, and finally *ice cream* became a properly generic label.

- When Sara was 10 months old, her family moved from a one-level apartment into a two-story house. Sara's father soon fell

into the habit of counting the steps every time he carried Sara
(or later she crawled) up the stairs. One day at about age 14
months, Sara toddled to the edge of the lowest stair rung and
proclaimed,

"Two!"

- From then on, Sara called stairs *two*. Since she referred to stairs
  by name only when talking about that particular staircase, there
  was no way of knowing whether *two* was her name for all stairs
  or only for "those stairs in the house that we always count
  when I go up and down." What is more, Sara's parents could
  not say whether Sara interpreted *two* as a homonym for the
  number or, like Alex with *go*, merely happened upon *two* as a
  substitute for the less easily pronounced word *stairs*.

- Ryan had a special fascination for vehicles. Whenever his family
  was out driving, his older sister, Cathy, would point out cars
  and trucks for him. One afternoon (Ryan was 20 months at the
  time), a Land Rover drove by, and Cathy identified it as a *jeep*.
  Ryan was delighted with the strange topless vehicle. A few
  weeks later, the family passed an old Chevy convertible, and his
  sister commented,

  "Ryan, look at that old car!"

Indignant that his sister had "mislabeled" the vehicle, Ryan
retorted,

  "Jeep!"

For Ryan, *jeep* meant "four-wheeled open-air vehicle in which
the driver sits outside" (hence properly excluding dump trucks
and pickups but mistakenly including convertibles), while *cars*
were fully enclosed vehicles.

How many words does the average child know by her second birthday? Somewhere between a dozen and several hundred, depending on
the child's physical maturity, personality and acquisition style, and
whether production or comprehension is being measured.

Even listing the productive language of a single child yields dubious
results, since early words tend to be evanescent. By age 1;6, Sara's
growing vocabulary included the word *fone* (for *saxophone*), learned

from watching Hoots the Owl (on "Sesame Street") sing to Ernie that "you have to put down the duckie if you want to play the saxophone." Yet after three weeks on summer vacation without television, Sara was no longer able to name the saxophone in her picture dictionary.

The fluidity of children's early vocabulary exemplifies a lesson learned by David Starr Jordan, the first president of Stanford University. An ichthyologist by training, President Jordan had vowed (so the story goes) to learn the name of each student on campus. However, the experiment was short-lived, for every time he mastered another student's name, he forgot the name of a fish. Given all the memory demands on young children (how to unscrew a jar lid, which end of the telephone receiver goes next to the ear, where the ice cream is stored), we can hardly expect toddlers to remember the name of every object they encounter.

Budding Conversationalists: The Art of One-Liners

Harnessing a growing ability to express themselves in words, toddlers begin to engage actively in conversation. Unlike a year ago, these children can now not only uphold their side of a dialogue but even engage in monologue, filling the role of both speaker and respondent.

Linguistically outgoing toddlers like Sara are likely to initiate conversation (with parents following her lead), while less outgoing children such as Ryan and Alex tend to respond to conversation initiated by others. Not surprisingly, Sara began constructing monologues nearly four months before Ryan and almost a year before Alex.

What level of conversational sophistication can we expect of a 20- to 24-month-old? With only a limited vocabulary and maybe the barest traces of productive syntax, there is need for ingenuity. Consider how young children answer questions that require a "yes" or "no" response (e.g., "Do you want some ice cream?"). As we have seen, *no* enters children's vocabulary fairly early, while *yes* is more troublesome because of its initial *y*. One solution is to stay silent (but miss out on the ice cream). The other is to improvise. Ryan's strategy was to answer "yes"/"no" questions affirmatively by repeating the essential word in the question:

Q: "Do you want some milk?"
A: "Milk."

versus

> Q: "Shall we get into the car?"
> A: "No."

Another conversational skill to emerge about this time is humor. Toddlers are beginning to understand that language can make people laugh. It takes considerable linguistic skill to make jokes, so again children exercise their creativity. Alex first used language humorously when he was exactly 24 months old. The family had been at a conference in Ohio and had just visited the Cincinnati zoo. Alex had enjoyed the outing enormously. He had seen tigers, peacocks, giraffes, and pandas. Best of all, he had ridden on the miniature train that runs through the property. At the end of the day, reflecting on the fun they had had, his mother gently prodded Alex with questions:

> "Did Alex see the tigers?"

His response:

> "No."

She tried again:

> "Did Alex see the peacocks?"
>
> "No."

A quick trip through the rest of the menagerie drew the same emphatic "No." Finally, his mother played her ace:

> "Did Alex ride the train?"

He could no longer maintain a straight face. Though his response was (naturally) "No," the utterance was smothered with laughter.

So far, we have been looking at how children converse with adults. How do children interact with peers?

To find out, I heartily recommend a visit to a nursery program for "young 2s" (children who are about to or who have just turned 2). Outside of sobs from the little boy who doesn't want Daddy to leave or gleeful squeals from the girl who finally managed to go down the slide by herself, you will be astounded at the silence. Teachers address the children. The children sometimes talk to or respond to the teachers, but little conversation goes on between the children themselves.

Of course, children don't do much else collaboratively at this age.

The term **parallel play** (I do my thing, you do yours) profoundly applies to the activities of toddlers. I have seen 2-year-olds literally walk over each other as if they were pieces of furniture or remove objects from one another's hands as if the victim were a wooden Indian in front of a cigar store. And the children who are walked over or relieved of their toys do not necessarily respond. While prior experience with other children (an older sibling, a twin, a frequent neighborhood playmate) commonly affords toddlers a developmental edge, sophisticated tools for interacting with other children socially and linguistically do not usually emerge until at least the third year of life.

The Origins of Grammar: Alternative Routes

In many people's minds, children "begin to talk" when they start combining words: "No want," "Fall down," "More milk," or "Tell me." The age span for beginning grammar is broad. Some children productively combine words as early as 14 or 15 months, most start between 18 and 24 months, and a small yet still normal group move into grammar as late as 28 to 30 months.

Sara represents the vanguard of the mainstream. At age 15 months, she stretched both arms out towards her father (who had just set her down from a piggyback ride) and demanded,

"More horsie!"

Sara's route to grammar was to link together within a single utterance words she had previously used independently.

Moving from one word to two and then on to many is the way most children make the transition into grammar. This passage rarely occurs in a vacuum. For weeks or even months before their first coupling of words, toddlers typically use one or more forms of **proto-grammar**. An obvious method is to combine a word with a gesture or other contextual indication of meaning. From age 13 months, Sara had expressed her desire for another round on her father's back by stretching out her arms and demanding,

"More."

A second form of protogrammar is to chain one-word utterances

84

together. Each word is spoken separately, with falling intonation at the end. Yet taken as a sequence, the words make up a connected thought. At age 14 months, Sara produced this chain of utterances:

"Sara. Milk. Cup."

Clearly Sara wanted to have some milk in her cup, but she lacked the wherewithal to combine the three elements into a single breath group (and therefore a sentence). The conceptual groundwork for forming sentences was in place, however.

Ryan's movement into syntax was more incremental. Since his first word at age 11 months, many of Ryan's new utterances seemed more like phrases—even sentences—than single words. Among his first 50 "words" were *tanku* [= *thank you*], *go 'way* [= *go away*], and *love you* (in direct imitation of his mother's farewell each day when she left him at the day care center).

Ryan's independent combination of words into sentences began when he was 24 months old. Like Sara, Ryan sometimes used transitional bridges into grammar that was beyond his grasp. His favorite devices were to combine a real word with a babbled sequence or to insert the syllable *uh* as a placeholder. By age 25 months, he would say

"Uppy go!"

"Waga home?"

"Fall uh down,"

which initially made no sense to his mother. Over the next two months as Ryan's pronunciation and understanding of grammar evolved, the utterances transformed into

"Up we go!"

"Wanna go home?"

"Falling down."

All three combinations originated as imitations of phrases heard from his mother or sister. Ryan gradually figured out how to parcel the sound stream into distinct words.

Alex's grammatical progress was hampered by the fact that all his words remained monosyllabic until he was 2½. If you cannot articulate two syllables in a single word (e.g., *daddy*, *cupcake*), there is no way of combining two words to form a sentence. Alex's first solid two-syllable utterance was a sentence:

"More ju [= juice]."

Over the next six months, polysyllabic words (and multiword utterances) tumbled out, helping Alex to catch up with his age-mates.

In his travels toward grammar, Alex had gone through a brief "false alarm" period (typical of many children) before grammar became solidly productive. At 18 months, Alex stood before the refrigerator one morning and requested,

"Ap ju [= apple juice]."

Two months later, while playing with a toy car, Alex proclaimed,

"Ca [= car] go."

At age 2;3, while watching a segment of "Sesame Street" in which a man was riding in an elevator, Alex spontaneously declared,

"Man go up."

Three days later, when sitting in the car, Alex pounded on the window and demanded,

"Up dow [= window]."

Outside of these four isolated utterances, Alex had no syntactic (or even multisyllabic) combinations until age 2;6.

■ IDEAS AND ALERTS

How Can I Help?

Continue to be an active conversational partner.

Engaging toddlers in conversation, even one-sided conversation, is the most important thing you can do to nourish your child linguistically.

Adult initiative continues to be especially important with quieter children. Structure your conversations as if your child is intelligent, listening to what you are saying, and understanding.

Ensuring adequate adult language stimulation to toddlers presents challenges regardless of your child care situation (parent is staying at home, other young siblings are at home, child is in the care of a nanny, child is in day care). Parents understandably rely on television or even slightly older children as baby-sitters. Nannies who speak little or no English sometimes hesitate to be active conversationalists. And even high-quality day care programs for toddlers can hardly provide the same rich language stimulation that an adult can offer a single child. At the same time, all of these situations can be used to advantage. The presence of a non–English speaking nanny offers a marvelous opportunity for children to become bilingual. Children who spend their days with other children have a social, experiential, and often conversational advantage over only children who spend their early years at home alone. The issue is always one of balance.

Remember to listen.

Many years ago, *New York* magazine had a cover of a grown man sitting in a wheelchair, with his proud mother poised behind him. The caption read, "Of course he can walk. Thank God he doesn't have to." Since toddlers' speech is often slow and laborious, parents are often tempted to supply words and thoughts for them, much as they did when their children were infants. It is especially important to encourage children to express themselves, no matter how painstaking the process or how much of a hurry you are in. When older siblings are in the house, these children need to learn not to speak for the toddler either.

**Use a language style with which you are
comfortable, but consider ways of
expanding your child's linguistic abilities
and horizons.**

A wealth of research data suggests that the style of language addressed to young children can influence their rate of linguistic development. While these findings in no way argue for eliminating baby talk features that help you and your child establish strong social rapport, they do suggest that conscious attempts at expanding your child's linguistic universe will bear fruit.

Here are some guidelines for shaping your conversational style:

- Don't be afraid to use ungrammatical language (e.g., "No eat") or to imitate your toddler's novel forms (e.g., *bozer* for *bulldozer*).
- Using long sentences need not be problematic, especially if you highlight one or two words through emphasis (e.g., "Is that your very own *apple juice*?").
- Using sophisticated vocabulary is also reasonable if you speak clearly and provide contextual definitions (e.g., "That worm is *humongous*; it's really *big*").
- Use rhymes (both that you read and that you make up).
- Ask questions that encourage answers other than "yes" or "no."
- Actively repeat, expand, and recast your child's utterances. Not only do these conversational responses indicate you are listening to and have understood what your toddler is saying, but they also provide natural avenues for correction.
- Introduce new topics, expanding your child's cognitive and linguistic horizons.
- Model humor in your own conversation.

Adjust to your child's idiosyncrasies rather than working against them.

Toddlers approach vocabulary development and early grammar in diverse ways. None has been shown to be superior in the long run to any other. Many parents worry that their toddlers are more prone to imitate the words of others than to use words spontaneously. Parents of highly imitative children should be reassured that imitation is very common among children developing language (especially through an expressive style) and provides a useful transition for learning new vocabulary and getting a beginning sense of syntax.

Many toddlers have difficulty pronouncing words and making themselves understood. Such difficulties often lead to mutual frustration. Whenever possible, make toddlers feel as if they are being understood. One ploy I have seen used successfully is to avoid saying "What?" over and again but instead respond to an unintelligible observation with,

"Oh really?" or "I see"—even though you don't. Later, when your child's pronunciation and vocabulary have matured, you can raise your standards for intelligibility.

Avoid sexual stereotypes.

Don't let your toddler's sex—or your own—unwittingly determine the amount or style of your conversation. As we have seen, many American mothers are prone to be more linguistically supportive of girls than boys—vocalizing more to infant and toddler daughters and using more linguistic patterns that encourage language growth (such as asking questions or repeating children's utterances). At the same time, a number of studies have shown that fathers tend to talk less with their toddlers and preschoolers than do mothers, while mothers seem less prone than fathers to use semantically correct and specific vocabulary. Active and cognitively enriching initiatives are beneficial from all available adults.

Resist making normative comparisons.

Be aware of the ages at which your child reaches specific milestones (first word, first 50 words, first grammatical combination), but be careful not to measure this development rigidly against children of neighbors or friends. Unnecessary anxiety from you can seep through in interactions with your child.

Should I Be Concerned?

What if my toddler isn't combining words by age 2?

Separating transient language problems from the potentially more serious ones can be extremely difficult in children this young. Many normal children tend to be late starters linguistically. Among the likely causes of such late starts are prematurity or presence of a twin or older sibling. Children who begin language with an expressive strategy may also appear to be (or actually be) later in starting syntax because they frequently combine identifiable words with what sounds like babble. Many "late bloomers" (who don't begin using syntax until sometime during the third year of life) display both good comprehension and the ability to use sequenced gestures.

What about problems that may be more serious? Combining together language delays or language disorders caused by a variety of factors (articulation problems, low intelligence, psychological disorders, and "unknown etiology"), between 5 and 10 percent of young children suffer from some kind of developmental language problem. The good news is that nearly half of the children diagnosed at age 2 or 3 as having a language problem will outgrow it by the time they enter school.

One of the most puzzling developmental language difficulties is **specific language impairment** (also called **developmental aphasia, childhood aphasia,** or **infantile speech**). Specific language impairment, which seems to affect roughly one child out of a thousand, is defined by what it is not: It is not a problem with intelligence, it is not a gross neurological problem, and it is not childhood autism. All that we know is that an otherwise normal child is not achieving language milestones at the expected time.

Most often, the diagnosis of specific language impairment is based on slow (or unusual) development of syntax, but the production and comprehension of individual words can be problematic as well. Children with specific language impairment show enormous variation in their language skills. Some 4- or 5-year-olds can produce fairly lengthy sentences but have trouble remembering the names of everyday objects. Others have problems with particular grammatical constructions or with mastering the rules of conversation. And yet others simply progress very slowly, still using the rudimentary syntax we might expect from a 2-year-old at age 3 or 4.

We don't know what causes specific language impairment. In all likelihood, the problem stems from a brain dysfunction, but it is not even clear what particular brain function is compromised (e.g., auditory processing, cognitive skills, motor abilities). It may well turn out that specific language impairment is really a cluster of problems, with many causes and differential outcomes.

What is the prognosis? We know that some "late starters"—even very late starters—rapidly catch up by themselves around age 3. Many older preschoolers and school-aged children benefit markedly from speech-language therapy, while others continue to have difficulties.

When do you decide that slow development warrants professional attention? It is extremely hard to say in the case of a language delay that has no obvious cause and no other symptoms. If a child has not begun combining words by age 24 to 30 months, parents may find it reassuring to get a professional assessment, although most times such children will very soon be using syntax spontaneously.

What if my toddler sometimes babbles instead of consistently using recognizable words?

Forming words is hard work at this stage (as forming individual letters will be later on). Continued use of babbling provides a welcome break. At other times, what sounds like babbling may actually be an attempt at words or phrases that your toddler cannot yet pronounce properly. A good way to check is to count the number of syllables in the target word or phrase (if you can identify it) and compare that number with the syllables in your child's utterance.

I can understand what my child is saying, but other people can't.

Pronunciation problems are common at this stage, especially with children following an expressive course of early language development. In most cases, the difficulty will resolve itself (with you playing the role of unobtrusive interpreter). If problems persist by the time your child is 3, it is appropriate to consider professional evaluation.

My son has older siblings, and I am a single parent. Should I be doing something special to enhance his language development?

We have seen that rates and styles of language acquisition are products of children's individual profiles plus the social context into which they are born. Children such as Ryan may seem to have several possible strikes against them: sex, birth order, limited access to an adult conversational coach and partner. There is no denying that many children born into these circumstances never develop the adventuresome relationship with language that a child such as Alex, or potentially Sara, does. While Ryan's mother can be taught natural and simple ways of encouraging her son's linguistic development, we should also remember that other adults Ryan and children like him encounter, especially teachers, can have a profound impact on children's linguistic skills and attitudes.

Does it matter in the long run whether my child begins language with a referential or an expressive style?

No. Regardless of the initial language learning strategies children begin with, all normal children end up mastering the basics of language—sound, meaning, grammar, and conversation—by about age 5 or 6. The important issue is not the *style* or the *age* at which children begin their linguistic journeys but the *orientation* toward language they develop.

While early differences in acquisition strategies tend to fade by age 3 or 4, individual attitudes towards language become increasingly distinct about the same time. As we will see in the chapters ahead, parents play a critical role in shaping these attitudes and orientations, which determine the eventual level of linguistic saturation children will reach as adults.

■ 4. Why You Don't Like My Chooses?

Grammatical Orienteering

THE HUNT for Matthew's present was on. Three-year-old Sara and her mother were combing the aisles of the local toy store, searching for an appropriate gift for a boy in the neighborhood who was about to turn 6. Sara was up for the challenge. Pulling from the shelves first a set of blocks, then a pop-up book, next a doll, she brightly presented each option for approval. Trying to temper Sara's growing desire to participate in decision making with the need for age and sex appropriateness of the gift, her mother enthusiastically welcomed each offering and then suggested perhaps they might look a little further.

After the third not-so-subtle rejection, Sara paused in her scavenging and reflectively asked,

"Why you don't like my chooses?"

Sara's challenge epitomizes the ingenious strategies preschoolers invoke in attempting to make sense of English grammar.

During a span of two or three years, children move from the simplest two-word combinations (appearing somewhere between 15 and 30 months) to basic linguistic saturation (typically by age 5 or 6), when they begin appearing to be competent language partners. Yes, some pronunciations and usages still need fine-tuning during the elementary years, and, no, 5-year-olds do not really understand all the language used around them. But by the time children enter kindergarten, the most intense linguistic growth period is over.

How do children accomplish this feat? Through **language orienteering**.

Language Orienteering

A popular outdoor sport currently is orienteering. Armed with a compass and map (and sometimes a few matches and an initial supply of food), adventurers set out into the woods to fend for themselves and then reconnoitre at an appointed spot. By making creative use of their tools (e.g., the compass, the matches), practitioners draw sustenance, shelter, and direction from the natural environment.

No path is inherently right or wrong. Nonetheless, participants may reach dead ends, need to double back, go hungry for stretches of time, and become frustrated. Individual paths share many similarities: the same magnetic North guides each compass, the same forest provides blackberries for all to pick. But in the end, each forager charts a unique path to the goal.

Language acquisition is fundamentally language orienteering. Each participant sets out with a basic set of tools: our genetic endowment that permits us to acquire language. The natural environment through which learners blaze a trail is the social community into which the child is born and the language modeled by that community. The goal is to join the group as a full-fledged member.

Grammatical Orienteering: Rules or Playdough?

The most dramatic linguistic transformation during the preschool years is in grammar—from gluing two words together to orchestrating complex sentences. In listening to the ingenious (and outrageous) utterances that typify children's attempts at grammatical orienteering, we get a glimpse of what sense children make (and do not make) of the language adults use and how children structure their own linguistic universe.

What strategies do children concoct for grammatical orienteering?

A language is a collection of pieces that can be combined following established conventions. The pieces are the sounds and words that make up words and sentences, respectively. The conventions are the guidelines defining which sounds or words can pattern with each other (e.g., *spring* and *I read the book*) and which cannot (e.g., *kpring* or *The read I book*).

When linguists talk about the makeup of human language, they speak in terms of **rules** that govern the construction of admissible (grammatical) combinations. A simple example is the rule for forming plurals in English. The average 3-year-old, for example, "knows" that the basic rule for pluralizing a singular noun is to add an -*s* (or -*es*), and many children create words like *childrens*, *mans*, and *fishes* (as in "Two little fishes are in the bowl").

Do children actually discover or construct such rules to get their linguistic ducks in the right rows, or are these rules really adult creations arising from 20-20 hindsight? An alternative to seeing language as a collection of pieces to be combined according to prefabricated conventions is to view language instead as a lump of playdough to be shaped by different hands in individual ways.

What might lead us to think of language as playdough? Consider how children learn notions of similarity or sameness. English has phrases like

These two things are *like* each other.

These two things are *similar to* each other.

These two things are *the same as* each other.

For a young child orienteering among such language boulders as *like*, *similar*, and *same*, the concepts of comparison and likeness may be clear long before the grammar comes into line.

By age 4, Sara, Ryan, and Alex were all laboring to make grammatical sense of comparative notions. Alex struggled valiantly with the linguistic markers for over a year, pushing and pulling, molding and pummeling, and coming out with questions like

"Are these two like the same?"

To Sara, comparison of size presented the same challenge. Standing on a chair and beaming across the room at her mother, Sara declared,

"I'll be so big than you."

Ryan, in a foot race with his older sister, called out,

"I can run so faster than you!"

To say that Alex's or Sara's or Ryan's syntax is "wrong" is to assume a model of language acquisition in which rules exist for children to learn and to conclude that none of the children had yet mastered the grammar of comparison. To say, alternatively, that Alex, Sara, or Ryan had actually constructed independent rules (later to be replaced by normative adult versions) is to read too much into utterances such as these. Certainly children create their own words and structures and hold on to them for long stretches of time. Yet a sizable chunk of these attempts at language are as ephemeral as this afternoon's playdough construction. Children use the materials at hand to create something that fills their needs. When they are done, they mush the raw materials back into the can so a new sculpture can be created the next time.

Language orienteering strategies run the gamut from rules to playdough. The three strategies we will focus on are **analogy, scissors and paste**, and **potshots**.

I Changed Up My Mind: Analogy

Four-year-old Alex was adamant. Sitting at the dinner table, he resolutely refused to drink the glass of milk set before him. "But Alex," pleaded his father, "you just asked for milk, and I brought it." Not missing a beat, Alex retorted:

"I changed up my mind."

If you can "make up" your mind, it stands to reason, by simple analogy, that you can "change up" your mind as well. Unhappily for Alex, English grammar often proves fickle, and promises of regularity are marred by unpredictable or abstrusely regulated exceptions.

Children striving for grammatical saturation seek out regularity like plants seek light. In most cases, learners' success at identifying regularity (and making analogies) goes unheralded. If Sara correctly uses *pans* as the plural of *pan*, we hardly notice. After all, both *pan* (singular) and *pans* (plural) might be individually memorized forms. Yet when Sara speaks of "two *mans*," our linguistic sensibilities are jolted. The only way she could have come up with the inappropriate (but wholly logical) *mans* is by noting the regularity in English whereby singulars like *pan*, *fan*, and *van* are pluralized by adding an -*s*. Whether we describe Sara as having a formal rule for plurals or as having developed a working principle based on analogy, Sara has discovered an invaluable tool for creating new language that bolsters her ability to describe experience.

Such analogies pervade preschoolers' attempts to learn English morphology and syntax. Yet Sara, Ryan, and Alex customized their use of analogy to suit their personal language acquisition strategies.

Sara, as usual, led the pack in derring-do. Always game to try out a new piece of language and see if it would fly, Sara began actively using language analogies by the time she was 2. Ryan was far more cautious. In fact, until past his third birthday, Ryan almost never coined independent analogies like *mans* or *goed*. Alex, also true to form, was very slow to begin creating his own grammatical analogies. His first neologism (*wented*) did not appear until he was 3;1. However, as with the rest of his grammatical development, Alex then rapidly made up for lost time, grabbing at any language component he found handy to get his meaning across.

What do children's grammatical analogies look like? A bevy of examples hinge on the sound *s*.

The *s* sound fills many roles in English, among which are markers of possession ("*dawn's* early light"), plurality ("two *dawns*"), and the third-person-singular of a present-tense verb ("day *dawns*"). It can take children months, if not years, to sort out these constructions, especially because of the irregularities of English morphology. Ryan, Alex, and Sara (all about age 3;6 at the time) offer a bounty of examples of the confusions that ensue:

- Ryan's aunt had sent him a splendid Mickey Mouse T-shirt from a Disney store. William, Ryan's best friend, already sported the same model. When their nursery school teacher commented on their shared couture, Ryan responded,

  "I'll wear mine, and William is going to wear hims."

  In the simple language of analogy,

  her : *hers* = *him* : *hims*

- From his school friends, Alex had recently picked up the word *guys* (as in "Come on, you guys!"), referring to a group of companions. One Saturday morning, Alex was feeling bored and abandoned because his mother had left him to play alone in the living room while she was preparing lunch. Alex marched into the kitchen and declared,

   "Hey guy! Come here!"

   that is,

   friends : *friend* = *guys* : *guy*

- Through the centuries, English has lost most of its inflectional verb endings. (A thousand years ago, the verbs of Old English resembled those of modern German.) One of the few remaining markers on English present-tense verbs is used when the subject of the sentence is a third-person-singular noun or pronoun (e.g., "He need*s* some apples"). That little -*s* caused no end of trouble for Sara. Initially she followed the analogy exactly:

   "He gots to go home."
   (*need* : *needs* = *got* : *gots*)
   "He gots something."
   (*have* : *has* = *got* : *gots*)

   However, once the final -*s* for verbs in sentences with third-person-singular subjects took root, Sara became yet more creative:

   "I'm hots."

   What began as the recognition of a morphological regularity took on a life of its own.

Another set of reasonable—but wrong—analogies involves comparative adjectives and adverbs. As we saw at the beginning of this chapter, the grammar of comparison proves very tricky for young children. The coping strategies preschoolers devise are rich and varied. Here are several analogies our 3-year-olds created for using the regular morphological marker of comparison, -*er*:

- Sara (3;3):

  "He went in the ambulance because he got hurter and hurter."
  (*sick : sicker = hurt : hurter*)

- Ryan (3;8):

  "Go down in the hole. Even downer!"
  (*low : lower = down : downer*)

- Alex (3;6) (responding to his mother's attempts to turn off the light, thereby making the room dark):

  "Turn it offer!"
  (*dark : darker = off : offer*)

A third venue generating a host of mistaken analogies centers on past-tense verbs. To understand how some very reasonable orienteering strategies can go awry here, we need a little background.

Preschoolers commonly put double morphological markers of number or tense on nouns or verbs. For example, many children add an extra plural marker to the word *children*, yielding *childrens*—presumably because they do not recognize *-en* as a plural marker (compare *ox/oxen; brother/brethren*). The irony is that *children* is already doubly marked for plural. In Old English, both *-en* and *-r* were common plural markers (the Old English singular of *child* was *cild*, and the plural was *cilder*). Perhaps some child a thousand years ago initiated the *-en* as a double marker, much the same way that preschoolers today add the redundant *-s*.

Learning the past tense of English verbs can be especially difficult since the modern English verb system patches together what used to be three very different methods for expressing past tense: **strong** verbs, which regularly changed the vowel sound from the present tense to form the past (e.g., *sleep/slept*); **weak** verbs, which simply added an *-ed*, *-d*, *-et*, or *t* to express the past (e.g., *want/wanted*); and **suppletive** verbs, which, for historical reasons, paired the present tense from one verb with the past tense of another (e.g., *go/went*).

Here are some examples from our three children of orienteering with past-tense verbs:

- Ryan's mother had come to pick her son up at nursery school one afternoon. Ryan, then 3;3, began talking about his friend

William. When his mother inquired whether Willliam was still at school, Ryan observed,

"No, he already leaveded."

Such double markers (*-ed* + *-ed*) are common among children this age, especially when the first marker is not phonologically prominent. Since the first *-ed* of *leaveded* is not pronounced as a separate syllable, it makes logical sense to add another one. Ryan demonstrated the solidity of this principle two months later when he declared to his sister,

"I yawneded."

- A few months after she turned 3, Sara built a snowman of sorts in her front yard. The next day (a Sunday) it rained, and Sara spent her time indoors. When she happened to look outside the window, she found a small lump where her snowman had been. Excitedly, she called her father to witness the snowman's demise:

  "Look, Daddy. It meltsed."

  Why the intrusive *-s*? Probably because Sara typically used *melt* as a third-person-singular verb ("The snow melts," "Ice cream melts"), not with first- or second-person subjects. She naturally took *melts* as the base form to which she added a past tense *-ed.*

- As an airplane buff, 3½-year-old Alex loved to watch and talk about anything that flew. One day he was deeply engrossed in a television rerun of *Star Wars*. His father happened by and asked Alex what was going on. Alex answered,

  "The bad airplane got blewned up."

  His father paused. "What was that?" Alex repeated his observation:

  "It got blewned up."

  Alex's orienteering process seems to have gone something like this:

present:	blow
past:	bl*ew*
past perfect:	bl . . . *n* (cf. flow*n*) or bl . . . *ed* (cf. mov*ed*)
therefore:	*blew* + *n* + *ed* = blewned

Blewned was not a one-time accident. Alex continued to use the word for nearly another year whenever he needed a past tense for *blow*.

While the preponderance of grammatical analogies deal with morphology (combining two or more elements of meaning to form a single word, as in *man* + *s* = *mans*), some of the most endearing analogies preschoolers use involve syntax (joining words together to make phrases and sentences). Most syntactic analogies in English center on verbs. Because verbs with related meanings often pattern with very different particles and objects (recall Alex's "changed up my mind" on analogy with "made up my mind"), the possibilities for reasoned but incorrect analogues are vast:

- By the time she was 3½, Sara had begun to assert her independence. She insisted on pouring her own juice, pulling off her own shoes, and brushing her own teeth—all with varying degrees of success. Fearing for her daughter's dental health, Sara's mother gently tried to extract the toothbrush from Sara's hand one evening during their nightly battle of wits. Grabbing the brush back, Sara warned her mother,

  "Don't cooperate me!"
  (cf. Don't help me)

- Ryan (3;9) was entering that special phase of realizing he had sufficient control over his bodily functions to urinate at will. A favorite game became spending long periods at the toilet, practicing his new art. His sister, needing the facilities, planted herself in the doorway of the bathroom to see what was delaying her brother. Oblivious to her impatience, Ryan explained his new skill:

  "You can stop it, and you can go it."

Why You Don't Like My Chooses?
Scissors and Paste

Most attempts at grammatical orienteering involve not straightforward analogies (like "changed up my mind") but cutting and pasting together words and phrases to express meaning. The resulting collage reflects the complexity of the task at hand. Not only must children get the words in the right order, but they need to figure out how the choice of one word early in a sentence affects words later on.

The examples we will be looking at of the scissors and paste strategy did not happen to result in grammatical English. However, it is the process, not the product, that intrigues us. As we already saw for plurals like *pans* and *mans*, the same strategy may lead to acceptable language in one case but not in the next.

This sense of process is unmistakably clear in the query with which this chapter began:

"Why you don't like my chooses?"

Chooses is itself a delightful innovation. Sara selected a verb (*choose*), anointed it a noun, and then pluralized it. (We'll see more of these word creations when we look at meaning in Chapter 5.) At the same time, she forged her own solution to the ubiquitous problem young speakers have in getting the proper word order, especially when asking questions or negating affirmations.

Two fertile areas for examples of preschoolers' use of scissors and paste strategies are in the ways they ask questions and negate sentences. Both of these processes are complex undertakings in English.

The first problem is getting the words in the right sequence. Most preschoolers initially approach questions and negatives very practically: start with a question word (or negative) and then tack on the active, declarative sentence. And so Sara (2;4) commented,

"*Not* door open."

[= The door isn't open.]

Ryan, at 2;8, demanded,

"*Why not* ball roll?"

And at 3;2, Alex asked his mother,

"*Why* you aren't sad?"

In each instance, the children simply pasted words (*not, why not,* or *why*) in front of an independently functioning sentence ("Door open," "Ball roll," "You aren't sad").

With negatives, the strategy of putting the negative word first gives way fairly quickly to embedding it somewhere in the middle. By 3;1, Ryan was noting,

> "That car not has a roof."

However, getting the word order right in questions can take much longer. Listen to Sara:

> 3;2 "Would-you-please don't do that."
> (pasting together the memorized phrase "Would-you-please" with "Don't do that")
> 3;5 "What are you are doing?"
> (realizing that a verb has to follow a question word but not yet venturing to violate the integrity of the affirmative "you are doing")
> 3;6 "Where is it can be?"
> (a curious mélange of the more mature "Where is it?" with the intended "Where can it be?")

The perversity of English—which reverses question word order when a question is embedded in another sentence—haunted Sara four months later:

> 3;10 "Could you get my lunch box? I don't know where is it."

But even if children manage to get the sentence order right when asking a question, they can still get bollixed up in locating the right question word to use. Many preschoolers understand that special words exist for asking questions (*who, what, where, when, why, how*) long before they puzzle out which word goes with which meaning. Their solution is to rely on scissors and paste.

Ryan's odyssey is by no means atypical:

> 3;0 (in response to his mother asking, "Do you know who is coming on an airplane today?"):
> "*What* [= *who*]?"
> 3;7: "*What* [= *where*] are we going?"

103

3;8:   "*Where* [= *what*] does it do?"

4;2:   "*How* [= *when*] are we going to be home?"

These substitutions recurred over several months, with the replacement of *how* for *when* lasting until Ryan was almost 4½.

An additional confusion—and a scissors and paste response—arises in negative sentences when children need to figure out whether to use *no, some,* or *any.* In English, the addition of a negative word (*not, no*) to a sentence has consequences for a subsequent word of quantification: *somebody* becomes *nobody, some* becomes *any.* Mastering this additional complexity takes time. In the process, children end up with scissors and paste solutions such as these:

- Sara (3;5):

    "I don't see nobody."

- Ryan (3;6):

    "How [= *Why*] this duck doesn't have no more bubbles?" [said of a plastic duck that once contained bubble bath].

- Alex (3;2) was in the playhouse that dominated the waiting room of his pediatrician's office. The 5-year-old with whom he had been playing hide-and-seek had recently been called in to see the doctor, leaving Alex by himself. Plaintively informing his mother that he was now companionless, Alex bleated,

    "There's no somebody but me [left in the playhouse]."

Scissors and paste strategies sometimes find their way across boundaries between words. Once children begin to understand morphology (that is, knowing they generally need to add syllables to mark plurals, past tenses, progressives, and such), they encounter an added dilemma: identifying the word to which the syllable should be added. When Alex (3;8) questioned what happened to the baby chicks that hatched at his school just before Easter, he answered his own query with a possible explanation:

"Maybe they grow upped."

At about the same age (3;9), Ryan was warned not to touch the hood of his mother's car, since the engine was very hot. Not to be dissuaded, Ryan extended his hand (the sky was now drizzling slightly) and calmly declared,

"That's OK. The rain is take caring of it."

Such misplacing of language parts is usually short-lived—perhaps a few days or weeks. Yet it illustrates how children creatively provide temporary shelter for stray grammatical markers.

In the even broader grammatical arena, scissors and paste orienteering can be useful when attempting complex constructions (like relative clauses) or simply long ones (like compound sentences). For all their good efforts, sometimes children say too little and other times too much. Performing for his sister one day on the jungle gym, 3½-year-old Ryan called out,

"Watch can I do!"

[= Watch what I can do!]

Ryan both omitted the all-important object *what* and neglected to realize that the word order of relative clauses ("what I can do") is not affected by the elusive *what*.

When do children "say too much"? In times like these:

- Sara (3;5):

  "I held everybody's hand [walking with her friends to the park] and they held my hand back *to me*."

- Ryan (4;0):

  "Something that somebody put *it* in the engine broke down."
  (Neither Sara's "*to me*" nor Ryan's "*it*" needs to be expressed.)

- Alex's syntactic redundancies more often arose from pasting together pieces from two constructions that expressed the same meaning. For over a year (from 3;1 to 4;2), Alex persistently asked,

  "Do you know what something?"

  chaining the direct objects in "Do you know *what*?" and "Do you know *something*?" in much the same way that he redundantly linked *like* and *the same* in

"Are these two like the same?"

(See the beginning of this chapter.)

Finally, much as analogies prove useful devices for handling past-tense verbs, a scissors and paste approach can come in handy for dealing with the future tense. Part of the difficulty in talking about the future is conceptual (envisioning things that are not now and perhaps never will be), and part is linguistic (figuring out the correct verb components).

Between ages 3 and 4, Sara devised an ingenious method for expressing the future: use a past-tense verb to indicate what you want *to have happened*. Her choice of the past tense was so regular that she clearly was not simply taking grammatical potshots:

3;3 "Mommy, I want to broke it [the necklace her mother was wearing at the time]."
3;6 "Abe [a child who had just gotten into his family's car] is going to drove away."
3;7 "I am going to ate it up."

And then, a few days later,

3;7 "I will ate it all up."

Not for another six months did Sara spontaneously use correct future-tense verb forms:

4;2 "I will eat my supper."

Are You Still Have Any of These Candies Before? Potshots

For his fourth birthday, Ryan invited a dozen of his school friends to his house for a party. In planning for the event, Ryan chose a special treat from the candy store to include in the goodies bags: pieces of marzipan shaped like little fruits.

The party neared an end, and on cue from his mother, Ryan distributed a parcel to each child. One of his buddies (two months Ryan's senior) promptly tore into the bag and liberated its contents. Encountering a yellow banana shape which, while strange, nonetheless seemed edible, friend Christopher exclaimed to the other party goers,

"Are you still have any of these candies before?"

Ignorance of the niceties of the English auxiliary and tense system ("Have you ever had . . . ") posed no obstacle for a child intent upon expressing an important semantic message. Christopher's "potshots" at English verbs illustrate a vital strategy for grammar orienteering: use whatever language is at hand to get your point across, and correct grammar be damned.

Besides the aberrant look of grammatical potshots, their most singular characteristic is that they are one-shot deals. Constructed on the fly, they generally do not reappear, even at parental bidding.

Ryan's way of handling the fact that he could not retrieve his own makeshift constructions was to blame his audience. Commonly when 4-year-old Ryan and his mother were traveling in the car (Ryan ensconced in the back seat, his mother driving), Ryan would attempt an involuted sentence that his mother was unable to hear, much less understand. She would reply,

"I didn't hear you. What did you say?"

and Ryan would retort,

"You know! You know!"

dissolving into tears.

Like most other young children, Ryan assumed his mother was omniscient. She was supposed to be able to understand and reconstruct Ryan's grammatical attempts even when he could not. In fact, Ryan displayed precisely the same expectation structure for reproducing his Duplo constructions. He would build an edifice, knock it down, and demand that his mother rebuild it precisely the same way. When she protested that she could not remember how his unique architecture had been configured, Ryan would insist,

"You know! You know!"

GROWING UP WITH LANGUAGE

It took Ryan until age 4½ to acknowledge that even he did not remember the Duplo (or verbal) novelties.

Probably all children take some grammatical potshots. Unlike grammatical analogies (which conservative children like Ryan and initially, Alex, tend to avoid), potshots provide a lifeline for preschoolers who have unique meanings to express but lack adequate control over the plethora of grammatical detail necessary to get everything right the first time.

Curiously, the literature on language acquisition, not to mention informal accounts from parents, contains little about preschoolers' one-shot stabs at grammar that still eludes them. Why? The conversational imperative. By virtue of the conversational imperative, listeners are likely to "hear" correct grammar from children, fitting what is actually said to the procrustean bed of the community language. Much as writers find it difficult to proofread their own work, speakers tend to hear language as if it conforms to the norm. And so grammatical potshots have tended to go unnoticed, even by people who spend a great deal of time with children.

When my son was a preschooler, I occasionally joined him for lunch at the nursery school run by the university where I teach. One day, as six of us sat around a lunch table, the children were comparing peanut butter and jelly sandwiches (the universal cuisine of choice):

"I've got grape jelly!"

declared Jonathan.

"I've got strawberry!"

boasted Emily.

"Hey, guys. I've got blueberry!"

countered Susan, as she admired the real fruit lumps on her bread. Jonathan quickly sought the dominant ground:

"I'll squish your blueberries, so it'll look just like grape jelly."

Susan pensively contemplated her sandwich and sighed,

"Then it won't be any more gooder." [= Then it won't be good any more.]

108

I bolted from the table to grab pen and paper; Susan's construction was too precious to risk forgetting. As I rejoined the lunch ensemble, I casually remarked to the teacher sitting with us that visiting a nursery school is a true busman's holiday for someone interested in language acquisition.

The teacher looked at me quizzically:

"Did one of the kids say something interesting?"

I shared with her Susan's "any more gooder."

"Are you sure?"

the teacher probed.

"I just heard them comparing jelly."

Children can take potshots at any piece of grammar that lies beyond their grasp. Pronouns offer a good example. Somewhere between ages 2 and 3, children begin to recognize that pronouns (e.g., *he, she, we*) can be used in place of nouns. However, many young children take some time to figure out which pronoun to use when. Alex (age 3;3 at the time), in reply to his father's inquiry about his mother's where-abouts, responded,

"He wented out."

Another active area for potshots is prepositions. As speakers learning English as a second language can attest, prepositions often appear illogical, and even capricious. Such problems are just as real for children learning the language as native speakers:

Sara (3;4):   "Wait *until* [= for] me!"
Ryan (3;11):   "I'm hungry *of* [= for] potatoes."

One of the worst linguistic labyrinths through which new speakers must wend their way is the system of verbal auxiliaries: forms of *be, have,* and *do,* plus progressive *-ing* and perfective *-ed* or *-en.* These pieces provide the grammatical putty necessary to express complex verbal meanings. Children initially go astray in a host of ways. For example, one day Alex (3;8) and his mother had been out visiting friends. As

109

the two returned home in the car, Alex called out to his mother from the back seat,

"Where *were* we *been?*"

[= Where *have* we *been?*]

A similar potshot was fired by Sara, the day of her fourth birthday. Sara had been given a Polaroid camera, and the family went off to the local zoo to try it out. In the bird house, Sara snapped a picture of a snowy owl. When the owl turned its head to avoid the sudden light, Sara observed,

"Snowy owls don't like *to be take* one of these."

[= Snowy owls don't like *to have* their pictures *taken.*]

But of all the auxiliaries, the one generating the most confusion is the deceptively innocent word *do* (as in "*Do* you want some cheese?" or "I *didn't* eat it" or "You want to go home, *don't* you"). The course of saturation in the use of *do* provides a synoptic case study of how children move from taking grammatical potshots, to engaging in coherent (though incorrect) strategies using scissors and paste, to mastering a construction.

Let's follow Ryan's development.

Around age 3, Ryan began dallying with forms of the auxiliary *do* as well as with concepts whose expression in English requires the use of *do*. Drawing together two memorized (but incompatible) phrases, Ryan declared to his mother,

"I love you, doesn't it?"

A few days later, in response to his mother's question whether he would like to finish his milk, the little boy declared,

"No me no."

[= No, I don't.]

Over the next three months, Ryan began actively attempting to use *do* but typically confused the correct distribution of *do* with that of the verb *be*. On the one hand, Ryan said,

"Don't car broken."

[= The car isn't broken.]

and

"I don't hungry."

[= I'm not hungry.]

On the other hand, in reply to the question, "Do you know what he did?" Ryan answered,

"No he aren't."

[= No, I don't.]

or in response to "Do you like the music?" Ryan exclaimed,

"Yes I am!"

Between the ages of 3;6 and 4, Ryan came to recognize that *do* can appear in the middle of a sentence as an auxiliary and can carry a past-tense marker (e.g., "I didn't want to leave"). In adult English, this use of *do* is appropriate with negatives. When it appears in declarative sentences (e.g., "I did want to leave"), the result is to lend emphasis. However, Ryan's forays into *do* at this stage suggest that he was using *do* strictly to carry the past-tense marker. In fact, for several months, *did* was Ryan's standard way of expressing past tense—sometimes in tandem with another past-tense marker on the main verb for good measure:

3;5   "He did catch a train."
3;6   "You did buy it for me."
3;6   "I did wanted to go."

and after a water taxi ride around Baltimore's Inner Harbor,

3;7   "I did went on a boat to [= in] Baltimore."

By the time he neared age 4, Ryan had largely figured out the mysteries of *do*, although proper placement of the tense marker and appropriate distribution of *do*, *be*, and *have* as auxiliary verbs and *-ed* as a

111

perfective marker occasionally remained elusive. At 3;11, while watching his neighbor haul a leaf blower out of the garage, Ryan inquired,

"What does this does?"

The same month, after viewing a chase scene from *Indiana Jones and the Last Crusade* in which Indy and his father are being pursued by the Nazis, Ryan asked,

"Did all the bad guys died down into the ground?"

Why Because? Adult Contributions

Besides children's self-generated strategies (such as analogy or scissors and paste), another crucial source of children's early grammatical patterns is the speech they hear modeled by parents. The conversational imperative that fuels the original language duet leads parents to indulge in baby talk when addressing their offspring and to adopt special conventions for carrying the conversational load.

Adult speech alterations are designed to facilitate children's acquisition of language and to strengthen the personal bond between parent and child. Yet as undiscriminating language consumers, children take adults at their word, and parents are treated to echoes of their own speech. For instance, in hopes of simplifying the words and sentences with which children must cope, parents often instruct 12-month-olds to wave "bye-bye" (rather than "good-bye") and ask 4-year-olds if they want to "go potty" (not "to the bathroom" or even "to *the* potty"). When a child repeats back the ungrammatical phrases she hears modeled, it is hardly fair to charge her with a grammatical error.

Even parental modeling of correct grammar can sometimes bear strange fruit when a child inappropriately analyzes the language he hears. When Alex was less than a year old, his parents conscientiously modeled both sides of conversations for their son. A typical monologue would go like this:

"Alex, do you see that plane in the sky? It's flying very low. Do you know *why*? *Because* it is going to land soon."

For reasons of clarity, both *why* and *because* carried special emphasis.

By age 2;11, Alex had entered the proverbial "why" stage, challenging why he had to eat his supper, why the sun was setting, and even why the cat had just fallen asleep. But given the persistently modeled adult structure of "Do you know why? Because . . . ," Alex's own question was never "why" but always "why because":

> Alex's mother: "It's time to go to bed now."
> Alex: "Why because?"

Through similar modeling, Sara (2;3) came up with the request

> "Please carry you." [= Please carry me.]

following her mother's constant refrain,

> "I don't always need to carry you, Sara."

More generally, how do adults—consciously or unwittingly—influence their offspring's emerging grammar? One especially important avenue is massaging children's own utterances.

The main role parents have in shaping their children's grammar is "massaging" the form or content of what children have already said. Sometimes the goal is subtly to correct children's half-baked linguistic attempts; at other times, the parent's intention is simply to further the conversation. In either case, the result is to provide a reinforcing model for the grammar appropriate to a conversational context.

To see how such massaging of children's own utterances works, let's look at some exchanges between Ryan and his mother. In the first instance, Ryan's mother molds Ryan's original comment by expanding it:

> Mother: "Ryan, finish your milk."
> Ryan: (2½-year-old Ryan picks up his milk and dutifully drains the cup)
> "Milk all gone."
> Mother: "Yes, the milk is all gone."

Ryan's mother retrieves her son's entire sentence ("Milk all gone"), adds to it the grammatical trappings of an adult utterance (a modifier for *milk*, i.e., *the*, and a verb, i.e, *is*), and affirms the correctness of the whole utterance by adding "*Yes*" to the front.

A second type of linguistic massage is not only to repeat what a child has just said but to introduce a correction at the same time:

Ryan (3;0): "Why we're going home?"
Mother: "Why are we going home?"

Ryan's mother takes her son's complete but grammatically incorrect sentence and repeats it back in a corrected form.

A third possibility is to use what a child has said as a springboard for more conversation:

Ryan (3;1): "You did be there before?"
Mother: "Yes, I've been there before. In fact, I've been there with you, silly!"

Rather than directly correct Ryan's grammar, his mother proceeds to answer his question. However, her answer also models the proper grammatical form for the auxiliaries (*have . . . been*).

Beyond massaging what children actually say, some parents take a more aggressive role in their children's grammatical saturation by attempting to teach constructions they sense are troublesome to their child. A clear example is the way Alex's mother undertook to help her son learn pronouns.

Alex's mother had initially practiced the common baby talk strategy of substituting nouns for pronouns ("Does Alex want to get into the car now?"). By the time Alex was 2;10, his mother's seemingly innocuous strategy backfired. Unlike his age-mates, Alex wasn't learning any pronouns.

Alex's mother swung into action. Her first move was to abandon proper names and restrict herself to pronouns wherever possible ("Do *you* want to get into the car now?"). The next step was to help ease Alex through the predictably rocky shoals of selecting the right pronoun. When Alex, describing his (female) teacher's new rabbit, announced,

"He got a new rabbit,"

Alex's mother gently coached her son:

"Boys are *he's* and girls are *she's*. Your teacher is a girl, so she is a *she*. *She* got a new rabbit."

Within three or four months, Alex not only actively used pronouns but began correcting many of his false starts:

3;4 "She went, *he* went to the bathroom."

In addition to linguistic massages or old-fashioned pedagogy, parents also have the option of directly correcting their children's mistakes.

Does correction work?

When I first began studying children's language acquisition in the late 1960s, my fellow classmates and I were taught that children learn language on their own, not through imitation or through correction by adults. Time and again the same conversational exchange between a little girl and her mother was cited to prove the point. The example went like this:

Child: "Nobody don't like me."
Mother: "No, say 'Nobody likes me.' "
Child: "Nobody don't like me."

. . .

[eight repetitions of this dialogue]
Mother: "No, now listen carefully; say, '*Nobody likes me.*' "
Child: "Oh! Nobody don't like*s* me."

The moral of the example, we were told, was that no matter how hard parents might try to correct a child's grammar (the offending aberration here being the double negative *nobody* + *don't*), corrections will not register until the child is ready.

Over the years, I have spent a good deal of time listening to parental corrections and children's responses (be they in grammar, or in meaning, sound, or conversation). To conclude that children ignore corrections is simply wrong. Rather, children seem to be fickle. Sometimes they accept a correction, other times not.

But why?

After much more observation and analysis, a pattern finally began to emerge. A preschooler's openness to absorbing a correction depends on whether the child has a "stake" in the construction adults are trying to correct—that is, the child has exerted effort in formulating the wayward construction (through analogy or scissors and paste) rather than taking a linguistic potshot.

Ryan, Sara, and Alex's responses to parental correction are highly predictable by seeing when they have a stake in their grammatical choices:

- Ryan, at 4;3, was recounting for his mother a recent class trip to the bakery:

    "Mommy,"

  he said,

    "it was very crowded. One person was buying rolls. One person was buying cookies. And two persons were buying cupcakes."

  His mother paused for a moment and replied,

    "Oh, so two *people* got cupcakes."

  Ryan shot back,

    "No, Mommy. Two *persons* got cupcakes."

- Sara's mother had come to tuck her daughter into bed one evening (the girl was 3;4 at the time), and Sara requested,

    "Lay down with me, Mommy."

  As she stretched out on the bed, Sara's mother murmured,

    "Sure, I'll lie down, Sara."

  Her daughter's "correction" was immediate:

    "No, *lay* down, Mommy!"

- And then there's the case of *allbody*. Just before turning 3, Alex began expressing social niceties such as "Hello" and "Goodbye" without being prompted. One evening, as he prepared to go off to bed with his visiting aunt, leaving a cluster of adults behind, he waved brightly and chirped,

    "Good night, allbody."

  In the months ahead, the locution held fast ("Allbody outside" or "Where allbody?"), despite repeated parental attempts to massage Alex's version (e.g., "Yes, everybody is outside" or "Where do you think everybody is?").

Ryan, Sara, and Alex's insistence on sticking to their linguistic guns reflects their stake in what they had said. By the simple rule of analogy (*apple* : *apples* = *person* : *persons*), Ryan's *persons* is a perfectly logical plural, just as Alex's *allbody* is a reasonable melding of phrases such as "all the friends" with *everybody*. Sara's rejection of *lie* in favor of *lay* reflects the fact that Sara did not yet have *lie* in her vocabulary and therefore assumed her mother did not know what she was talking about. (Granted, many speakers of American English do not make the traditional distinction between "to *lie*" and "to *lay*," though Sara's mother did.) And the little girl who would not relinquish her double negative in "Nobody don't like me" was also reasonably clinging to her strategy for handling negatives (paste together a subject and verb—who said anything about counting how many negatives you have in one sentence?).

When are children open to correction? When they have nothing to lose by relinquishing their own (incorrect) attempt. Consider some of the grammatical potshots we looked at earlier. When Sara (3;4) said to her mother,

"Wait until [= for] me!"

her mother countered with the recast

"Shall I wait for you?"

Sara's response was a naturally compliant

"Yes, wait for me!"

In the same vein, when Alex (3;3), referring to his mother, explained,

"He wented out."

Alex's father queried,

"Oh, she went out?"

Alex's answer revealed his grammatical cards:

"She wented out."

117

While quite willing to accept a correction on the pronoun, Alex was not yet prepared to relinquish his principled construction of *wented*.

Not surprisingly, children's openness to correction is subject to additional conditions. The two most important are, Is the grammatical construction at issue truly beyond the child's grasp? and Is the child on the verge of abandoning a previously active strategy?

Take Sara's

"Snowy owls don't like to be take one of these."

[= Snowy owls don't like to have their pictures taken.]

At age 4, Sara used very few passive sentences. The ones in her repertoire were limited to simple subjects and verbs (e.g., "I got hit," "The car was mushed by the train"). A complex passive verb phrase such as "have their pictures taken" was much beyond her control. While Sara might have been able to imitate the correct version immediately following parental modeling, there's no reason to believe such imitation of a corrected sentence would lead directly to language learning.

Are immediate imitations of adult corrections ever productive? Definitely yes—when the child is on the verge of abandoning old analogies or scissors and paste strategies that yield logical but incorrect results. We see this kind of evolution in Ryan's approach to word order in questions and in Alex's loosening stake in his old favorite, *allbody*:

Ryan (4;0)	"Why we aren't going home yet?"
Ryan's mother:	"Why aren't we going home?"
Ryan:	"Yeah. Why aren't we going home?"
Alex (3;8)	"Allbody come here!"
Alex's aunt:	"Do you want everybody to come here?"
Alex:	"Everybody come here!"

As we will see in Chapter 6, children's growing ability to absorb correction (delivered either overtly or more subtly) is itself an important step in their awareness of language as a malleable system.

■ IDEAS AND ALERTS

How Can I Help?

**Become aware of the grammatical features
of baby talk you use with your child that
yield unusual or ungrammatical language.**

As preschoolers expand their grammatical skills, they increasingly benefit from hearing standard grammar modeled. Many baby talk features that initially were used to enhance social rapport or facilitate communication can now be jettisoned. These include:

- Using nouns in lieu of pronouns ("Daddy wants Alex to brush his teeth.")
- Using plural pronouns in place of singular ("Shall we brush our teeth?")
- Intentional ungrammatical usage ("No eat!")

**Reinforce, build on, and correct your
preschooler's grammatical efforts.**

Actively model the kind of grammar you want your children to be learning. Repetitions, expansions, and recastings provide a natural way of building on your child's interests and current focus of attention.

Recognize your child's orienteering strategies (analogies, scissors and paste, potshots) as signs of grammatical growth, not as errors. Offer corrections (e.g., through repetitions and expansions), but don't be judgmental if the correction is not taken. Fluent 2-, 3-, or 4-year-olds can be driven to stutter if they sense you are dissatisfied with their grammar. Remember that children who still have a stake in analogies or scissors and paste constructions have genuine difficulty in abandoning their strategies.

**Encourage entire sentences (not single
words) in requests and in answers to
questions.**

Without turning pedantic or generating stress in your child, encourage preschoolers to exercise their growing grammatical knowledge.

Less verbal children can especially benefit from gentle urgings to articulate "Please may I have more juice" in lieu of simply "Please" or "Juice."

Should I Be Concerned?

My 2-year-old has started using a few word combinations, but his sentence length doesn't seem to be increasing.

Many children who are linguistic late bloomers go through a sharp growth spurt some time between ages 2 and 3, and about 50 percent of children who appear to have a delay in their expressive language at age 2 show spontaneous "remission" of the problem by age 3. Additional research suggests that although a 1½- or 2-year-old may go for even half a year without producing progressively longer sentences, he may well be acquiring other linguistic skills during the same period (e.g., conventions of conversation, intonation markers). Such children have been known to double or triple their average sentence length within a few months.

The older a child becomes, the greater the likelihood that delayed syntactic development may warrant professional attention. Three-year-olds who are not spontaneously using three- or four-word sentences should probably be evaluated.

Many of my child's sentences are simply imitations of other people's sentences, not spontaneous creations of her own.

Children who are late talkers and those who initially began using syntax through an expressive strategy (the groups are often the same) commonly imitate language they hear from others. As a 3-year-old, Alex was more likely to imitate the speech of adults and other children around him than he was to create his own multiword utterances.

For many children, such imitations provide a linguistic stepping-stone for launching into independent constructions. However, if a toddler or preschooler is only imitating the language of others, or if imitation continues to predominate past age 3, professional assessment is in order.

My child seems to be developing grammar but rarely makes use of analogies or scissors and paste strategies.

Many shy or linguistically cautious children (especially during the early preschool years) avoid language experimentation. These are the same children who tend to be heavy imitators of other speakers' vocabulary and grammar. Most of these children reach a takeoff point between age 3 and 4, when they launch into analogies and scissors and paste strategies.

What about children who do not reach this takeoff point? Continuing shyness may be the explanation. Lack of such creativity may also be a sign of slow (though still normal) language development. And with yet other children, the problem is a genuine developmental language disorder. In his landmark longitudinal study of language acquisition, Roger Brown and his colleagues at Harvard University described the syntactic and morphological development of three children. No morphological overgeneralizations were reported for the child who was slowest to learn grammar. In my own studies of grammatical development in children with specific language impairment, I found that among the 4-, 5-, and 6-year-olds I was observing, none produced any morphological overgeneralizations (such as *mans* for *men* or *goed* for *went*).

■ 5. Bags on the Banks

Orienteering in Meaning, Sound, and Conversation

RYAN and his mother were driving home from the post office one afternoon. As they waited at a red light, the little boy (then 4;1) had a question:

"Why they put bags on the banks?"

Ryan's mother was stumped.

"What do you mean? I don't know what you're talking about."

Ryan persisted:

"Bags on the banks. You know!"

But of course she didn't. Ryan's mother put out a cautious feeler:

"Where were the banks, Ryan?"

The child described the location precisely:

"Right in front of the post office. On the street."

Ryan's mother imagined the scene, and, in an epiphany, her son's cryptic question became clear. The "banks" were the parking meters in front of the post office, all of which were temporarily covered with plastic bags bearing the warning "Emergency—No Parking."

Why *banks*? Ryan didn't yet know the term *parking meter*. However, he did know about putting money into little machines and turning knobs, thanks to the small plastic bank he had been presented a few months earlier. *Bank* was a highly reasonable label for the familiar but nameless parking meter.

During the same two- to three-year period that children engage in active grammatical orienteering, they are also edging toward saturation in their control of meaning, sound, and conversational formats. In all three areas, preschoolers exhibit ingenuity and effort as they struggle to make language serve their communicative and social needs.

Last Night in the Morning: Strategies for Expressing Meaning

Preschoolers soak up new meanings at an astounding rate. Estimates have put the average number as high as 10 or 20 new words a day, although parents would be hard pressed to compile actual lists, since children rarely utter all the words they learn—at least not in hearing range of their parents.

How do children attribute meanings to words and find words for expressing meanings? In the earliest stages of language development, word use is directly tied to objects and events in the immediate environment (like *daddy* and *dogs*, *juice* and *jeeps*). With time, children begin learning words for abstractions and ways of talking about what was or might yet be. From toddlerhood up through old age, people continue to learn new words for meanings and new meanings for words. The fundamental motivation underlying this effort is the drive to make sense of the world of experience—and of language—that we encounter.

Children's personal experiences and interests guide their early meaning interpretations. Alex's fixation with trains, for example, led to an amusing piece of meaning orienteering. For his second birthday, Alex had been presented with a Brio train set—a wooden track and a dozen wooden cars that attached to one another magnetically. Although Alex could hardly keep the cars on the track (much less connected to one another), he fell in love with trains on the spot, a fascination that was to last for many years.

When Alex was about 2½, his mother started toilet training him, keeping him in diapers but sitting him on the potty at regular intervals. Alex enjoyed the attention, although he did not seem to get the message. When he was 2;8, his mother took a more aggressive tack, abandoning diapers altogether. To herald the event, she purchased a supply of thick training pants. Trying to entice Alex to embark on this new adventure, she whipped out a pair of pants and proudly displayed them:

"Alex, shall we put on your new training pants?"

Alex skeptically sized up the strange cotton bloomers and grasped them at arm's length. Suddenly he broke into a smile:

"Choo choo trainee pants!"

he declared and clutched them to his body. If these contraptions had something to do with trains, they had to be OK.

Sara's love of the zoo accounts for one of her attempts at meaning orienteering. Since her family lived within walking distance of a large zoo, she went often and came to know the names of many animals—many, but not all. One day as she and her father strolled into the primate house, her father leaned over and asked,

"Do you know what baboons are?"

Sara, who was 3;6 at the time, hesitated for only a minute:

"Panda bears eat baboons!" [i.e., bamboo]

Ryan made one of his own forays into meaning orienteering a week before Halloween. His mother was trying to nail down a costume for her son, but her suggestions (a doctor? a fire chief?) fell on deaf ears. It was 1990, and all the kids at school (including Ryan) knew just what they wanted to wear.

"What?"

asked his beleaguered mother. Ryan's prompt answer:

"I want a teenage-and-a-turtle suit."

[= a Teenage Mutant Ninja Turtle suit]

125

Parental influence is evidenced in much of the vocabulary toddlers and preschoolers use: their names for bathroom functions (is it *pee pee* or *wee wee*), minor cuts and scrapes (*boo boo* or *ouch*), and even for parents themselves (e.g., *Mommy, Mom, Ma, Mama*). Parents—or their modern surrogate, television—also account for some esoteric vocabulary, as when Alex (3;2) picked up the word *puce* (describing Maria's shoes in an episode on "Sesame Street").

Much as the meanings of words naturally evolve with time and experience, the words themselves that children choose for labeling meanings can shift. The changing words parents use and the new contexts they create often contribute to this evolution. Alex's labels for "telephone" illustrate the process.

Like many other parents, Alex's mother and father developed several affectionate names for their son. The name with the greatest longevity was *Clue*, derived from their own imitation of Alex's earliest consistent vocalization back at age 3 or 4 months, when the expected *coo* or *goo* had come out sounding more like *clue*.

By the time he was 1½ years, Alex had developed a fascination for the telephone. Whenever it rang, he insisted on having the receiver immediately placed by his ear. When members of the family called, they fell into the habit of opening their conversation with,

"Hello, Clue,"

knowing he would be the first to hear their voice.

Alex clearly needed a name for the apparatus in order to summon adults to pick up the receiver when the phone rang. *Telephone* was far too complex. (Recall that Alex used only monosyllables until he was 2;6.) The solution was obvious: he called it *coo*. (Now that Alex had passed the cooing stage, he no longer could produce the *cl-* in *clue*—or any other consonant clusters, for that matter.)

Phase two came when Alex was 2;2. He had begun to refer to himself by name (*Uh*), and the family had dropped *Clue* in favor of *Alex* as well. Therefore, calls home now began with,

"Hello, Alex."

Alex's new name for the telephone? *Uh.*

Over the next few months, a minor family crisis generated a large number of telephone calls from Alex's aunt, Sheila. The phone would ring, and Alex's father would announce,

"I'll get it. It's probably Sheila."

Alex's new name for the telephone became *she* (his version of *Sheila*).

Finally at age 2;6, Alex began to master polysyllabic words. One of his earliest three-syllable utterances was *telephone*.

Beyond their influence on specific vocabulary choices, parents exert more subtle and far-reaching semantic sway as well. A classic example is the role parents play in shaping children's very language (and perhaps notions) about what is inert and what is alive. Common lore has it that young children are animistic, attributing living qualities to lifeless objects. The evidence? Comments like Sara's

"The chair tripped me,"

when she stumbled over its legs and fell down.

Did 3-year-old Sara really believe that a chair could strike out like an untamed lion? Given that Sara never tried to feed the chair or take it for a walk, it's hard to take this hypothesis seriously. What is Sara really saying—and where did she learn to say it? Listen to her parents:

"Sara, please don't hit the table. It will cry."

"Take your feet off the chair. Would you like the chair to put its legs on you?"

"Don't drop that music box. If you break it, it can't sing to you any more."

Or consider this scene from the dinner table at Ryan's house. Ryan was refusing to eat his vegetables. His mother played her last card:

"But Ryan, the spinach will be very sad if you don't eat it."

Sara's mother and father are gamely trying to protect the furniture from the excesses of a healthy 3-year-old, while Ryan's mother is struggling to ensure her son adequate nutrition. But like many other well-meaning efforts, these lead to unintended (though harmless—and transient) consequences. Does Sara really believe the chair is alive? When Ryan replies,

> "I don't care about how the spinach feels. It make me feel yucky,"

does he really believe that spinach has feelings? Hardly. When Sara and Ryan join in on these animistic conversations, they confirm how the conversational imperative draws us to harmonize with our interlocutor's language patterns. Logical meaning takes a backseat to conversational repartee.

Another common lexical strategy of children is to use existing words in their vocabulary to stand in for names they do not yet know (like Ryan's *banks* in lieu of *parking meters*). With younger children (whose sentences tend to be no more than a few words in length), adults sometimes have initial difficulty figuring out what words their children's stand-ins are intended to replace. Close attention to context, coupled with multiple repetitions (often accompanied by frustration from the child), eventually leads to decipherment. Such was the case with Sara's idiosyncratic use of *bye*.

By the time she was 2, Sara had learned both the words *bye* (as in "good-bye") and *no* and used them appropriately. However, unlike most of her age-mates, Sara had not adopted the habit of using *no* as an emphatic form of refusal.

Make no mistake. Sara possessed the same stubborn streak that most other children do, but she expressed it differently. When she absolutely did not want something to happen (like being given medicine), she would cry out,

> "Bye!"

(as in "Get thee gone, oh medicine!"). As her likes and dislikes became increasingly defined, Sara embellished the imperative and would yell,

> "No, bye, no!"

when she truly wanted to suspend an impending action. (In the same vein, the 2-year-old son of one of my colleagues used to refer to his baby-sitter as "Maria-Bye-Bye," hoping she would take the hint.)

Ryan's early lexical stand-ins centered on repairing damage he felt his mother had done to the status quo. At age 2;6, he was especially sensitive to having water spill on him or on anything else. He would demand of his mother that she dry the moistened object (a shirt, the floor, his face) immediately. With obvious logic, Ryan soon began using the word *dry* to mean "undo damage" (of whatever origin). If a spoon fell on the floor or a glass broke, Ryan's immediate demand was

"Dry!"

One evening at bedtime, when Ryan was 2;8, his mother was sitting on Ryan's bed reading him a story. All of a sudden Ryan bellowed,

"Dry poo!"

(*Poo* was Ryan's word for "pillow.") His mother was perplexed. The pillow wasn't wet; nothing had broken. Puzzled, she declared,

"But the pillow isn't wet, Ryan."

Ryan ignored the irrelevancy:

"Dry poo! Dry poo!"

Tears of anger began to fall. Still his mother did not understand. In desperation, Ryan yanked the pillow away and began to smooth the case. In a slightly calmed, affirmative voice he declared,

"Dry poo."

Ryan's mother had been sitting on the edge of the pillow (causing, in Ryan's eyes, incalculable damage). Ryan had been making the reasonable (though initially incomprehensible) request that his mother offer reparations.

As children get older and their grammar becomes more advanced, the stand-ins they invent become more immediately interpretable. Here are some samples:

- Sara (2;8) was staring at the bathroom mirror, which had become fogged over after her father's shower:

  "Let's *erase* the mirror."

- Sara's family had just returned from a Middle Eastern grocery store, where they had purchased the traditional thin, folded

129

Lebanese bread known as lavash. Sara (3;8) unfolded a piece and declared with glee,

"It's *napkin bread!*"

- Ryan's family was on its way to the beauty parlor. His sister, Cathy, began describing how she would like her hair to be cut. Ryan (3;6) asked,

"Where's the *cut shop?*"

- Alex (age 3;5) had been learning procedures for sequenced activities: nighttime rituals, directions for baking bread, instructions for operating a small robot. However, he did not yet know the word *instructions*. This gap did not dissuade Alex from describing how to carry out a procedure that held great fascination for him:

"Hey, I know the *ingredients* for driving. You put both hands on the wheel. Push it round and round, and then it goes."

Another major source of children's novel vocabulary is words derived from other words. In each case, these new forms might logically belong in the language but do not happen to. A large number of children's new words arise by deriving verbs from nouns, or the reverse:

- Shortly after his fourth birthday, Alex informed his aunt (whose birthday celebration he was attending),

"When I get big, I can *match* [= light with a match] the candles myself."

- Ryan (3;8) was watching an episode of "Sesame Street" in which Big Bird was being his usual ungamely self in a tennis match:

"Why Big Bird can't *tennis* the ball [= hit the tennis ball]?"

- Sara (3;8) was going through an intense phase of independence. Not only was she adamant that she could do everything herself, but she refused to let anyone act in parallel. Whenever her parents seemed to err, Sara was quick to call a halt:

"Don't *copy cat* me [= don't be a copy cat of my actions]!"

- Ryan (4;2) had been watching his sister sharpen a pencil in a small hand-held sharpener (of the sort with a transparent plastic dome to hold the shavings). Ryan ran off with the sharpener to the nearest wastebasket and dumped out the contents. Upon returning, he proudly announced to Cathy,

"I emptied the *sharpens*."

Other active transformations are of prepositions into verbs:

- Alex (3;8) and his mother were reading a book in which on the current page a large fish was swimming in the opposite direction from the page before. Alex informed his mother,

 "The fish is *towardsing* this way [moving towards this direction]."

verbs into adjectives:

- After much anticipation, Ryan (3;2) and his older sister were allowed to go out and play in the newly fallen snow. As they dashed out the door, Cathy exclaimed to her brother,

 "It's snowy out here."

 Ryan rushed past his sister. Running as fast as the drifts would allow, he called back over his shoulder,

 "I'm *runny*."

adjectives into verbs:

- Sara's mother always took extra care when driving in the car with her children. Often she would comment,

 "That's a bad driver!"

 when she found herself applying the brakes quickly or swerving suddenly to give another vehicle wide berth. Sara (3;6) was at the height of her "Why?" phase and naturally wanted to know why her mother had identified the drivers of certain cars as "bad." Grasping for an abbreviated explanation, her mother replied,

 "Because they have empty heads."

 Sara paused for a moment and then brightly volunteered,

 "Let's *full* them."

and nouns into nouns:

- As she neared age 4, Sara took increasing delight in imaginative play. Not only did she create new objects, but she invented words for them as well. One afternoon she rolled up a piece of paper, held it to her shoulder, and announced,

"This is my *gunner*."

(apparently similar to—but not the same as—a gun). Several weeks later, while standing outside in bright sunlight, she squinted and placed a rock in front of each eye. Matter-of-factly she informed her mother,

"These are my *sunners*. They throw the sun."

Children's creativity in meaning orienteering is often evidenced in the ingenious methods they devise for talking about time. Preschoolers often understand basic concepts of past and future but do not yet control the appropriate linguistic tools for expressing these notions (recall Sara's "I want to broke it"). Even when children have mastered essential grammatical markers of the past tense (e.g., *-ed*) and indicators of future intent (e.g., "I will break it," "I want to break it"), they still must learn to distinguish events in the immediate past, the far past, the near future, and the more distant future.

While English lacks standard grammatical forms for differentiating these points on a time line, the language does offer such phrases as "a little while ago," "yesterday," "a long time ago," "in a few minutes," "sometimes," and so forth. Children take several years to learn linguistic labels for these nuances. In the meanwhile, how do they talk about specific points in the past and the future?

One solution is to capitalize on words already in their repertoire, relying on context (or modifiers) to clarify their meanings. The scheme Alex created between the time he was 3 and 4 illustrates one such strategy for talking about the past.

At age 3;1, Alex learned the word *yesterday*. However, within days, it became clear that he did not define the word to mean "the day before today." Rather, it meant "any time in the past"—yesterday, several minutes ago, or several years back. And so he would declare,

"I went to see the trains *yesterday*,"

when he actually had seen them but a few hours before.

Five months later, the universal past time marker *yesterday* was replaced by the phrase "last night." In talking about a visit to the pediatrician six months earlier (during which he was asked to produce a urine sample), Alex reminded his mother,

> "*Last night* when I was a little tiny baby I pee peed in a cup."

(The family had devised the phrase "when you were a little tiny baby" to reinforce the message that Alex was a big boy now, and big boys do not whine, cry, and so forth.) The next month, Alex refined his use of "last night" by adding modifiers that were more specific:

> "*Last night in the morning* my friends played at the playground."

(Alex's description to his father of the adventure Alex and his friends had had earlier that day).

By the time Alex turned 4, he was using *yesterday* and *last night* with their normal adult meanings. The problem was that Alex now lacked a generalized term for marking the past. (He still did not command phrases like "a long time ago" or "in the past.") His solution, while unorthodox, filled the bill. Any event that happened further back than yesterday was now labeled "the day before this day," for example,

> "*The day before this day* [four months ago] we went to Vermont."

Over the next several months, Alex simplified his past-tense marker to "a few days ago," as in

> "A few days ago [eight months ago] we built a snowman."

The Aunt from Ami: The Sounds of Language

The family was off for a Saturday outing to Annapolis, Maryland. As they drove along Route 50, heading out of Washington, Sara's mother counted off the adventures that awaited them in Annapolis—lunch at a restaurant overlooking the harbor, a boat ride along the Chesapeake, a visit to the Naval Academy.

Sara, who was 3½ at the time, listened attentively and then asked her usual,

> "Why?"

> "Why what?"

queried her mother. Sara explained the obvious:

"Why are we going to Apolis?"

Her mother paused and recast her daughter's truncated nomenclature:

"You want to know why we are going to Annapolis?"

Sara cut off her mother immediately:

"To *Apolis*. Why are we going to *Apolis*?"

Sara's confusion over the name *Annapolis* was understandable and ingenious, revealing important (though not fully consistent) knowledge of the way English works. Sara recognized that names of things often are modified by (have stuck before them) words like *the*, *a*, or *an*. At the same time, she knew that proper names (like names of people or places) do not carry such initial baggage. When she heard they were traveling to "an Apolis," she discarded the unwanted *an* and held fast to what she assumed was the real name of the place.

Sara's interpretation of *Apolis* is but one example of a common strategy preschoolers use. When Ryan was 4;7, he came to school accompanied by an aunt who was visiting. Ryan's teacher asked the boy to share with the class where his aunt was from. Suddenly shy, Ryan fell mute. His aunt supportively leaned over to Ryan and whispered,

"I'm from Miami."

With new confidence, Ryan addressed his friends:

"She's from her Ami."

Apolis and *Ami* illustrate preschoolers' orienteering strategies in sound. As the canister of meaning, sound is a vital component of linguistic expression. A continuing source of frustration for many preschoolers is that their cognitive abilities outstrip their control of phonology. Sometimes the problem is speed: getting your tongue to keep up with your mind. Other times, persistently problematic sounds (or sound combinations) throw up obstacles that slow the communication process and generate considerable frustration. Fortunately, a combination of context and the conversational imperative usually enables children to make themselves understood, even when their linguistic tools are still in need of honing.

Many children whose command of grammar and meaning is fairly sophisticated nonetheless have difficulty pronouncing certain sounds. Among the most infamous culprits are the two liquids (*l* and *r*) and the two glides (*w* and *y*).

Why are *l*, *r*, *w*, and *y* so problematic? Because their construction in the mouth is elusive. If you stand before a mirror and make first an *r* and then a *w*, you see little difference, other than a slightly greater pursing of the lips for the *w*. To make a *y*, you part your lips and then curl the tongue just so towards the roof of the mouth—hardly something you can detect in the mirror or children can see from the faces of adult speakers. Producing an *l* is even worse. Not only are you unable to see what the tongue is doing, but placement of the lips shifts, depending upon what sound follows. The *l* of *liquid* is made with the lips spread wide, while the *l* of *larceny* is generally formed with the lips more rounded—in fact, more like a *w* or *r*.

The result is that preschoolers commonly speak of "pet wabbits," describe the sun as *wellow*, or call a *lamp* a *ramp*. Young children sometimes initially avoid the word *yes* altogether because of the troublesome *y* sound. Such confusion among liquids and glides can extend into the early elementary school years.

The choice of sound substitutions is often predictable by looking at where in the mouth the sound following the liquid or glide is formed. Ryan's struggles with the *l* sound over a two-year period illustrate the process.

One of Ryan's favorite teachers at nursery school was named Lawrence. When Ryan first met up with Lawrence—Ryan was 2;8 at the time—he refused to attempt Lawrence's name. (Ryan's means of getting Lawrence's attention was to grab his leg.) Shortly after his third birthday, Ryan ventured his first name for Lawrence:

"Warence"

The sound *w* soon became Ryan's universal substitution for all *l*'s and *r*'s. In fact, Ryan's own name for himself was *Wyan*.

Warence continued as the name of choice for Lawrence for nearly eight months, when it was replaced by

"Yarence"

Most other *l*'s retained their original *w* substitutes, as in,

(at 3;8) "Yarence, I'm teasing you a *w*iddle."

The exception was words with the *a* sound in *bat*, where Ryan substituted an *r*. And so Ryan would say *rand* for *land*, *rast* for *last*, and *ramp* for *lamp*.

The distribution of substitutions was remarkably consistent: any *l* followed by a vowel formed at the top or in the middle of the mouth was replaced by a *w*:

little => *widdle*

let => *wet*

Sheila => *Sheiwa*

loop => *woop*

low => *wow* [rhymes with *go*]

For *l*'s followed by low vowels (the vowels in *bat* and *bottom*), the substitution was either an *r* or a *y*: *r* if the vowel was formed in the front of the mouth—

last => *rast*

and *y* if the vowel was formed in the back of the mouth—

Lawrence => *Yarence*

The month of his fourth birthday, Ryan began attempting a real *l*. Some days Lawrence was *Lawrence*; other days he was back to *Yarence*. The deciding factor was the level of Ryan's concentration. When Ryan was tired or trying to talk quickly, *Yarence* reigned. In calmer moments, *Lawrence* prevailed. Ryan did not master *l* completely until he was nearly 4½.

Besides the challenges children encounter with individual sounds, they can also run into trouble with sound combinations. The biggest problem is that sounds in one syllable tend to influence sounds in an adjacent syllable. This symbiotic relationship appears in several guises: **syllabic consonants, assimilation,** and **dissimilation.**

What are **syllabic consonants,** and what is so problematic about them for children? In grammar school, we were taught that every syllable must have a vowel in it, with the exception of words in which *n* or *l* takes the place of a vowel (that is, functions as a syllabic consonant). Words like *button* and *hospital* are good examples. In normal adult conversation, we don't say "but-ton" or "hos-pi-tal" but rather "but-n" and "hos-pi-tl," where the *n* and *l,* respectively, serve double duty as consonants and vowels.

If you listen to young children utter words like *button* and *hospital,* you find they are generally more articulate in their pronunciations than adults. Many 3-year-olds enunciate "but-ton" even though their parents regularly say "but-n." Why? Because the principle of the syllabic consonant is beyond their ken.

Other children, such as Alex, invent alternative solutions to the problem of syllabic consonants. When one of his friends asked Alex why his father (a physician) wasn't coming to a Sunday afternoon birthday party, Alex (then 3;10) matter-of-factly replied,

"He's at the hospididil."

The addition of the extra -*di*- syllable (hospi*di*dil), along with the introduction of the *i* in the final syllable (hospidi*dil*) provided Alex a smooth way of breaking up the consonants (*p* . . . *d* . . . *l*) bunched at the end of the word. Alex's creation had lasting stability. Despite repeated attempts at correction by his parents, *hospididil* persisted over eight months.

Assimilation is a process whereby the sounds in one syllable are made to approximate those in another. Assimilation can involve making two sounds more alike in any of several ways, including the **place** in the mouth the sound is formed (e.g., in the front or the back), the **manner** in which the sound is produced (e.g., *t* and *ch* are formed in the same place but with different tongue configurations), and the presence or absence of **vocal cord** activity.

Take a simple word like *dogs*, which we pronounce as if it were

137

spelled *dogz*. Back in Chaucer's day (around 1400), the word was spelled *dogges* and was pronounced the way it was spelled. Over time, when the vowel *e* dropped out of plurals, the original final *s* was **assimilated** to the preceding consonant *g* with respect to voicing. Some consonants in English (e.g., *b, d, g, z*) are pronounced with the vocal cords vibrating, while others (e.g., *p, t, k,* and *s*) are formed with the vocal cords still. (Put your fingers over your Adam's apple, pronounce first *p* and then *b*, and you will feel the difference.) In the case of *dogs*, the plural *s* sound (which is "voiceless") assimilates in voicing manner to the preceding *g* (which is "voiced"), and so the *s* sound turns into a *z* sound.

Assimilation is very common among children struggling to handle polysyllabic words. Take the word *pasketti* (which is the way many 3- and 4-year-olds pronounce *spaghetti*). The word presents two difficulties:

> The initial *s* is formed in the middle of the mouth, the following *p* is produced in the front of the mouth, the next consonant, *g*, is made way in the back, and the final *t* returns to the middle.

> While *s, p,* and *t* are all voiceless consonants, the *g* (which is stuck between the *p* and the *t*) is voiced. To pronounce the word correctly, you must initially keep your vocal cords still, then have them vibrate, and finally hold them still once again.

Such rapid movements become second nature to saturated speakers, but these oral gymnastics prove too much for many inexperienced language users. A logical solution is to keep all sounds voiceless (thereby changing the *g* to a *k*) and to move in only one direction (from the front of the mouth—*p*—to the middle—*s . . . k . . . t*). The result is *pasketti*. (Note that in English, when an *s* sound precedes a *k*, the *k* is formed in the middle of the mouth rather than in the back, where *k* and *g* are usually formed. Try saying aloud *comb* and then *skidaddle*.)

Sara, Ryan, and Alex all made use of assimilations:

- Sara (2;10) "That's my *mazagine!*"
  As in the example of *spaghetti*, Sara breaks up the long trek from the front of the mouth (*m*) to the back (*g*) and then returning to the middle (*z*) by switching the second and third consonants (the *g* and the *z*).

- Alex (3;7) "Where's my *dump trunk?*"
  Although Alex consistently pronounced *truck* correctly when it appeared in isolation, as soon as the modifier *dump* was added, assimilation of nasal sounds (*m*, *n*) set in. Following the pattern of *u* + *m* + *p* from *dump* (where both *m* and *p* are formed with lips closed in the front of the mouth), Alex inserted an *n* into *truck*, yielding *u* + *n* + *k* (with both *n* and *k* formed in the middle of the mouth).

- Ryan (3;11) "Can I have a new *toofbrush?*"
  Rather than shuttling back and forth in the mouth to pronounce first a *t* (formed behind the teeth), then an open *oo*, then back behind the teeth for a *th*, and next up to the lips for the *b*, Ryan took a shortcut and assimilated the place of articulation of the *th* up front with the *b*, yielding *toofbrush*.

Sometimes instead of making two sounds more similar to each other, we make similar sounds distinct (**dissimilation**). Many people pronounce the word *library* as *libary* (dropping out the first *r*) because the two *r*'s in succession prove unwieldy. Others talk of "*bunking* [= *bumping*] into things," dissimilating the identical places of articulation of *b*, *m*, and *p* into two areas (*b* in the front of the mouth and *n* + *k* in the middle).

Children learning the sounds of language sometimes rely on dissimilation as well. When she was 3½, Sara announced one late afternoon that she was hungry.

"What would you like to eat?"

queried her mother. Sara thought for a moment and politely replied,

"Can I have a hangburbon?"

Sara's mother was bewildered. Obviously her daughter wasn't making historical reference to a French ruling family. Her mother asked for clarification, and Sara tried again:

"I want a hangburbon for supper."

Eventually Sara's meaning came clear. She wanted to eat a *hamburger*. Her difficulty was in tackling the juxtaposition of *m* + *b* and then the distance between *b* and *g*. Sara's solution was to **dissimilate** the place of articulation of the first two sounds by changing the *m* (formed in the front of the mouth) to an *-ng* combination (formed in the middle of the mouth) and then **assimilate** the original *g* (of -burger) up front with the *b* of -burger. The result: *hangburbon*.

No Thank You!
Becoming a Conversational Partner

Orienteering in grammar, meaning, and sound helps preschoolers develop the essential ingredients for conversing with people. In addition, however, children need to learn conversational rules of the road through which their utterances become timely and meaningful.

Conversational orienteering is the hardest of the language components to chart. Many speakers never master conversational etiquette and appropriateness. The precise nature of a person's conversational competence reflects a host of variables—from parental training in social expectations ("Say 'Thank you' ") to preparation for dealing with communication technologies (e.g., learning to use the telephone or leave a message on an answering machine). Regardless of the specific endpoints reached, the orienteering strategies children use to make sense of and enter the conversational stream are similar across situations. The overriding principle is always to capitalize on the linguistic tools you have available (words, grammatical constructions, memorized phrases) to accomplish your conversational goal—be it to make yourself understood, capture someone's attention, or halt an unwanted action.

The power of conversational orienteering becomes clear from the creative use Alex made of the simple phrase "thank you."

Alex's mother and father were intent upon raising a polite child. Whenever a desired item was proffered, Alex was reminded that a "thank you" was in order. Moreover, if Alex was offered an item or option ("Would you like some more milk before you go to bed?"), he was similarly reminded that an acceptable response was not "No" but rather "No thank you."

Alex was about as interested in saying "thank you" as he was in going to bed at night. However, when the phrase appeared to serve his own ends, Alex was quick to use it. In response, for example, to his mother's request,

"Shall we brush your teeth now?"

Alex (age 3;8 at the time) had a ready answer:

"No thank you!"

Alex had learned—only too well—that an invitation ("Shall we . . . ") can be declined with a "No thank you." His mother was checkmated.

The force of Alex's understanding that "No thank you" is an acceptable conversational vehicle for refusing an option at hand became clear two months later on a family vacation to Francophone Canada. Alex, who was highly allergic to insect venom, had been bitten by a common mosquito. Within a day, the puncture on his thigh was red and puffy. Home remedies (hotel style) proved useless. By the evening of the second day, the entire leg was swollen, and Alex was extremely uncomfortable. Not knowing any physicians (it was a Sunday to boot), the family went to a nearby hospital emergency room. The diagnosis was unclear: Either this was a simple allergic reaction to the mosquito venom or a very serious infection might have set in. Alex was promptly admitted to the hospital, and a series of tests was immediately ordered.

Alex tolerated the basic X rays of his leg quite well. His mother, trying to suppress her own concerns (and to calm her son), explained that the doctor was so impressed with Alex's leg that he wanted to take a picture. Leaving her son on the X-ray table and moving with the technician behind a metal shield, Alex's mother called out,

"Say 'Cheese'!"

which the brave little boy obediently did.

The next test, however, was more problematic. Alex was wheeled to nuclear medicine for a bone scan. Initially confident, Alex became traumatized when a heavy metal disk, nearly two feet in diameter, was suspended over his head. (The test necessitated scanning the entire body from head to toe.)

"No thank you!"

he called out to the new technician. Not understanding English (but used to children being fearful of the apparatus), she continued positioning the machine.

"No thank you! No thank you!"

the terrified child wailed, his voice rising and the tears beginning to flow.

Unable to bear her son's psychological ordeal, Alex's mother halted the test. As things turned out, the boy's swelling subsided within twenty-four hours, and he was released soon after. In the months ahead, Alex frequently recalled the incident—and often brought forth "No thank you" when an impending situation did not suit his liking.

Appropriate use of "thank you" is just one example of the myriad of conversational formulas that pervade everyday language use. Children learn many of these phrases by observing and imitating other speakers in their surroundings.

The power of conversational imitation came home to me several years ago when I was observing a class of 2-year-olds. One linguistically advanced little girl, about age 2;2, was happily playing with a large toy truck. As she explored its components, she called out to me (the closest audience at hand),

"Look at the wheel!"

"Look at the wheel!"

"Look at the wheel!"

"Look at the wheel!"

"Look at the wheel!"

"Look at the wheel!"

Six times she repeated the same message. Did she think I was deaf? Suddenly it dawned on me that adults do the same thing with children—what I have called playing "language tour guide." If repeatedly pointing out objects in the environment is an appropriate way for adults to converse with children, this little tyke reasonably assumed she might follow suit.

As children get older, their awareness of conversational rituals becomes more sophisticated. One day, Sara's father had come to pick up his daughter at nursery school. As he strapped Sara into her car seat, the 4½-year-old casually asked,

"What did you do at your office today?"

Sara's father was taken aback. To his knowledge, he had never spoken about his job with Sara. But of course, since Sara had begun attending nursery school a few months ago, *he* had regularly asked *her*,

"What did you do at school today?"

Sara's unexpected reformulation revealed her sophisticated ability to generalize a conversational protocol.

In his attempts at conversational orienteering, Alex sought to make sense of physical as well as verbal components of conversational exchange. When he was 4;1, the boy walked into the living room where his father was sitting and reading and announced,

"Daddy, I want to talk to you."

Alex's father welcomed his son into his lap and said,

"What's on your mind?"

Alex then lifted his right hand, formed a fist, and pounded his forehead three times.

"What's that all about?"

asked his father. Alex replied,

"I'm thinking."

Alex's father tried to assure him that you do not need to pound your head in order to think.

"But *you* do, Daddy,"

his son retorted. At that moment, Alex's mother entered the room and confirmed that yes, her husband did (unbeknown to him) tend to press his fist to his forehead (very gently) before replying to a serious question. As with the Miranda rights policemen read to suspects about to be arrested, parents should be warned that anything they say (or do) can be used against them.

Learning conversational rituals also entails understanding the range of situations to which a conversational formulaic applies. The importance of grasping such nuances became clear to Ryan (age 4;3) the Sunday after Christmas. Ryan had gone to his friend William's house to play. After hours of romping in the snow and then warming up inside with hot chocolate, it was time for Ryan to leave. While Ryan's mother (who had come to collect him) began pulling on her son's boots and gloves, William's mother thrust a small package into her son's hands (a Christmas gift for Ryan) and whispered instructions into William's ear.

At the time, Ryan was sitting on the floor by the Christmas tree, with his back to William. On cue from his mother, William boomed to Ryan's back,

"Merry Christmas!"

Not bothering to turn around, Ryan replied,

"Good bye! See you later!"

William grew perplexed—while the adults burst out laughing. Ryan knew "Merry Christmas" as a special farewell said at Christmas time, not a phrase to accompany a Christmas gift. Since the only bearer of Christmas presents Ryan knew of was Santa Claus, he had no reason to expect that William's "Merry Christmas" portended a gift in the way that "Happy Birthday" often does.

During their first years of life, children are often as much pawns as participants in conversational exchange with adults. In Chapter 2, we saw how parents of very young children typically take both sides of the conversation. As children get slightly older, the parental tendency to control dialogue takes the form of modeling and recasting children's incomplete or ungrammatical utterances, insisting upon politeness rituals (like "Please," "Thank you," or "May I"), and chastising children for interrupting adult conversation.

Not surprisingly, by the time they get to be preschoolers, children seek out acceptable ways of taking control. The best known is the constant refrain of "Why?":

Mother says to daughter that it's time to put her shoes on. Daughter asks,

"Why?"

Mother explains that if she doesn't put her shoes on, they cannot go outside. Daughter says,

"Why?"

Mother, slightly irritated now, continues that if daughter goes outside without shoes, she might catch cold. Daughter:

"Why?"

And on, and on, and on. Such "Whys" occasionally signal genuine curiosity, but overwhelmingly they are a conversational stalling tactic.

Besides the old standby "Why," Alex, Ryan, and Sara developed unique conversational power tools as well:

- Alex's ploy for stopping unwanted action was to dramatize the consequences. One day, at age 2;9, he tired of waiting for his mother to get off the telephone. Alex first tried talking to her, but she repeatedly asked him to please be quiet until she was done. Alex needed a new strategy. After remaining silent for nearly a minute, he excitedly warned,

    "Don't do that [talk]! Please don't do that! Danger!"

    She got off the telephone.

- Ryan's method of getting an adult's attention was more physical. Recall that before he attempted to hail his teacher Lawrence by name, Ryan had simply grabbed Lawrence's leg. At 3½, Ryan had become more subtle in his body tackles. Whenever he wanted to seize the conversational floor, he walked up to the adult with whom he wished to speak, clasped one hand on either side of the person's chin, turned the immobilized victim's face in his direction, and began talking.

    Ryan's strategy for controlling conversations also worked in reverse. When an adult uttered something Ryan did not wish to hear, he placed one hand on the speaker's chin and turned the offending message off in another direction.

- Sara took a more indirect approach to conversational power plays. Using variations on the "Why?" ploy, she manipulated her way to become the initiator of conversation (and often managed to halt action she did not want to take place). Her most common technique was to ask,

  "Do you know what?"

  whenever she sensed something was about to happen that she didn't want (such as turning out the light at night). In her wisdom, she knew that her parents always encouraged her conversation and would likely let her come out with her question or comment before they insisted that she carry out their wishes.

  Sara's alternative ruse was the phrase,

  "But first I have to tell you something."

  Her father would say,

  "It's time to brush your teeth,"

  and Sara would immediately counter,

  "But first I have to tell you something."

  When her skeptical father asked, "What?" Sara would sigh deeply or stall with an extended "Ummmmmmm" until she thought up something to say.

Besides mastering conversational rituals and learning how to control the conversation itself, children must learn how to speak with people they cannot see or who cannot see them. This skill is intrinsically necessary in any society (e.g., for talking with someone in the next room, with someone who is blind), but it also becomes critical as technology has made first the telephone and now the computer ubiquitous modes of communication.

When we speak with a person who can see as well as hear us, we have at our disposal many channels for getting our message across: words and sentences (and the sound patterns and intonation structures that shape them), facial expressions, body postures, and often our hands. We gesticulate (pounding tables, dismissing an issue with a flick of the hand), indicate sizes ("it was *this* big"), differentiate between possibilities ("Take this one"), and note directions ("It's over here").

Simple logic dictates that when speaker and hearer cannot see one another, there is no point in adding (much less relying upon) nonverbal cues. However, since face-to-face conversation is our quintessential way of communicating with one another, even fluent adult speakers typically fall into face-to-face habits when addressing people whom they cannot see. An exercise I give my linguistics students is to observe people talking on the telephone. The amount of gesticulation they see—gesticulation that the person on the other end of the line does *not* receive—never fails to amaze students. What is more, these observers report that when they try to monitor their own telephone behavior, they find it extremely difficult to still their hands and faces.

If fluent adults blur the lines between face-to-face conversational techniques and communication at a distance, imagine the problems young children have.

The Swiss psychologist Jean Piaget argued that before at least age 5 or 6, children are strongly **egocentric**. They tend to see the world only from their perspective, unable to consider how the same information looks from another person's point of view. This theory of egocentrism explains why toddlers literally walk over one another or play in parallel (rather than cooperatively). It also has been used to explain why preschoolers often fail to provide adequate information to ensure their meanings are successfully conveyed.

Many years ago, some Princeton psychologists did a series of experiments with nursery school–aged children designed to explore how children learn to communicate about objects in the world. Two children were seated, one at either end of a table divided by a partition, making it impossible for the children to see one another.

The experimental materials consisted of two identical sets of six wooden blocks (each of which had a hole drilled in the middle) plus two 14-inch stacking pegs. Each of the six blocks in the sets had a novel design printed on the vertical faces. For the child who played "speaker" in the experiment, the blocks were dispensed one at a time from a vertical device (of the sort that holds paper cups). For the child playing "listener," the six blocks were spread out before him in random order.

The goal of the experiment was for the speaker to communicate to the listener which block came out of the dispenser so that the listener could retrieve the same block from his own set. Both children then stacked their respective blocks on their posts. At the end of the experiment, the two children—if successful—would have six blocks stacked on their posts, each set in the same order.

The children set about their task. The challenge was for the speaker to explain to the listener which block to select. More often than not, the children identified the blocks by name (rather than by descriptive features):

"Take Mommy's hat."

the first child would say, and the second child would comply. (These experiments were done back in the days when mommies still wore hats.) The problem, of course, is that the listener typically grasped a *different* piece than the speaker, since the children had different mommies who wore differently shaped hats! However, neither child apparently sensed any problem in communicating his meaning.

Traditional Piagetian theory explains the results by describing the children as egocentric—seeing communication only from their individual perspectives. However, rethinking the scenario in the light of the conversational imperative, it becomes clear that the children here were simply functioning like any two speakers and hearers. They proceeded as if the other person understood what they were talking about. Much as the conversational imperative drives adults on the telephone to persist in gesticulation (pointless though it is), the children in this experiment extended to one another the conversational benefit of the doubt.

Yet for all our willingness to behave as if we understand each other, the pragmatics of conversation at a distance demand that speakers learn basic conventions for sharing meaning when they cannot see one another. For over one hundred years, the prototypic example of conversation at a distance has been talking on the telephone.

The first challenge in mastering conversation by telephone is to figure out the limits of the technology. Despite our tendencies to gesticulate while on the telephone, adults do not actually believe the person on the other end of the line can see what the speaker is doing.

Today's children often go through a transitional period of treating the telephone as a multichanneled device. When she was 2, Sara would often "talk" with her grandmother on the telephone. Her grandmother would ask,

"Have you been good today?"

and the little girl would smile and nod her head, not realizing that she had to speak for her grandmother to understand. Two years later, following her trip to the zoo with her new instant camera, Sara had brought home a dozen photographs. Her grandmother called that evening, and Sara excitedly narrated her afternoon adventure. Grabbing her photos, Sara enthused,

"Grandma, look at the pictures I took!"

and thrust the pile in front of the receiver. True to the conversational imperative, her grandmother replied,

"They're lovely, Honey. I'll see them close up when I come to visit you."

Watching (and listening to) Sara on the telephone, it is hard to figure out what is going on in the little girl's head. Does she really believe her grandmother can see what is in Sara's physical environs, or is such conversation akin to children (and adults) talking about chairs tripping people or spinach feeling sad?

At this stage, Sara's approach to telephones and images falls in the same realm as her attitude towards multiple Santa Clauses at shopping malls. Logically, telephones do not carry pictures (at least not the ones in common use), and by standard convention, there is only one Santa Claus. However, the pragmatics of living (the conversational imperative, the reality of commercialism) often lead children to suspend disbelief just far enough for them to cope with—to orienteer in—the world in which they live.

Conversational orienteering amid modern technology is neatly illustrated by Sara's first encounter with a speaker phone. When she was nearly 5, Sara visited her father's office. Like most other modern businesses, her father's accounting firm had telephones with a hands-free option. Sara's father demonstrated the device by calling home.

"Look, Sara,"

he said,

"you can talk with no hands,"

and proceeded to show her how. Turning to his daughter, he invited Sara to speak.

Sara looked at her father and then stared at the small grid on the telephone console. Leaning forward, her lips hovered just an inch shy of the black molded plastic.

"Hello, Mommy!"

she bellowed at the top of her lungs. Sara's father quickly scooped the girl up into his lap, fearing for his wife's eardrums.

"Why are you shouting?"

he inquired. Sara's answer was immediate:

"Because Mommy's a long way off, and if I don't shout, she won't hear me."

As long as Sara was using a conventional telephone, it never occurred to her to speak extra loudly, even to be heard by her grandmother in Florida. But with the unknown technology of the speaker phone, all bets were off, and Sara was taking no chances.

A second challenge children face with telephones is puzzling out the conventions of conversational give-and-take. Young children gradually learn to uphold their side of a conversation in face-to-face exchanges and to alternate turns with another speaker. In telephone conversations, however, a whole new set of conventions comes into play. Many protocols that are desirable (though not imperative) in face-to-face conversation now become indispensable.

Conversations typically include an opening greeting (such as "Hello," "Jones, here"), a main body, and a closing ("See ya" or "Bye"). When people meet on a daily basis (e.g., at an office or at school) or live with one another (spouses, parents, and children), the greetings and closings usually occur at most once a day.

Parents socialize their children from early on to use opening greetings and closings in face-to-face encounters ("Say 'Hi,' " "Wave bye-bye"). But these openings and closings are more social niceties than necessities. If a 3-year-old walks over to a visitor and announces she has a new sweater on, no one stops to remind her to say "Good morning" first.

When talking on the telephone, however, openings and closings become obligatory. Preschoolers are afforded a grace period when their parents (or elder siblings) do the dialing and the hanging up. However, once children are granted sole responsibility for initiating, carrying forth, and concluding a telephone conversation, the necessity of learning all the pieces becomes clear.

Ryan's experiences typify the difficulties unsaturated telephone users can get into. When he was 4;5, Ryan asked if he could call his friend William "all by himself." Ryan's mother reluctantly agreed. In her wisdom, however, she first telephoned William's mother to be sure he was home and to alert his family that a momentous communicative act was about to take place.

With a clear sense of purpose, Ryan punched each of the digits on the telephone as his mother called them out. Immediately following the last number, Ryan roared,

"Hello! Hello! Hello!"

not realizing that he had to wait for the telephone to ring in William's house and for someone to pick up the receiver. By the time Ryan's mother had finished explaining the procedure, William had (luckily) already picked up the telephone and begun "hello-ing" back.

Ryan panicked:

"What do I do now?"

he whimpered, literally not knowing what to say after he had said "hello."

"Talk about anything you like,"

Ryan's mother prompted, only to realize that preschoolers don't know how to make small talk.

"Tell him what you had for supper,"

she then suggested.

"Hot dogs and apple cider,"

Ryan announced into the telephone, not recognizing that this message, out of context, made no sense.

The "conversation" proceeded in this fashion for a few more rounds, with both mothers coaching and each child, in turn, uttering responses to questions unheard by the other party. The turning point finally came when Ryan announced to his mother that he had to go to the bathroom:

"What do I do now, Mommy?"

Absentmindedly, she counseled,

"Say 'good-bye' and hang up."

Ryan took his mother at her word. He said "good-bye"—to his mother, not into the telephone to William—slammed down the receiver, and trotted off to the bathroom. Like a computer that can only follow the specific instructions programmed into it, a child learning the rules of telephone conversation needs to have each step explicitly laid out, including what explanations must precede a "good-bye" and even to whom the "good-bye" must be directed.

■ IDEAS AND ALERTS

How Can I Help?

**Use a conversational style appropriate to a
budding conversational partner.**

Emphasize interactive rather than directive language. Work at tempering the use of imperatives through open-ended questions that invite thinking and new information in the response. Incorporate your preschooler's conversational topics into your own replies.

Continue to monitor the amount of adult language stimulation your child is receiving. Such monitoring may be most important for children raised at home, since preschoolers who are in nursery programs (especially those with low child-to-staff ratios) often have the linguistic advantage over age-mates cared for at home. Nursery school teachers are not distracted by housework, errands, or other obligations on their time. And the language that child care professionals use in addressing young children is often more sophisticated than the language style children hear at home. Family circumstances motivating affective features of baby talk (e.g., high pitch, echoing of children's incorrect words or pronunciations, repetitions) are largely absent in a preschool setting.

Remember to listen.

Give preschoolers time to figure out (even stumble over) the words or sentences they need to express what they want to say. Avoid the temptation of completing children's sentences in order to move the conversation along. Parental interruption of children's speech can sometimes lead to stuttering.

Be aware of your own pronunciations, meanings, or conversational formats that are no longer appropriate for addressing preschoolers.

Begin to wean yourself of baby talk features that, while once innocuous or even beneficial, can now hold back your children's linguistic development—for example:

Continuing high pitch, wide frequency modulation, loud volume, and echoing of child's incorrect pronunciation;

Meaning substitutions or diminutives (e.g., *choo choo*, *kitty*), semantically inappropriate words (e.g., calling an orangutan a *monkey*), echoing the child's invented words (e.g., *ish* for *water*);

Restricting topics of conversation, giving both questions and answers, having questions predominate over declaratives, repetition of own utterances.

Reinforce and expand your preschooler's development in sound.

Actively model the kind of pronunciation you want your child to be learning. Offer corrections of pronunciation, but don't be judgmental if the correction is not taken. Fluent 2-, 3-, or 4-year-olds can be driven to stutter if they feel you are dissatisfied with their pronunciation.

Reinforce and expand your preschooler's development in meaning.

Actively model the kind of vocabulary you want your child to be learning. Introduce more advanced vocabulary into the speech you address to your child. Continue to play language tour guide, but make your role more sophisticated (e.g., point out things your child doesn't yet know; provide definitions as appropriate; seek definitions from your child). Offer corrections of word choice, but don't be judgmental if the correction is not taken.

If your child has put creative effort into devising a name for an unfamiliar object (e.g., Sara's *napkin bread* for Lebanese lavash), combine praise for the ingenuity (e.g., "That's a very good name for the bread") with correction ("but the people who made it call it *lavash* instead"). Similarly, if your child creates a word that might have been (but isn't) a part of the language (such as Alex's "The fish is *towardsing* this way"), gentle modeling rather than direct correction is in order (e.g., "That's a really good way of talking about the fish, but most people say, 'The fish is moving this way' ").

Reinforce and expand your preschooler's development in conversation.

Actively model the kind of conversational style you want your child to be learning. Children gradually begin using politeness formulas if you incorporate them into your own conversation with other adults (as well as with your child). Similarly, children learn to look at other people when they are speaking, not to interrupt the conversations of others, and to modulate their volume to suit conversational circumstances if they see these behaviors in others.

Ask for clarification when you don't understand what your child is saying.

Preschoolers benefit from parents gently but firmly asking for clarification. Children need to learn how much information to provide about an object or event with which the listener is unfamiliar. Unless parents let children know their communication efforts have failed, children have no reason to change course.

Should I Be Concerned?

Should I worry about stuttering?

Children need to learn correct pronunciation of individual sounds and sound combinations. At the same time, they also strive to develop into fluent speakers who don't stumble over their words.

Nearly all of us are disfluent in our speech at some time. We prolong our pronunciation of a sound, repeat a word or syllable, can't remember the name of a familiar object, or generally get tongue-tied. Many of us are prone to get into such trouble when we are tired or under stress. But for some speakers, these problems are perennial. Such people are said to stutter.

The line between "normal" disfluencies and stuttering is hard to draw. Even experts don't agree on how to define stuttering, and no one is sure what causes it. However, we do know that at some time during their lives, about 4 percent of people will stutter and that most stuttering begins in childhood.

Roughly 1 percent of children below the age of puberty stutter. The onset of stuttering is most common in children during the preschool years (between ages 2 and 5). Nearly three times as many boys stutter as girls. (Curiously, when children first begin to stutter, the ratio of boys to girls is about the same. However, the balance soon tips because girls who start stuttering are more likely to recover than boys.)

Although we don't know what causes stuttering, researchers have been able to correlate the problem with some biological and environmental factors. The possibility of a genetic basis is suggested not only by the greater prevalence of stuttering in boys than girls but also by the fact that among twins, the coincidence of both twins stuttering if one of them does is much higher among monozygotic (identical) twins than among dizygotic (fraternal) twins. Moreover, the chances of stuttering are greater among children who have a close relative who stutters. Many researchers believe the problem is rooted in the system controlled by the larynx, perhaps exacerbated by a delay in the normal auditory feedback speakers receive from the words they utter. These are just hypotheses, however.

Children who stutter often have other language problems as well. Studies indicate that young stutterers average about six months behind other children in passing language milestones such as first words and first word combinations. Stutterers also are more prone to have articulation problems and to be slower in developing vocabulary and grammar.

People used to believe that children's stuttering is caused by emotional disorders. While that theory has been discounted, stuttering can be *triggered* (though not necessarily *caused*) by stress on a child. Stress can stem from normal events in growing up (moving from one house to another, entering a new school, birth of a sibling) or from special strains, such as divorce, serious illness, or death in the family.

As mysterious as the causes of stuttering are, so is its prognosis. By the time early stutterers reach junior high, nearly 75 percent of them spontaneously recover. We have no accurate way of predicting which children will recover and which won't.

Parents of toddlers or preschoolers who begin stuttering understandably agonize over what to do. Is the problem a transitory disfluency, caused by social or family stress (or even by rapid development in another cognitive area)? Or does it portend a more serious problem? Even for the 75 percent of children who will spontaneously stop stuttering, the social and communicative strain on both children and their families is considerable.

Traditionally, pediatricians and popular lore have counseled against therapy for stutterers younger than age 5 or 6. However, contemporary advice from stuttering experts is that families of young children who persist in repeating or prolonging speech sounds—even for only a few weeks—seek preventive intervention. A model therapy program aimed at preschoolers and developed by a team at Temple University exemplifies the kind of preventive intervention used with young children and, significantly, their parents. The Temple University program identifies a cluster of adult language behaviors as contributing to stuttering in preschoolers and counsels parents to limit their use. The list includes parents

- indicating concern over the child's stuttering through their affect
- speaking rapidly
- interrupting the child when he or she is speaking
- asking many questions
- using complex vocabulary and syntax
- correcting the child's pronunciation or grammar

Some of the program's recommendations are useful in addressing any child but especially in speaking with children who stutter. Parents who grimace, stare, or look away when their child is stammering his way through a sentence telegraph a searing message that the child's behavior (over which he has no voluntary control) is unacceptable. Slowing down your own rate of speech and waiting for your child to complete sentences himself (however long or painful the process) are eminently commonsensical as well.

But the last three recommendations on the list form an anomalous set because they seem to fly in the face of advice I have been offering in the previous chapters on natural mechanisms for facilitating toddlers' and preschoolers' linguistic growth. Prolific use of questions is a ubiquitous feature of baby talk that provides young children an obvious and simple means of entering a conversation. Yet if a child has difficulty formulating words and sentences, the pressure to "perform" in a dialogue can contribute to stuttering. In much the same way, while intentional use of complex vocabulary and syntax can provide excellent models to children with normal fluency, those with existing or potential stuttering problems can have difficulty figuring out what is being said and in replicating such language themselves.

What about corrections? As we have seen in recent chapters, children who have an orienteering stake in an ungrammatical (or mispronounced) construction are not likely to heed corrections (be they explicit or through repetitions, expansions, or recastings). Many children who feel pressured to correct their language in ways they cannot yet handle understandably lapse into stuttering.

What should parents do about asking questions, using more sophisticated language, and offering corrections? Decisions must be individual and flexible. In many cases, temporarily switching to a less challenging language model for children showing signs of linguistic stress provides the breathing room necessary for linguistic novices to gain a firm grasp on fluency.

My child is starting to use profanity. How do I handle it?

First, be certain that the profanity isn't learned from you. (Children can hardly be chastised for picking up language modeled at home.) If the source is external, explain to your child that some behaviors other people engage in (such as dangerous driving—or using bad language) are unacceptable in your family. If the source is another child (or a teacher) at preschool, inform the director of the school, who may be unaware of the problem.

If all efforts fail, the best strategy is often to ignore the language and let it die from neglect. Remember that children this age have little, if any, understanding of what they are saying when they use profanity. When Ryan was 4;1, he greeted his mother one day with a booming

"Oh shit!"

After some probing, it became clear that Ryan had picked up the phrase from an assistant at his nursery school. When his mother queried Ryan as to what the phrase meant, he promptly replied,

"That's what you say when you want attention."

■ 6. Zuckerman's Famous Airplane

Language Awareness

IT WAS a few minutes after 10:00 A.M. on a blustery Sunday in January. Alex and his parents had arrived soon after the doors opened at the National Air and Space Museum in Washington, D.C., one of Alex's favorite haunts. Since the usual crowds had not yet gathered, Alex was free to romp from one exhibit to the next, first gaping at the Wright brothers' plane and the *Spirit of St. Louis*, then dashing off to tour the cutaway DC-7.

During past visits, the clan had developed a game of asking what each plane was "called" (a takeoff on their habit of naming city buses by their numbers—N4, 34, D2, H8). Passing various aircraft, Alex's father would inquire,

"What's this plane called?"

and Alex would answer, "6062" (the Bell X-1 that was the first plane to fly faster than the speed of sound) or "SS-20" (a Soviet Saber rocket in the main entranceway).

On this particular morning, the family came upon a new display—a bright yellow "Grumman Goose," the amphibious commuter plane designed by Grumman Aircraft in the 1930s. The plane before them, labeled NC 702A, was handsomely parked on a special wide-planked wooden floor, surrounded by a neat red metal railing. After reading aloud the brief text describing the creation of the Grumman Goose, Alex's father asked his usual,

GROWING UP WITH LANGUAGE

"What's this plane called?"

The little boy, who was two months past his third birthday, hesitated for a moment and then announced,

"Zuckerman's Famous Airplane."

Alex had recently become an avid fan of a video rendition of E. B. White's classic, *Charlotte's Web*. In the story, a pig named Wilbur (owned by Farmer Zuckerman) narrowly escapes being turned into bacon by impressing the farmer with his intelligence. Zuckerman capitalizes on his good fortune by showing off his wondrous Wilbur. Positioning the animal in the barnyard behind a neat fence, the farmer mounts a sign heralding "Zuckerman's Famous Pig." The visual gestalt of an object (and hadn't his father said something about "goose"?) situated within the confines of a barnyard-like fence was too tempting to resist. The laughter in Alex's eyes established that he knew "Zuckerman's Famous Airplane" wasn't really the vehicle's name but rather an intentional joke.

Beyond saturation in the essential building blocks of speech lies another dimension of language children must learn to handle. This is the domain of **language awareness**—of seeing language as a set of possibilities to be manipulated and explored rather than exclusively as conventions to follow. Language awareness also entails treating language as an integrated system rather than an unstructured collection of individual elements.

When Alex dubbed the Grumman Goose "Zuckerman's Famous Airplane," he revealed his awareness that language is as much a game as a predefined set of rules. By juxtaposing diverse contexts (the Air and Space Museum versus the farm in *Charlotte's Web*; a plane versus a pig) joined by a common thread (a barnyard-like fence), Alex engaged in the kind of language play that marks conscious language control.

Language awareness—the ability to control rather than be controlled by language—permeates all four basic linguistic components. Saturated language users are able to fine-tune, reflect on, and play with sound (e.g., making up rhymes), meaning (e.g., requesting definitions for words), grammar (e.g., correcting your own mistakes), and conversation (e.g., recognizing that you must call your mother "Mommy" while your father can address her by first name).

How do children become aware of language?

Why Are There No Lady Holes?
Language about Language

Many of the first stages of language awareness are unconscious. Children as young as 2 or 3 sometimes complain when adults address them in ungrammatical language ("Go bed") or with names reserved for babies, without being able to articulate what they are objecting to. Just so, 3- or 4-year-olds begin to correct their own mispronunciations or faulty grammar, though when queried, most vehemently deny making any emendation. Conscious control over language as a system with multiple possibilities emerges only gradually.

How much awareness of language do children develop? Youngsters vary widely in the degree and direction of conscious control over their native tongue. Every healthy child acquires the basics of sound, meaning, grammar, and conversation. But the ability to talk about language, to play with individual components, to select the right word, to craft a powerful sentence reflects a child's personality and, most important, his opportunities. Parental influence on children's growth in language awareness is profound. Adults model language attitudes and skills and in the process help shape how early (and easily) a child learns to talk, whether a child loves jokes involving word play, whether a child is intimidated by foreign languages, and the extent to which spoken and written language become powerful tools for self-expression.

How do children develop an awareness of the building blocks of spoken language? Let's look at three conversational contexts: correcting other people (and yourself), playing with language, and overtly reflecting on language use.

Correction and Self-Correction: "But Potatoes Can't Talk!"

The sounds of language are highly subject to mispronunciation (or idiosyncratic treatment), and so sound is a natural and early domain for correction. By age 3, most children have begun to correct some of their own phonological fumbles. Ryan's case is typical:

- Dominating the living room in Ryan's home was a large grandfather clock. An heirloom handed down from Ryan's great-grandmother, the clock marked the quarter hours with traditional Westminster chimes.

  A weekly ritual in the household was winding the clock. From the time he was 6 months old, Ryan had delighted in helping his mother crank each of the weights back up to the top. By the time he was 2½, Ryan had begun to alert his mother when he saw the chimes needed winding. One day (he was then 2;9), Ryan trotted up to his mother and declared,

  "Wind the clop up."

Spontaneously, he tried again:

  "Wind the clock up."

Having muffed the first attempt (with an assimilation of the final *k* in *clock* to the *p* of *up*), Ryan corrected himself without external prodding.

Overt correction of children's pronunciation by parents is also common. Preschoolers become increasingly open to correction at all levels of language, so long as they have no stake in a formulation they have worked out for themselves and as long as they can handle the complexity of the correctly modeled version. When we saw Alex at 3;10, he was not ready to relinquish his pronunciation *hospididil*, despite adult attempts at correction. Six months later, Alex still used *hospididil* in spontaneous conversation but would switch to *hospital* when the correct word was modeled:

Alex:	Is Daddy still at the *hospididil?*
Alex's mother:	He's due back from the *hospital* very late tonight.
Alex:	I'll wait up until he's back from the *hospital.*

As children become more mature, they decree that linguistic turnabout is fair play. If another person can correct their speech, why not correct the speech of others? One afternoon, Sara (barely more than 3 at the time) declared verbal war on her grandmother. The two were ensconced in a restaurant, having lunch. The little girl had been demanding ice cream, and her grandmother was resisting until Sara finished her main course. Eventually abandoning principles in hopes of avoiding a public scene, her grandmother sighed,

"O.K."

Sara immediately stopped crying but refused to loosen her juggernaut:

"Not O.K.'. O.'K."

Not only did the judgment have to suit her liking, but it had to be delivered with the same stress pattern Sara was used to hearing and using.

Getting a controlling grasp on meaning requires a little more sophistication, and so children do not generally begin to comment on word meanings until after their third birthdays. Examples from Ryan and Sara are typical:

- Ryan continued to be a finicky eater from birth up through puberty. His mother's litany of "the spinach will be very sad if you don't eat it" had become part of the normal dinnertime routine. One evening when Ryan was nearly 4, the abandoned-food-of-the-day was a baked potato. Ryan's mother pleaded,

    "The potato is saying, 'Eat me. Eat me.' "

    This time, Ryan (still ignoring the potato) had an answer at the ready:

    "But potatoes can't talk. They don't have mouths."

    Ryan's mother had been bested at her own game.

- Four-year-old Sara and her parents were walking in the neighborhood. Her father pointed out a fire hydrant that some of the local children had painted a bright pink. With a literal streak worthy of a lexicographer, Sara retorted,

    "That's not a *fire* hydrant. It's a *water* hydrant. It doesn't have any fire in it."

By age 3, most children have begun spontaneous correction of their own grammar. (Correcting the grammar of others is usually a year or two further off, given the complexity and seemingly limitless number of exceptions found in English.) In some cases, spontaneous self-corrections herald transitions to correct morphology or syntax. When Alex (3;4) said of his mother,

> "*He . . . she* is on the telephone,"

his self-correction resulted in an appropriate syntactic construction.

Other times, a sequence of self-corrections is actually a string of grammatical potshots, often marking a transition from a principled (though incorrect) analogy to a quest for the correct form. Ryan's attempts at 3;2 to talk about the snowmen he was building illustrate this still-wavering process:

> "I'm building *snowmans. Snowmen. Snowmens.*"

The fact that Ryan's second attempt (*snowmen*) was correct English is of no relevance, since he failed to recognize when his potshot hit the bull's-eye.

Conventions for conversation offer a fourth context for language awareness to emerge. In talking about how children acquire the rudiments of conversational saturation (Chapter 5), we saw that anything adults say or do can be used against them—recall Alex's pounding his head to "think," in imitation of his father. As children learn not only to converse but to converse *about* conversation, the warning becomes increasingly apt:

- Ryan was seated at the dinner table (not eating, as usual). His mother, deciding to concentrate on her own nourishment for the moment, turned to her daughter and requested,

  > "Cathy, pass the green beans."

  Four-year-old Ryan came alive:

  > "Don't do it! Don't do it!"

  Hungry and impatient, Ryan's mother demanded,

  > "Why not?"

  Ryan's answer was squarely on target:

  > "Because you didn't say 'please.' "

- Sara's complaint was not about a word but about a whole manner of speech. As an older sister (her brother, Michael, had been born when she was 2), Sara lived in a household filled with baby talk for as long as she could remember. Among the most distinguishing traits of baby talk is the prevalence of diminutives: *doggy* for *dog*, *kitty* for *cat*, even *milkie* for *milk*.

  By the time she was 4, Sara had temporarily abandoned her initial sibling rivalry and begun playing big sister to her little brother. In return, she now expected to be treated like a "big person." And generally she was. However, her mother occasionally slipped, addressing Sara in the same language style she now used with Michael. Sara's correction was swift and blunt:

  > "Don't talk to me like a baby. Say *duck*, not *ducky*. You should only say *ducky* to Michael."

As part of conversational saturation, children also learn to correct false starts. Just as Sara recognized *ducky* as a word appropriate only for younger children, she became aware of differences in the ways young children speak in comparison with adults.

Five-year-old Sara was telling the story of "Goldilocks and the Three Bears" to her 3-year-old brother. She had gotten to the part where each of the bears asks in turn, "Who's been sitting in my chair?" With a deep voice, she echoed the words of the father bear and mother bear and then launched into the baby bear's line with the same basso voice. Halfway through she switched to falsetto:

> "Who's been sitting in my chair?"

she squeaked, correcting her earlier intonation in order to match the voice of a baby.

Language Play: Rainsets and Snowsets

Corrections and self-corrections are common occurrences in the linguistic landscape of nearly all families with young children. Differentiation among children in their language awareness skills surfaces in more subtle arenas such as language play and using language to talk about language overtly.

Emerging differences in language awareness have little to do with a child's precosity in initial language learning and almost everything to do with the amount and style of direct talk about language going on in the household. "Sesame Street" has almost singlehandedly raised the language awareness level of preschoolers (poor and middle-class alike) from that of children a generation before. However, without reinforcement of language play and talk about language from other adults, the positive effects of television easily evaporate.

The three families we have been following illustrate the gamut of language environments in which language awareness stalls or flourishes. Sara's family typifies the middle-class norm. Two college-educated parents (one staying at home) could afford their firstborn child the luxury of captive conversationalists for her first two years, both to hear what Sara had to say and actively to nurture her linguistic explorations. Yet Sara's parents never saw the language they used themselves as particularly relevant to Sara's development. They read their daughter books of rhymes, but their own language was not particularly marked by rhymes, puns, or other word play. Although Sara had begun using recognizable words and then grammar before either Ryan or Alex, this relative precosity gave way to solid (though unexceptional) language development (including development of language awareness) by the time Sara was ready to enter kindergarten.

Ryan's paucity of language play strongly reflected his upbringing. We know that younger siblings (especially boys) and twins typically lag slightly behind older or only children in developing basic language skills, though invariably, younger siblings and twins catch up with their peers in handling sound, meaning, grammar, and conversation. However, for the same reasons that Ryan's mother found limited opportunity to nurture her son's basic language, she did little to stimulate Ryan's language awareness. Not surprisingly, Ryan engaged in relatively little spontaneous language play, despite some pedagogical efforts from his nursery school teachers.

Alex's personal history reveals the impact that concentrated parental attention to language can have on a child's development. Of the three children, Alex had gotten off to the slowest linguistic start. A premature child, he used his first words at almost 12 months, but his utterances were exclusively monosyllabic until he was 2;6. Before age 2, Alex did little spontaneous vocalizing, and his earliest grammar did not appear until over a year after Sara had begun combining words (2;6 versus 1;3). Yet throughout it all, Alex's parents never stopped talking and listening, joking and coaxing. By the time Alex was 3½, his vocabulary and grammar were laced with locutions more typical of a 6- or 7-year-old (although his language orienteering was otherwise commensurate with that of his peers). Even more noticeable was the ease with which he played with language.

A child's most natural entrée into language play is to mix and match the sounds of language through rhymes. Whether adults begin with standard nursery rhymes ("Hey diddle diddle the cat and the fiddle . . .") or with homemade productions ("Touch the sink in a wink or you will shrink"), the very act of rhyming teaches children that words are only combinations of sounds, and the possible combinations are limitless.

From the time Alex was a few months old, his mother made up rhymes—sometimes meaningful, other times not—in the normal course of talking with her son. By age 2, Alex took clear delight in hearing rhymed poetry read aloud, but he produced no rhymes himself until age 3. Then Alex's rhyming spiggot switched on full. His mother would say,

"Eat your peas, if you please!"

and the little boy would answer back,

"Eat your peas on your knees!"

When Alex had no conventional word at the ready, he resorted to nonsense:

"Eat your peas, wees gees!"

By age 4, Alex was declaring,

"Hey, that rhymes!"

and taking considerable delight in his accomplishments.

Many preschoolers love to play with word meanings. With Alex and Sara, you could always tell when they were teasing because their word play was accompanied by giggles and grins. (When engaged in serious language orienteering, such as Alex's "The fish is towardsing," they would continue their conversation without a smile.) Here are several examples of Alex's and Sara's jokes with meaning:

- One winter night about five o'clock, Alex (who had just turned 4) was getting out of the car. It had been raining, and dark clouds covered the sky. As Alex stood staring into the distance, his father asked what he was looking at:

  "The rainset. It's raining, so there's no sunset tonight."

  Two weeks later, Alex sat in the living room on a Sunday evening, watching heavy flakes of snow cover the street and sidewalk. Alex ran up to his mother and dragged her to the window:

  "Hey, Ma, look at the snowset."

- In the Washington, D.C., area, a favorite restaurant chain for families with young children is Hamburger Hamlet. The food is familiar but well prepared, the prices are reasonable, and, best of all, the tables come complete with large sheets of white paper and a collection of crayons. Roughly once a month, Sara's family treated themselves to an hour of sanity by having dinner there.

  One particularly trying Sunday afternoon when Sara was 3;9, her parents looked at one another and spontaneously agreed this would be an excellent night for a pilgrimage. Sara's father broached the subject with his daughter:

  "Would you like to go to Hamburger Hamlet tonight?"

  The girl paused, and a smile crept across her face:

  "No, I want to go to Hamburger Omelette."

- Like many other preschoolers, Alex engaged in a lot of symbolic play, using hats as pretend cereal bowls, brooms as horses, sticks as rifles. However, unlike most of his age-mates, Alex enjoyed commenting as he crossed category boundaries. One morning when he was 3;6, his mother was struggling to comb his hair. Alex grabbed the comb from her hand and poised it between his knees:

  "You can't comb hair with a bridge!"

  he chortled.

Language play also sometimes spills over into broader conversational contexts. One especially rich area is naming.

Just as children initially have difficulty learning pronouns (the person I call *me* you call *you,* and so on), many children have problems figuring out which proper names to use when addressing family members. Daddy calls Mommy *Alice,* but Junior is supposed to call her *Mommy.* Once children get the system straight, they often delight in tweaking the rules. Sara, nearly 4½ at the time, announced to her parents one day,

"I'm the mommy,"

and promptly began addressing her father by his first name, a name she knew very well but never ordinarily used.

Reflecting on Language: "What Did I Call 'Popcorn'?"

A defining trait of cognitive maturity is the ability to reflect upon one's life and actions. This skill not only enables us to see errors in our ways but also to mark our own growth and development. To this end, American nursery schools commonly have children bring in toys and clothing they used as babies, along with pictures of themselves in their first years of life. Watching a 3- or 4-year-old with tokens of her former self reminds us how sophisticated even young children can be in recognizing change and alternative possibilities.

Learning to reflect upon language is another way in which children gain purchase on a community and their place in it. These reflections on language take many shapes, including language practice, word decomposition, explicit requests for definitions, queries about how you used to talk when you were very young, and the glimmerings of linguistic guile.

One of the clearest signs that a child is reflecting upon language as a system is that he overtly practices a construction. Many 2- or 3-year-olds practice or play with language in solitary monologues. Some children engage in the whimsical equivalent of grammatical babbling, juxtaposing words for the sheer pleasure of creating new combinations (e.g., "blue block, green block, yellow block, white block"). Other children, such as Ryan, devote their practice time to constructions whose makeup they are still puzzling out. At age 3;7, while he played by himself one afternoon, Ryan carefully repeated to himself,

GROWING UP WITH LANGUAGE

"Can't, cannot. Can't, cannot. Can't, cannot."

During this same age, he was also prone to use *cannot* in his everyday speech (rather than *can't*), even though his mother and sister nearly always said *can't*. Why? Because the grammatical structure of *cannot* is much clearer than the contracted *can't*, and Ryan was still trying to sort out the usage of words such as *can't*, *don't*, and *won't*.

Another way children reflect upon language is by spontaneously decomposing words. Sara began playing with word components when she was about 4½. One day while grocery shopping with her mother, she pointed to a pile of mushrooms and inquired,

"Where's the room in *mushroom*?"

That evening, while her mother was unpacking the grocery bags, Sara complained,

"But there's no cake in these pancakes!"

(said while contemplating a new box of Bisquick). A few months later, Sara asked her father,

"Why are there no lady holes?"

—a logical question for a little girl who had just learned what manholes are.

Learning to reflect on language can also entail focusing on individual words as units of meaning that are sometimes interchangeable and always definable. This awareness of verbal subtlety and definition was especially well developed in Alex.

Alex's mother, in defiance of common wisdom, had used fairly sophisticated vocabulary with her son from the time he was around a year old. Instead of declaring,

"That's a great big elephant,"

she might say,

"That elephant is enormous,"

or

"Now that's a humongous elephant."

As a result, by the time he was 3, Alex was using words like *hysterical* (meaning "funny") or *actually* (when other children might say *really*)—

"Actually I would like some juice, not milk."

Alex's mother was generally careful to ensure that such words were not used in a vacuum. Whenever she used a word she thought Alex might not understand, she slipped in a definition:

"That elephant is *enormous*. He's really big, really huge."

Not surprisingly, Alex learned very early on to ask for definitions himself ("What does *ridiculous* mean?"). He naturally came to realize not only that words are labels for meanings but that the same real-life situation can be described in more than one way. This realization is invaluable for saturated speakers and writers attempting to be euphemistic, humorous, or simply lucid.

Another form of linguistic reflection is to talk about language used in other times and places. Such "talk about talk" was particularly common in Alex's household.

Like a family looking at baby pictures together, when Alex was around 3, his parents began reflecting on the language Alex had used when he first learned to talk. Alex's mother had started the game one evening while teasing her son that he used to call the telephone *coo* when he was "a little tiny baby" (see Chapter 5). One story led to another, and soon his mother was chuckling with Alex over his name *ish* for all objects associated with water (water in a glass, fire hydrants, hoses, fountains). These descriptions of language-gone-by unleashed a flood of questions:

"What did I used to call 'trucks'?"

(The answer was *truh*.)

"What did I used to call 'dogs'?"

(*Duh*.)

"What did I used to call 'popcorn'?"

The answer, of course, was that he didn't call it anything at all—babies don't eat popcorn!

Finally, children come to express their awareness of language through conscious linguistic guile. They learn that language can be used not only for communicating information but for manipulation and obfuscation as well. Listen to Ryan and Alex:

- Ryan's first trace of linguistic guile surfaced as a comment on one of his least endearing habits: whining. His mother's policy was to insist Ryan stop whining before any request of his was honored. Like any other fallible parent, she occasionally gave in prematurely, although she naively assumed Ryan had not spotted her foible.

  One morning when his mother was attempting to get Ryan (then 3;10) dressed and out of the house, Ryan was in a particularly whiny mood. Repeatedly she asked her son to stop whining, to no avail. Exasperated, she moaned,

  "Why do you whine so much?"

  Ryan took her rhetorical comment as a real question and had a ready answer:

  "Sometime I don't get what I want, and so I whine."

  Not only had Ryan learned to use whining as a power play. He had also developed the linguistic sophistication to describe his strategy.

- By the time Alex was 4½, he had came to understand that language can be used to cover a multitude of shortcomings. Reminiscent of Ryan, who used to demand of his mother,

  "You know! You know!"

  whenever he could not reproduce one of his own grammatical potshots, Alex discovered a handy linguistic device to save face when he did not know the answer to a question.

  One week his friend Owen was slated to embark on a family trip to Oklahoma, and Alex's mother inquired of her son,

  "Do you know where Oklahoma is?"

  Like a seasoned politician, Alex whispered back,

  "Yes, but I'm keeping it a secret."

Look at the Chien:
Functioning in Two Languages

Language awareness goes beyond reflecting on the essential building blocks of one's mother tongue. For millions of children around the world, growing up with language includes confronting more than one linguistic system.

Consider the case of Peter, the young son of one of my colleagues.

Five-year-old Peter stood silently before the window of a pet shop, admiring a puppy at play. A shy child, Peter had now been in France for four weeks, accompanying his parents who were on a four-month academic sabbatical. Although he and his parents had been staying with a French family (including children ranging from age 3 to 10), Peter hesitated to make forays into the French language. Contrary to popular lore, not all young children spontaneously begin learning new languages.

The boy's parents, recognizing that their son's natural shyness contributed to the continuing language barrier, gently urged Peter to try out some French:

> "Look at the dog, Peter. You know what you call a dog in French? You call it *chien. C'est un chien.*"

The child pressed his nose against the window then stood back and quietly repeated,

> "*Chien.*"

The following week, the three moved on to Germany. Again, they resided with a local family (German speaking, of course). Their hosts had one child, a girl almost exactly Peter's age. This time, Peter resolved to gather his courage and try talking with his German playmate. Since the family had a dog, Peter latched onto a topic of conversation he could handle comfortably:

> "Christine, can I play with your *chien?*"

he ventured. She gazed at him quizzically:

> "*Was ist ein 'chien'?*" [= "What is a '*chien*'?"]

she reasonably asked. Nothing in Peter's sentence made any sense, for in German, the word for "dog" is not *chien* but *Hund.*

GROWING UP WITH LANGUAGE

Undoubtedly children who encounter multiple systems of spoken language are faced with more linguistic challenges than their monolingual age-mates. However, the confusions and frustrations inherent in juggling more than one system of sound, meaning, grammar, and conversation are balanced by invaluable opportunities for nurturing language awareness.

Multilingual experiences for children arise in several venues. The most familiar is to grow up bilingual with two languages spoken in the home (a truncated variant is Peter's situation in Europe—more limited immersion into a new language community). A second multilingual context is being raised with two distinct dialects (such as traditional American "broadcasterese" versus Brooklynese, or standard English versus black English). However, there is also a third context for multilingual experience: becoming *aware* that different languages and dialects exist and *aware* that they express similar messages in diverse ways. Such prospects for awareness are open to all children, regardless of the availability of more obvious multilingual opportunities in their immediate language communities.

Growing Up Bilingual: Do Children Benefit?

As a professor of linguistics, the most common question I am asked by international students is whether they should raise their children bilingual. The query has always struck me as odd, given that the students themselves are generally fluent bilinguals and typically hail from countries where bilingualism is the norm, especially among educated citizens.

Nearly every country in the world has some degree of bilingualism. Fluency levels range from core survival skills of peasants attending regional markets where vendors come from linguistically diverse tribes, to the near-native command of English demonstrated by many Europeans.

The United States has always had an ambivalent attitude towards bilingualism. Although our Founding Fathers rejected calls to establish a national language, gradually English became the accepted norm. Each wave of immigrants—Poles, Chinese, Italians, Portuguese, Arabs, Hmong—has needed to learn English (or have their children learn English) to function effectively in American society. With some notable exceptions (such as Swedish in the upper Midwest or Spanish in south Texas), the language of the old country typically fades with the first or second American-born generation.

Despite—or perhaps because of—its immigrant heritage, the United States has developed an "English-only" attitude in its educational and political policies. Compared with their European counterparts, American children have only a glancing exposure to other languages in school. The country is highly ambivalent about supporting bilingual education programs and quick to judge anyone who cannot function in English. A grass-roots movement to make English the exclusive official language in the United States is now being spearheaded by S. I. Hayakawa, sometime linguist, educator, and politician.

American predilections against use of multiple languages have sometimes been justified by the curious claim that children who grow up bilingual are intellectually disadvantaged. This rationale traces back to the turn of the last century, when a number of injunctions against bilingualism began appearing in the British psychological and educational literature. The spirit of these warnings was captured in an educational tract published in 1890: "If it were possible for a child or boy to live in two languages at once equally well, so much the worse. His intellectual and spiritual growth would not thereby be doubled but halved."

By the 1920s, a steady flow of researchers began offering "scientific" evidence on the dangers of bilingualism. D. J. Saer's work is representative. Studying Welsh/English bilinguals, Saer declared that in rural districts, monolinguals "show a considerable superiority over bilingual children . . . when tested by the Binet scale of intelligence," a discrepancy that Saer said persisted even among university students. Subsequent studies in the 1930s, 1940s, and 1950s continued to report serious linguistic disadvantages to bilingualism, including poorer vocabulary, worse articulation, inferior writing abilities, and a larger number of grammatical errors.

Occasionally a researcher would question the by now standard assumption that children coping with two languages were mentally inferior. In the late 1930s, a public school official from Nogales, Arizona, performed the simple experiment of administering not one but two IQ tests to children whose native language was Spanish:

the first in English and the second in Spanish. Not surprisingly, the scores averaged 13 IQ points higher when the test was given in Spanish. Yet this seemingly obvious lesson failed to penetrate all quarters. As late as 1979, the *New York Times* still could run this front-page story:

> A few years ago Olivia Martinez, then a guidance counselor for the San Francisco public schools, was asked to look at a 10-year-old girl in a class for mentally retarded children.
>
> "Her name is Elena," the teacher of the class said, "and I know she's higher than a 45."
>
> "I went over to Elena and asked her in Spanish where she was from," Mrs. Martinez called, "and her whole demeanor changed. She sat up very straight and her eyes sparkled. She told me she'd been in the country six months from Nicaragua."

Given such a linguistic climate, it is hardly surprising that parents (or parents-to-be) wonder if raising children bilingual is a wise move. Yet contemporary research argues that children who become fluent in more than one language are intellectually *advantaged* (not disadvantaged) in comparison with their monolingual peers.

The watershed study was published in 1962 by a team of researchers at McGill University in Montreal. Their carefully designed investigation of Canadian 10-year-olds revealed that bilingualism (here, in French and English) proved an intellectual boon. The bilinguals performed significantly better on cognitive tests, verbal tests, and even nonverbal tests.

In the ensuing decades, a growing number of studies have substantiated the McGill findings. Researchers have reported that bilingual children outperform monolinguals in a variety of specific cognitive and language-based tasks, including knowing how to use language to guide their reasoning processes, understanding that names of objects are distinct from the objects themselves, and being able to classify words on the basis of semantic similarity. More generally, investigators now speak of bilingual children as having more "cognitive flexibility" than their monolingual counterparts.

Why the vast discrepancy between findings before and after the

1962 Montreal study? The problems with the initial research were methodological. Nearly all of the earlier studies confounded bilingual issues with questions of socioeconomic status. The bilinguals being tested at the time tended to be children of recent immigrants (the majority of whom held unskilled positions), while the monolinguals were far more likely to be children of economically and educationally established families. Perhaps even more important, the so-called bilingual children often knew little English, and tests administered in English invariably underreported their abilities. Fortunately these errors are now largely problems of the past.

Most of the studies showing bilingualism to be a cognitive boon were done in French-speaking Canada, where, despite long-standing tensions between English speakers and Francophones, both French and English command official and community support and respect. This delicate balance is not true everywhere, especially in the United States. The appropriate question for parents, then, is not *whether* bilingualism is both possible and beneficial (it is) but *how* to raise a child bilingually in a particular sociopolitical context.

Here are some guidelines for parents considering raising their children bilingual:

Given family and community support, any normal child can learn two languages and benefit from the experience.

In principle, the earlier the second language is introduced, the better. Many families begin addressing children in two languages from birth. However, if the infant or toddler is under physical stress or appears slow in developing language (e.g., due to prematurity, temporary or permanent hearing loss, protracted illness, family tension), there is no hurry to introduce the second language. Up through at least age 10 or 12, most children can learn to speak a second language like a native. However, unless the child encounters the second language through extensive residence in an area in which the language is supported by the community, social pressures often make it difficult for children beyond age 4 or 5 to acquire native fluency in a second language used only at home.

GROWING UP WITH LANGUAGE

**The higher the family's socioeconomic
background is, the easier it is for children
to become fluent bilinguals.**

The 4-year-old daughter of a Spanish diplomat in Washington, D.C., has a greater chance of quickly becoming fluent in both Spanish and English than the 4-year-old daughter of a Salvadorean who has migrated to the same city. In addition to her educational and cultural advantages, the diplomat's daughter receives continual reinforcement that both her languages—and cultures—are valued. The Salvadorean's daughter is more likely to grow up sensing that Spanish is the language of poor, uneducated immigrants and English the language of the enfranchised.

**Regardless of social circumstances, most
children growing up bilingual go through
periods of linguistic confusion.**

Any speaker attempting to cope with more than one language system is prone to mix them from time to time. Even children growing up in supportive bilingual environments typically go through phases of juxtaposing vocabulary or syntax from one language into the other—

"*Je suis tres kalt*"—"I am very (French) cold (German)."

Such language orienteering is both natural and transient. Potentially more problematic are children's linguistic rebellions, typically against the language of the home that is not spoken by the larger community. Most families weather these challenges, though some school-aged children eventually reject the home language entirely.

**Families successful in raising their children
bilingual often make use of one or more of
the following techniques:**

- Have the same adults consistently speak the same language to the child (e.g., the father uses only Spanish and the mother exclusively speaks English).
- Travel, even for brief visits, to countries in which the language not supported by the community at home is now the primary spoken language.

- When international travel is not possible, find local activities or people to support the language not used by the local community (e.g., find a cable television program in Spanish or a radio program in Greek; visit ethnic grocery stores where the second language is spoken).
- Enroll the child in a school that supports the non–local community language. Increasingly, public and private schools are adding foreign language classes to the elementary school curriculum. In addition, many larger cities in the United States have special schools in which a language other than English (typically French, German, or Spanish) is the basic medium of instruction. Although these schools are typically designed for children from the international community (e.g., sons and daughters of diplomats, employees at the United Nations or the World Bank), they also draw a large number of students from monolingual American homes whose parents wish their children to grow up bilingual.

Is bilingual education always successful? No. For children from socially or culturally disadvantaged backgrounds, pressures in the United States to adopt not only American English but American folkways often lead to educational as well as linguistic failure. For all their good intentions, bilingual education programs rarely provide ample linguistic and social support for both languages. American cities that actively countenance two languages (such as San Antonio, Texas, which is heavily bilingual and bicultural) are the exception.

But even children from middle-class or privileged backgrounds may founder when cast into bilingual circumstances. Children raised in English or French school systems in former colonial countries sometimes report they do not feel at home in either their native language or their school tongue. The problem largely stems from their country's ambivalence to the European language: The British (or French) are locally hated for past political oppression, though parents believe their children will have better opportunities if they are fluent in a European language. The language and values of the school, while officially condoned at home, receive no familial support.

A second type of problem may develop for children whose parents move every few years to a new country (and language community). In a city like Washington, D.C., there are many such families. Their stories of acculturation are remarkably similar: When the family is transplanted, one child takes to the new language (and culture) like a duck to water, while another has considerable difficulty adjusting. More often than not, the child with problems is a boy. I particularly remember the 10-year-old son of one of my students, the wife of a World Bank officer. Dutch by birth, her son had lived in Germany, Indonesia, East Africa, and now the United States. While very bright, the child stuttered badly and did not feel at home in either Dutch, German, Swahili, or English. Fortunately, such cases are relatively rare.

Growing Up with Two Dialects: "Watch Out for the Be-ad Guys"

Any sizable language community develops local variants (or **dialects**) of the basic language. Sometimes the dialects are spoken in geographically close areas (such as Liverpudlian English, Scots English), and sometimes dialect speakers of the same core language are found scattered across the globe (American English, Australian English, South African English). Within the United States, American English itself is divisible into dialects. Natives of Biloxi, Mississippi, and Albany, New York, both speak "American English," but their sound patterns, cadences, vocabulary, and conversational styles have unique characteristics. In learning their native language, children become native speakers of a particular dialect of that language.

By definition, a dialect is a language variety that is understandable to speakers of other dialects of the same language. Preschoolers from Biloxi can essentially understand the speech of children from Albany, though each may say of the other, "They talk funny." In many countries of the world, one dialect is dubbed the standard, while others are judged colloquial. In the Arab world, for example, the Arabic of the Koran ("classical Arabic") sets the official standard. However, across the Middle East, the language has evolved into distinct dialects (e.g., Egyptian Arabic, Lebanese Arabic, Syrian Arabic), which are learned as native tongues and function in daily use. In the United States, black English differs markedly from standard American in sound, meaning, grammar, and conversational conventions. Speakers of colloquial Arabic and of black English learn that their dialect is not the same as the standard, although those who are less well educated frequently never master the standard system.

Speakers of regional dialects in America generally do not perceive themselves as sounding different from people around them. I'll never forget the scene one fall evening in a Boston drugstore when a young woman (probably a new student at an area college) approached the counter with her purchases, wanting to write a check. Politely she asked the clerk behind the counter if she could borrow a "*pin*."

"A what?"

he demanded.

"A *pin*, please; I don't have one,"

she responded.

The verbal exchange went several more rounds—the clerk becoming frustrated and impatient and the young woman growing ever more embarrassed. Finally, I intervened and handed the hapless woman a pen. She was obviously from the South or Southwest, where *pin* and *pen* are both pronounced "*pin*."

Young children who are exposed to dialects other than the one spoken at home often unwittingly pick up dialectal elements from friends or teachers. One of my colleagues, a British transplant to California, had enrolled her daughter in an all-day preschool in the San Francisco Bay area. The child's favorite playmate was an African-American girl from Oakland. Within four months, my colleague's 3-year-old was speaking black English like a native, temporarily abandoning standard American English, not to mention her earlier occasional Britishisms.

Ryan had a similar experience though on a more restricted scale. One of Ryan's nursery teachers, Joanne, was from upstate New York. Although a resident of Maryland for many years, she had retained some of her characteristic pronunciations, such as "*be-ad*" for *bad* and "*se-ad*" for *sad*. Three-and-a-half-year-old Ryan, who basically spoke a fairly nondescript mid-Atlantic dialect, was playing one afternoon when his mother came to fetch him from school.

"Watch out, Mommy,"

he yelled as he tore around the room, fleeing make-believe pursuers.

"Watch out for the be-ad guys!"

Neither Ryan nor the young girl in California was aware of these dialectal intrusions. With time, the little girl came to sound like any other middle-class Californian, and Ryan began saying "*bad*." In both cases, the parents simply ignored the appearance of these "nonnative dialects" and waited for them to fade. A hands-off policy is perfectly reasonable. However, as an alternative, parents can turn multidialectal (or multilingual) situations into ideal laboratories for nurturing language awareness.

Multilingual Awareness: "Aga Doodoo Bubu Petit Garçon?"

Learning tools are everywhere—if you know where to look. A savvy parent (or nursery school teacher) sees a wealth of crafts in empty paper towel tubes, stray buttons, and leftover aluminum foil. The same kind of savvy enables parents to capitalize on language opportunities for developing children's awareness of multiple linguistic systems. A child need not actually be bilingual or bidialectal to recognize that multiple languages and dialects exist and, in the process, to play with language possibilities like a composer writing a theme and variations.

In originally planning their bittersweet vacation to Quebec (see Chapter 5), Alex's family thought about how to orient Alex to living in a city where people did not speak English. "Sesame Street" provided an obvious jumping-off point. Alex already knew how to count to ten in Spanish (and that *uno* meant the same as *one*, *dos* the same as *two*, etc.). He also knew words like *adios* ("good-bye") and *hola* ("hello").

Several weeks before the trip, Alex's parents (both of whose French was minimal) gradually eased a few French words and phrases into everyday conversation. When his mother left the house in the morning, she might say,

"Do you know how they say 'good-bye' in French? They say *au revoir*. *Au revoir*, Alex. See you tonight."

Another favorite was to establish how Alex might be referred to in French:

"Do you know what they will say when they see you in Quebec? They'll say, '*Vous êtes un petit garçon.*' That means, 'You are a little boy.' *Petit.* That means 'little.' *Garçon.* That means 'boy.' You're a *petit garçon.*"

When the family arrived in Montreal, they mostly heard French but could manage to make themselves understood in return with a combination of pidgin French heavily peppered with English. Quebec City was a different story. Almost no one spoke English. Alex's mother led the troops with her fractured French, while Alex, on cue, would say "*au revoir*" to the waiter in the restaurant or "*bonjour*" to the hotel concierge.

Then Alex landed in the hospital because of his allergic reaction to a mosquito bite. Besides the terror of long needles and threatening machines, he was enveloped in a world devoid of English. After the initial traumas of admission and testing were over, Alex found himself isolated and bored in a hospital room with three French-speaking children. Like Coleridge's Ancient Mariner with water everywhere but not a drop to drink, Alex was surrounded by children he couldn't talk to. He ventured a few volleys of English ("Do you want to see my teddy bear?"), but was met with blank stares. Obviously English was not going to work.

Alex knew his roommates spoke French, and knew he could handle only a few words in the language, at best. Nonetheless, it was worth a try. Sitting up in bed and turning to address the 5-year-old girl on his right, he articulately inquired,

"Aga doodoo bubu petit garçon?"

Alex's "*petit garçon*" got a rise from his would-be playmate, so he continued:

"Mugu gugu wugu petit garçon?"

Throughout the remainder of his stay in Quebec City, a string of babbling ending in "*petit garçon*" became Alex's method of "conversing in French."

Upon returning to the United States, Alex displayed heightened interest in foreign languages he heard and frequently would ask,

"How do you say [such-and-such] in [French, German, Spanish, etc.]?"

In fact, he even invented his own "language"—which he called Jivanese—to keep up with his father, who had begun to learn Japanese.

Raising a child's awareness of other languages and dialects requires relatively little effort. Foreign language programs on cable television or radio, French or Spanish versions of familiar children's books (e.g., *Babar*, *Curious George*), matching up languages with countries on a globe, highlighting dialect variation ("Joanne says '*be-ad*' but I say '*bad*'—that's because she's from New York and I'm from Maryland") are but a handful of the ways in which parents raising monolingual, monodialectal children help their offspring acquire some of the natural benefits of growing up bilingual.

Media and Messages: Sign and Script

We have been looking at how children come to see spoken language not as a rigid set of rules but as sounds, words, and sentences that can be mixed and matched to express meanings through conversation. But speech is not the only channel through which societies interact. Other modes of communication include conventionalized gesture systems and written scripts. Just as speaking more than one language enriches language play and understanding of language possibilities, knowledge of multiple communication channels (e.g., sign and speech, speech and writing) affords opportunities for growth in language awareness.

Signing in a Hearing World: Goldilocks and the Three Bears Revisited

Everyone has probably encountered some version of signing systems. Former Boy Scouts may remember learning a few Amerindian hand signs. More probably, people have seen sign language interpreters—on television, at professional meetings—or perhaps taken a course on American Sign Language at a local college or school for the deaf.

A number of years ago, I received a grant from the U.S. Department of Education to investigate ways of improving the reading abilities of deaf adolescents. After some initial research, it quickly became obvious that the linguistic ramifications of deafness go far beyond not being able to hear the sounds of spoken language. The deaf students I observed generally did not conceive of speech (or writing) as anything other than a straightforward system for communicating information. Differentiating among literary styles made little sense to them, and domains of conversational appropriateness and language awareness seemed all but unknown.

The fault was hardly the students' own. Most instructors of the deaf focus on teaching sounds, words, and sentence structure. Stylistic variation, humor, or audience appropriateness seem topics far too arcane for students who have difficulty producing simple, active, declarative sentences that are intelligible and grammatical.

Unfortunately, the more subtle skills that the teachers ignored often prove critical when functioning in the hearing world. I remember one especially poignant story of a young man of 16, quite bright and with good lip-reading skills, who had landed a summer job as a stock clerk in a hardware store. With great enthusiasm, he reported to work and discharged his duties with a deep sense of responsibility.

Three days later he was fired for insubordination. He persistently had addressed his boss by his first name.

In the school for the deaf the boy attended, the teachers were addressed as "Mr. So-and-So" or "Ms. So-and-So." But the new boss had introduced himself as "Alan Fischer," and the youth had called him "Alan." No one had thought to teach the boy that when an older person (and an employer to boot) introduces himself by first name plus last name, the correct way to address him is by title plus last name.

Out of experiences such as these I launched the Language Awareness Project. Our goal was not simply to help teach deaf adolescents to read but to give them the more fundamental awareness of language as a system of expression that can take shape through speech, writing, or sign. The task facing our staff was to instill such awareness in both the deaf students themselves and their teachers, who could then rethink pedagogical approaches to language.

We began with two experiments. The first was designed to see if young adolescents (ages 12 to 15) were aware that different language registers are appropriate for different audiences (to wit, that "Mr. Fischer" should not have been called "Alan" by his new employee). We sensed the teenagers did not understand much about registers in spoken or written language, but what about registers in signing? If the students in fact recognized that their choice of signs depended on the age, sex, status (etc.) of the person they were signing to, why not build on this sign-based knowledge when teaching speaking and writing?

We asked our subjects to "tell" (sign) "Goldilocks and the Three Bears" to three different audiences: a child from the nursery program, a 7- or 8-year-old, and a peer. (All three of the "listeners" were also deaf.) The results were unmistakable. When signing to preschoolers, the teenagers incorporated a wealth of familiar baby talk techniques: short sentences, clear—even exaggerated—"articulation," simple vocabulary and syntax, much repetition. When addressing slightly older children, muted versions of the same kinds of techniques were invoked. In signing to peers, the stories went very quickly and were filled with shortcuts and slang. When we shared our finding with the teachers, they were amazed. It had never occurred to them that signing could provide a bridge for explaining linguistic subtleties in another modality.

The second experiment looked at grammaticality. In English classes, teachers had little success in explaining what it meant for a sentence to be ungrammatical. Not surprisingly, since the potential number of sentences is infinite, the job of figuring out which ones are grammatical and which ones are not seemed impossible to the students.

This time our subjects were 15- and 16-year-olds. Their task was to describe in sign the large tiled mural in their school's lobby. Each of the five students' descriptions was videotaped. In the next part of the experiment, the tapes were played to the other members of the group, and students were asked to identify who was a good signer and who was less skilled, and why.

The teenagers went about their task with considerable skill—and relish. Like grammarians at work, they immediately pointed up such traits as sophisticated vocabulary, subtle grammar, and traces of humor. They were also quick to note whose signing was awkward or ungrammatical—typically because the student had grown up in an oral household or school and had only recently learned signing from new school friends. Once again, the teachers were surprised to learn that their students had a lucid understanding of grammaticality and style issues—only in a different language modality. By referring to skills already developed in sign, the teachers discovered a valuable avenue for addressing these same issues in spoken and written English.

From Speech to Script: Emerging Literacy

For hearing children, the main challenge with language modalities is to make sense of writing as an alternative to speech. Their advantage over deaf children is that the broader community is intensely geared to easing children into literacy. ABC books, "Sesame Street," and public libraries help smooth the way. From the first alphabet blocks to the first story book, from initial attempts at writing their own names to the first letter penned to Grandma, children come to understand the unique uses and challenges of writing. In Chapter 7, we'll see how literacy emerges.

■ IDEAS AND ALERTS

How Can I Help?

**Emphasize rhymes in language you use
with your child.**

The more rhyming you do—reciting nursery rhymes, reading poems, making up rhymes, playing rhyming games—the better. Rhymes provide a perfect avenue for helping preschoolers understand that words are comprised of sounds and that new words can be formed with a simple sound change. Research shows that young preschoolers who can recite nursery rhymes like "Humpty Dumpty" or "Twinkle Twinkle Little Star" have the advantage a year or two later in reading-readiness skills such as forming alliterations or breaking words into syllables, and later, in reading itself.

**Enhance your child's understanding of
words by talking about homonyms, word
components, and definitions.**

By the time children are around 4, they have many homonyms in their vocabulary (e.g., *saw* [noun]/*saw* [verb]; *bark* [on a tree]/*bark* [sound a dog makes]). Children like Alex spontaneously notice homonyms (e.g., "There are two kinds of saw. One that you do with your eyes and the other that you do with a saw"). Other children can naturally be brought to such realizations with a little adult guidance.

187

Just as preschoolers like to build and take apart Lego or block constructions, they are ready to take an interest in word composition. The interest may be spontaneous (like Sara's "Where's the room in *mushroom*?"), or it can be initiated by adults.

Four- and 5-year-olds often spontaneously ask what words mean. Besides responding to direct inquiries, try accompanying a new word your child doesn't know with an informal definition or a synonym (e.g., "That's astounding. It's just unbelievable. I don't believe it!").

Talk about how your child's language has changed.

Reminding children what kind of language they used to use (such as Alex's *ish*) provides awareness of how much they have grown and motivation for facing new linguistic challenges.

Seek opportunities to tell jokes and riddles and to play word games.

Parents are often amazed to discover that 3- or 4-year-olds can understand many jokes and riddles (sometimes with minimal explanation) and genuinely enjoy them. A wealth of joke and riddle books are available for children even at this age.

The possibilities for word games are limited only by imagination (augmented by ideas gleaned from friends, preschool teachers, or books). Here are but a few ideas:

- opposites games ("I say *high*, and you say . . . ")
- number games ("I say *one* and you say *first*; I say *two* and you say . . . ")
- derivation games ("What do you call a boy from Texas? A *Texan*. What do you call a boy from California? A . . . ")

Use, or at least talk about, other dialects and languages.

If you have the opportunity, seriously consider raising your child bilingual. Barring that option, you can still do much to develop your child's understanding and awareness of other forms of speech.

In most parts of the United States, families have access to more than one dialect or language. Often the speaker is a teacher (such as Ryan's teacher Joanne from upper New York State) or a classmate (Sara's preschool included a little girl who had just arrived from Brazil and spoke only Portuguese). Actors or newscasters with regional or foreign accents, cable television, and vacations provide other avenues.

Preschoolers are adept at learning new words, greetings, or songs in other languages but can respond only if the opportunity is offered. Whenever possible, follow up the language "lesson" with reinforcements and reminders (e.g., finding Japan on the map, visiting native American exhibits in a museum of natural history, practicing counting to ten in Swahili long after the nursery school has completed its unit on Africa).

Introduce your child to sign language.

Not only will an awareness of sign as a system of communication expand children's linguistic horizons, but it will encourage them to appreciate the rich diversity of linguistic and social communities.

Should I Be Concerned?

I make up rhymes and play rhyming games, but my child refuses to join in.

Never press language on your child. Try games with other members of the family, and your child will participate (at least as a spectator) when he or she is ready.

Our family just returned from a year abroad, where our 3-year-old heard and used French exclusively. Now she seems to have forgotten her English and hesitates to speak at all (even in French).

Just as the 3-year-old learned French through total immersion, she will regain her English in short order. The transition back to the United States involves not only a language shift but cultural and social reorientation. At this age, significant changes of any sort (including moving to a new house down the block) can require a period of readjustment.

■ 7. Beyond Elemeno

Emerging Literacy

THREE-YEAR-OLD Alex was insistent. Pleas from his mother (hungry, tired, and eager to go home) were of no use. That Saturday afternoon, Alex had accompanied his mother to her law office to pick up some documents. On the way out, they passed the law firm's glassed-in library. Alex wanted at all those books.

Eventually she yielded, and Alex made a beeline for the multivolumed West's *Federal Digest*. Mustering all his strength, he extracted a volume and wrestled it to the floor. With focused concentration, the boy turned clumps of pages at a time, until reaching the back inside cover. Triumphantly, he beamed up at his mother, announced,

"The end!"

and emphatically slammed the back cover shut.

Alex had just "read" his first adult book.

The process of becoming literate unfolds gradually and idiosyncratically. Some children revel in written symbols, while others remain perplexed well into the elementary school years. Parents and the surrounding community are crucially influential in shaping the path through which literacy emerges. That influence includes overt efforts to nurture letter or word recognition, along with less tangible ingredients such as parental reading habits.

For the past two decades, family and community involvement in literacy training has been supplemented and often supplanted by educational television for preschoolers. The centerpiece of this effort has been "Sesame Street." Over the years, the program not only has generated a wealth of auxiliary teaching materials but also has spawned other educational programming, from "The Letter People" to "Reading Rainbow" and Bill Cosby's "Picture Pages."

How does literacy emerge?

Finding S's in Spaghetti: Recognizing Letters and Numbers

Children of all ages relish discovering needles in haystacks. Some of these buried objects dwell only in our minds—animal shapes in clouds, mythological figures in celestial constellations, an old man's profile in the rock face of a mountainside. Other objects actually exist—a camouflaged snake in the woods, a curious little fellow on a page in *Where's Waldo?* This search for hidden visual treasure drives imagination, artistic creation, and even the early stages of literacy.

The groundwork for literacy is laid in American households before children utter their first word. Crib blankets, wall hangings, baby clothing, and toys are as likely to be decorated with letters or numbers as with bunnies or teddy bears. This initial visual familiarity (heavily reinforced in the years ahead) gradually leads to recognition and eventual mastery, much as the early sounds and sentences directed at infants and toddlers slowly begin to make sense.

Sometime between first words and first grade, American children typically learn the letters of the alphabet and the rudiments of counting. (In societies using nonalphabetic scripts such as Japan or Korea, the process is more difficult and follows a very different timetable.) Unlike the natural enveloping presence of spoken language, the extent to which toddlers and preschoolers encounter writing depends overwhelmingly on conscious external nurturing. The stages and ages by which children connect sounds with squiggles are largely shaped by overt efforts from literate members of the child's immediate world.

Children's differing experiences with the familiar "ABC Song" illustrate how strongly the surrounding community influences children's mastery of the alphabet—the foundation of literacy in English. When I was growing up, few adults assumed children should learn to read before entering first grade. Kindergarten was optional, nursery school was the exception, and television broadcasting was restricted to a few hours of evening programming.

As the child of two working parents, I did attend nursery school, where we learned the fabled "ABC Song." Like most of my friends, I sang it this way:

"A, B, C, D, E, F, G

H, I, J, K, Elemeno, P"

and so on. Had you asked me what letter preceded "*P*," I would have told you, "*Elemeno*." Despite my familiarity with some of the individual letters, I hardly knew the set of 26.

Today's children live in a world with much stronger early literacy expectations. As a result, they develop a markedly different relationship with the alphabet. Although teaching reading is still normally a first-grade activity, most first graders arrive with the rudiments of text decipherment already under their belt. Day-long nursery school and kindergarten programs have become commonplace, and ubiquitous television programming provides a ready medium for early instruction. Likely as not, today's middle-class 3-year-olds can recognize all 26 letters and count to 15 or 20, sometimes even before mastering the "ABC Song."

In Ryan's preschool, the children had been focusing on individual letters since they were 2—playing with sandpaper *B*'s, stenciling *D*'s, doing puzzles with *Z*'s. A year later when the group was finally taught the "ABC Song," not a single child fell into the "*Elemeno*" trap. For these preschoolers, the alphabet was first a set of individual elements and only later an aggregate.

How do children come to know letters (and numbers) as individual entities? The growing torrent of alphabet books—museum alphabet books, wildlife alphabet books, zoo alphabet books, even caribou alphabet books—prod young book "viewers" to take the alphabet one letter at a time. Beyond the formal exercise of pointing up "*A*" is for *aardvark* and "*B*" is for *bison*, parents have the vast world of everyday print in which to unearth letters and numbers. Alex's father read out, character by character, the letters and numbers displayed on the backs of buses. While grocery shopping, Sara's mother challenged her daughter to find aisle 4 or to locate a product whose name began with a "W." Ryan's teachers took their charges on walks past shop windows, giving each child a letter to find in the store's name.

Some children spontaneously look for meaningful shapes in everyday objects. Ryan, the finicky eater, took more interest in playing with his food than eating it. A few of his games proved educationally redeeming. A knife, fork, and spoon became the two sides and crosspiece for constructing a capital letter "A." An uneaten strand of spaghetti quickly earned the name "S." Much as preschoolers naturally engage in symbolic play (making hats out of pots or horses from brooms), children immersed in a world of letters and numbers easily discover symbols in everyday objects.

Recognizing letters and numbers as symbols ("That's an 'A,' " "That's a '7' ") requires two steps: pairing sounds with squiggles, and then understanding what the squiggles stand for. For both letters and numbers, children generally connect up sounds (*s-e-v-e-n*) with shapes (7) before understanding what the symbols mean.

The second phase (attributing meaning) is conceptually simpler for numbers than for letters. "Number literacy" entails learning only one meaning principle, while "letter literacy" requires learning 26 sets of correspondences. With numbers, children need to recognize that any number symbol ("1," "2," "3," and so on) can represent a distinct number of objects (or, of course, numeracy in the abstract). The only difference between "2" and "3" is the number of objects at issue.

In the case of letters, the symbol-meaning correspondence is far more complex. In fact, connecting up letters with sounds presents three distinct challenges for young learners. The first challenge is to learn that the name of a letter is not pronounced the same way as the sound the letter stands for. The **symbol** "*E*" is pronounced "*ee*," but the **sound** that "*E*" represents is "*eh*." Compare the situation with numbers. Number symbols (e.g., "7") have names and stand for objects in the real world, while letter symbols (which also have names) stand for disembodied sounds.

The second challenge with letter symbols comes in learning a different symbol/sound pairing for each letter. While "*E*" is called "*ee*"— but represents the sound "*eh*" (as in *pet*)—the letter "*I*" is called "*aee*" and stands for the sound "*i*" (as in *pit*).

194

As if this were not madness enough, children eventually need to learn that sound/symbol pairings are themselves elusive. The same symbol may represent more than one sound (e.g., _a_pple and w_a_s) and the same sound may be represented by more than one symbol (e.g., _self-c_entered). No wonder children have trouble learning to read English.

Perhaps not surprisingly, adults whose disabilities have hampered their acquisition of language can sometimes nonetheless handle the rudiments of arithmetic. Susan Schaller, in her account of an uneducated deaf Mexican who acquired no language until he was 27 years old, reports that the man learned to handle simple addition before he understood a single gestured sign.

How can parents or preschool teachers help children bridge the gap between letter names and sounds? A vast array of teaching strategies has been developed for kindergarten and first grade. But now that preschoolers are increasingly introduced to the rudiments of literacy long before their fifth birthday, which of these strategies make sense for younger children?

One good example comes from Ryan's nursery school experience. By the time Ryan was 3½, his teachers began playing a game we might call "What Does This Letter Say?" Each letter was paired with a word in which the letter bore its most typical pronunciation. For example, when the teacher asked, "What does 'E' say?" the answer would be "_eh_" (as in _elephant_ or _pen_). "What does 'B' say?" It says "_buh_" (as in _buffalo_ or _bubble_). When they reached the first grade, Ryan and his playmates soon learned the world of sounds and symbols was more complex (even devious), but by then the basic connection between sounds and squiggles was firmly established, and the children were ready for new challenges.

Parents and teachers can do a great deal to help guide children on the path to literacy. Yet in contemporary times, the most effective guides are often not people but puppets.

Television and Modern Literacy: The "Sesame Street" Generation

In the mid-1960s, television pioneer Joan Ganz Cooney and puppeteer Jim Henson forged a new kind of quality educational programming.

The result of their efforts was "Sesame Street," a program originally designed for disadvantaged 3- to 5-year-olds. Now more than twenty years later, "Sesame Street" is a staple in middle-class homes across America and around the world.

The designers of "Sesame Street" set explicit educational goals: teaching about the physical and social environment, fostering a variety of cognitive skills, and, perhaps fundamentally, building an understanding of symbolic representation. Eight goals were defined for teaching letters:

- Given a set of symbols, either all letters or numbers, the child knows whether those symbols are used in reading or in counting.
- Given a printed letter, the child can select the identical letter from a set of printed letters.
- Given a printed letter, the child can select its other case version from a set of printed letters.
- Given a verbal label for certain letters, the child can select the appropriate letter from a set of printed letters.
- Given a printed letter, the child can provide the verbal label.
- Given a series of words presented orally, all beginning with the same letter, the child can make up another word or pick another word starting with the same letter.
- Given a spoken letter, the child can select a set of pictures or objects beginning with that letter.
- The child can recite the alphabet.

"Sesame Street" has done more to redefine literacy goals for young children than any other single force since education became compulsory in America. Goals designed for 5-year-olds are frequently reached by 3- and even 2-year-olds. Viewers as young as 12 months may spend several hours daily watching intently, thanks to repeat programming, multiple Public Broadcasting channels, and the wonder of VCRs. Such intense viewing from an early age can significantly accelerate the beginning stages of literacy.

Alex was an early viewer, watching up to three hours of "Sesame Street" in a single day during his second year of life. Around age 18 months, Alex (who at the time did little spontaneous talking) began counting to 10 and saying the alphabet by himself. He missed some numbers and letters (and many of the letters sounded the same, e.g., "S" and "X"). But as his phonology improved, so did his counting and alphabet. By 24 months, he had mastered most letters, and his counting skills were edging towards 20.

Was Alex exceptional? Hardly. A study of children who began reading before age 4 (which Alex did not) reports that typically "the child had learned [to read] independently, largely as a result of watching SESAME STREET." A number of these children were regular viewers by age 1, and many watched the program up to two or three hours a day.

"Sesame Street" aims to teach preschoolers letters and numbers, not to teach them to read. With the exception of a handful of word vignettes (like a charming sequence on the word *exit*), the show concentrates on single letters (and sounds), sometimes presented individually, other times in words. While "Sesame Street" provides young viewers an early boost toward actual reading, we need to look elsewhere to understand the process by which children learn to decipher written words.

Decoding the Written Word

In 1955, a freelance writer named Rudolf Flesch declared that American children were failing educationally because we were not teaching them to read properly. Instead of relying upon the **whole-word** approach (whereby children sight-read memorized words without decomposing them into parts), we should (Flesch argued) instill the **phonic** approach, through which children learn to sound out each letter in the word.

In the ensuing decades, the great literacy debate has raged over the relative merits of the whole-word versus the phonic approach. Depending upon whom you read, one side or the other comes out the clear winner. Nearly all the arguments have centered on appropriate pedagogies for children of elementary school age. But what about preschoolers? Should 4-year-olds be taught to sound out words? Does a 3-year-old "reading" each word in Dr. Seuss's *Green Eggs and Ham*, a book she has memorized, have any skills relevant to literacy?

Memory or Decomposition? Deciphering Words

Unlike orienteering with sound, meaning, grammar, and conversation (where strategies are primarily created by the children themselves), preschoolers' orienteering with written words typically reflects adult maneuvering (e.g., parents pointing to each word as they read a book, sounding out individual words slowly, asking the child to find a particular word on the page). Combining individuality with adult influence, children develop distinctive styles for coping with print before actual reading begins.

Ryan typifies the whole-word approach of recognizing individual words by sight. At school, the names of individual children were everywhere: on their cubbies, on each piece of artwork, on the "chores" board for the day (William is lunch table setter, Britta chooses the story before naptime). It is hardly surprising that after multiple exposures to the same dozen words, Ryan could recognize the written version of each classmate's name. Through similar repetitions, by age 4 Ryan had learned to "read" about a dozen words in his books at home, including *yes*, *zoo*, and *Babar*.

Sara memorized greater stretches of text. By age 3 she could "read" short books by heart, knowing just when to turn the page. Sara was quick to point out any deviations from the printed text when an adult read these books to her. If her mother accidentally replaced "large elephant" with "big elephant," Sara would chide,

> "No, Mommy! You did it wrong!"

Although Sara did not yet recognize *large* or *big* on the printed page, she knew from the spoken cadence which word belonged in the story.

Alex's approach was more eclectic, in part because of his own personality but also because of his parents' pedagogical style. Like Ryan, by age 3½ Alex recognized a number of individual words by sight. Besides recognizing the written versions of his friends' names from school, Alex could "read" the names of some of his favorite authors (Dr. Seuss, Eric Carle), along with about two dozen words his parents had taught him (including *plane*, *train*, *the*, and *end*). Like Sara, Alex had memorized some of his favorite books and had the overall gestalt of several others. For books in the latter category, Alex would challenge his mother,

"Did you read all the words on the page?"

if she attempted to shortchange him in the nightly ritual of reading three books before lights out.

Unlike Ryan or Sara, Alex was also learning to decompose individual words. Pausing at the written name for an animal Alex especially liked (such as an elephant), Alex's mother would ask,

"What does this word say?"

to which Alex predictably replied,

"I don't know."

On cue, his mother would suggest they sound out the word together, letter by letter. Her success rate hovered around 50 percent. Half the time Alex would play along, while the other half he impatiently demanded,

"You tell me"

—which she did.

Which strategy best fosters eventual reading: whole word, memorized text, or early decoding? The question itself is wrong-headed, for it presupposes exclusivity, homogeneity, and learning out of context. Most children, like Alex, draw from all three approaches although in differing proportions. As children get older, their needs and interests change, and an orienteering strategy well suited to a 3-year-old often yields to a strategy more appropriate for a 5- or 6-year-old, especially if parents and teachers help nurture the transition.

Even as seasoned readers, adults do not rely on an exclusive reading strategy. We often need to absorb words quickly without analyzing them—making out highway signs as we zip by at sixty miles an hour, scanning names in a telephone directory. While as saturated readers we rely on decomposition skills to make sense of new words, whole word recognition enables us to handle the wealth of text that assaults us daily.

The particular *route* by which children learn to read turns out to be less relevant than many specialists once thought. What about the *age* at which literacy begins?

The Doman Legacy: Does Age Matter?

Nearly thirty years ago, Glenn Doman, a physical therapist, wrote *How to Teach Your Baby to Read*. The book, which became a long-running staple in the parenting literature, argued that children as young as 2 or 3 have the capacity and motivation to begin learning reading, if only parents will help guide the process.

Doman's ideas about early literacy derived not from a desire to press children ahead academically but from his professional wonderment why children's natural curiosity and ability were not being fostered. A member of a research team working with brain-damaged children, Doman found that severely brain-damaged children as young as 3 years old could learn to read. Doman logically reasoned that if brain-damaged preschoolers could be taught to read, surely neurologically intact preschoolers could as well.

In the years that have followed, early reading in children has become a family status marker among the upwardly mobile. Middle-class parents—and aspirants—have sought to teach their preschoolers to read (or jealously eyed families with literate tots). At the same time, with the crescendoing success of "Sesame Street," parents and educators have realized that nearly all preschoolers can understand a great deal more about letters, sounds, and numbers than previous generations of mainstream educators believed.

Does it matter at what age a child learns to read? Generally no. Intelligent children vary enormously in the age at which they are ready to encounter printed language seriously. Becoming literate requires a whole collection of skills: visual ability to distinguish easily between letters like *b*, *d*, and *p*; cognitive ability to relate the shape of a letter to its name and to the sound it stands for; patience to work through the linear decoding process. Learning to read also requires motivation. Preschoolers who know the alphabet, can identify the main sound associated with each letter, and can even recognize several dozen words may feel little drive to read on their own, especially if they enjoy being read to by adults.

Considering the range in normal speech development—with first steps in grammar coming anywhere between 15 and 30 months—it is hardly surprising that children vary widely in the age at which they start to read. Differences may reflect variation in physiological development, amount of home nurturing, or personality.

Should children be allowed to determine the age at which they are taught to read? While a number of preschoolers spontaneously begin deciphering words by age 3 or 4, other children do not settle comfortably into reading until age 7 or 8. Understandably, parents with children at the later end of the spectrum are prone to worry. When difficulties do arise, they are reported more often in boys than in girls. Problems in spoken language development (especially stuttering— again, a problem plaguing more boys than girls) often portend problems with early reading.

Is early reading a sign of inherent intelligence? Probably, but not necessarily. As we saw in Chapter 3, children who are early talkers do not inevitably score well on IQ tests. On the flip side, a significant (but indeterminate) amount of intelligence as measured by early speech or reading is itself a response to active nurturing by parents.

Does early reading, in turn, foster cognitive development? Of course. The printed word reveals boundless information about the world that is, was, or might yet be. Early readers cannot help but benefit from this head start. However, since the time interval between an early reader (e.g., age 4), an average reader (age 6), and a late reader (age 7 or 8) is only a few years, what matters most is not the age at which a child begins to decode text but the positive experience she has in encountering the written word.

Learning to decipher someone else's words is a gradual process, reflecting both adult input and the individual child's personality. What about children learning to write their own words?

First Strokes

Sara (4;1 at the time) was sprawled on the living room rug, intently scribbling on a piece of paper. After a few minutes she called out to her father in the next room:

"Daddy, I need an envelope."

Her father, busy feeding his younger son, replied long distance that envelopes were in the bookcase, next to the front door. Picking herself up off the floor, Sara fetched what she needed, folded the paper she had been working on, and inserted it into the envelope. Proudly she marched into the dining room and announced,

> "I wrote a letter to Grandma. Let me read it to you
>
> [Sara whips the page out of the envelope]:
>
> 'Dear Grandma. I love you very much. Please come visit me soon. Love, Sara.' "

Like reading, children's writing is built up in several layers. The first (which Sara had nicely mastered) is understanding that thoughts can be represented in a durable medium by creating marks on a page. The next level—far more complex—is grasping how that representation must be done.

This second level has both mental and manual dimensions. Cognitively, children must learn that letters (which stand for sounds) are the standard means for expressing words (which, in turn, represent ideas). Scribbles or even pictures cannot convey the same information or precision. Many preschoolers understand in principle that letters and words are the accepted currency for written language and demand that adults produce the same, even though the child is still at the scribbling stage.

Why scribbling for writing? The problem is largely motor control. Children below age 5 or 6 often lack the fine motor skills needed to form letters with any degree of ease. Many children learn to "write" (or, more accurately, "draw") their names by age 4 but find the process so difficult that they do not begin writing other words for another year. Much of the story of how children learn to write is really an account of how they overcome obstacles of mechanical production.

Preludes to Writing: Art, Maps, and Graphic Fonts

Preschoolers learning to form letters typically pass through a series of stages that begin as drawing and end in language. Stage one—learning that marks on a page can represent objects (events, feelings) in the world (or imagination)—is part of the broader development of representational art.

Pictures that look like the things they stand for begin to appear some-where between age 3 and 4. Younger children produce scribbles and lines, blobs and dots, which, to the adult eye, are flights of imagination, not pictures intended as representations. Yet inevitably parents prime their youngsters with the idea that their pictures are meaningful:

"What is this a picture of?"

they ask, and 3-year-old Ellen or Earl volunteers,

"A duck,"

regardless of whether the child had a duck in mind when actually pro-ducing the drawing. In the process, parents teach their children that marks on paper have specific meanings, just as many adults "teach" children their first spoken words by lending meaning to infant babble.

Sara was the first of the three to begin creating drawings of recogniz-able objects. By age 2;10, she was producing four-legged animals, suns, and fish. Ryan did not venture into recognizable art until well over a year later (age 4;1). However, much as children often continue bab-bling for months after they begin articulate speech, both Sara and Ryan were more prone to scribble than to do representational drawings for at least six months after producing their first representational art.

Alex's journey into drawing was mercurial. Before his third birth-day, Alex produced—and described—only scribbles. On Thanksgiving Day (he was 3;2), Alex spontaneously turned out a recognizable engi-neer sitting on a locomotive, which, in turn, rested on a train track. Two weeks later, he painted a startling self-portrait, complete with hair, facial features, and an engineer's cap. Over the next month, an outpouring of trains appeared, along with a series of dinosaurs.

Two months later, Alex's representational drawing ceased, not to reappear in any serious way for another full year. This strange pattern mirrored Alex's development of initial grammar. A few phantom syn-tactic constructions had appeared around age 2 and then vanished. Productive grammar did not reemerge until age 2;6.

A second stage in learning to write is recognizing that visual repre-sentation can convey not simply an idea but a linear narrative. Such narratives can tell stories or provide sequential instruction. Alex illus-trates this stage through his production of maps.

A vocal backseat driver since age 3, Alex was fond of giving directions to his parents as they set out in the car:

> "You go down here. Then you turn that way. Then you go along that road. Turn right, and you're there."

By the time he was 3;9, Alex began offering his directions "in writing." What looked like a maze of tangled lines was always accompanied by an articulate explanation of where his house was on the map, what sequence of roads to follow, and where the destination lay. For Alex, these maps (created before he had sufficient motor control to produce many letters) provided a natural transition from "snapshot" art (portraying a single scene at a time—albeit in scribbles) to representation telling a story of how to move from one place to another.

In stage three, children actively form letters, but the forms are created as individual pieces of art, more like the initial letter in an illuminated manuscript than a character of type. Ryan's final transition to basic writing typifies this stage. Although he could identify all 26 letters by age 3, Ryan did not begin crafting letters himself until a year later, just a month before he undertook representational drawing. The coincidence of the two activities reflects the growing development of fine motor control that underlies both skills. Not surprisingly, the first four letters Ryan learned to form were "R," "Y," "A," and "N."

Watching Ryan produce these letters, what you saw was a young artist—not a young writer—at work. Ryan's challenge was to produce four letters, each different, collectively presenting a myriad of straight lines and curves. Watching over Ryan's shoulder during the initial months when he began attempting to construct his name, we get a sense of the artistic roots of writing.

We immediately notice that Ryan has no understanding of where to start in on a letter. Each of us, long ago, learned that to form an "R," you begin with a vertical line, next do the curved part on top, and end up with the half-length diagonal. Ryan, innocent of instruction in penmanship, started with the diagonal (moving from lower right to upper left), next did the half loop (starting at the bottom and circling up to the top), and only then ended up with the anchoring vertical. For adults who have learned a non-Roman script such as Cyrillic, Hebrew, or Japanese, the struggle to move from art to writing may still be vivid. In modern parlance, these early crafted letters are more like graphic computer fonts built each time they are printed than like a ready-made character set (analogous to the keys on a typewriter).

This "artistic" phase in writing is a direct response to the enormous effort children (or newly literate adults) must exert in creating individual letters. But times are changing. Given modern technology—first typewriters and now computers—letters can be produced with the flick of a finger, even a very little finger.

How does the proliferation of contemporary writing technology alter the very process by which children learn to write—and, derivatively, to read?

Type First, Read Later: Pragmatic Routes to Literacy

When Ryan was 3½, the mother of one of his classmates donated an old electric typewriter to the nursery school. Instantly the children were drawn to the machine. After waiting their turns (not very patiently), each youngster banged away for a glorious sixty seconds, generating the typewritten equivalent of scribble.

The novelty soon wore off for many, but a small contingent continued to work the machine day after day. Instead of firing at will, these children began studying the keyboard. Within a few weeks, several, including Ryan, were able to type out their names, using the tried-and-true hunt-and-peck method. By the time he was 3;7, Ryan could reliably type his name, fully five months before accomplishing the same feat using a pen on paper.

Alex was yet more fortunate, having a computer at home. Like Ryan, Alex began with a scribble stage, extending from age 2;2 (when he was first allowed to play with the family Macintosh) up through 4;5—long after he had initially begun to identify letters on the keyboard. By 3;5 Alex was typing his name, interspersed with strings of random letters. By 4;1, two months before he could write his name "by hand," Alex was able to type out (with coaching from his mother) the names of other family members, along with several of the words he had learned to recognize by sight (e.g., *plane, train*).

Alex's experience with typing letters on the computer enhanced his progress in creating letters manually. Producing a letter on a computer does not require painstaking art. Instead, each letter is formed with a single stroke. The concept of letters as standardized shapes, not individual constructions, provides the conceptual impetus for conquering the motoric barrier and producing written language, not calligraphy.

In simplifying the formation of individual letters, typewriters and computers enable children to forge a vital link between two otherwise out-of-phase language components: the rich spoken language skills they already possess and the still formidable system of writing that enables people to record what they have to say and to decode the written thoughts of others.

For centuries, the standard sequence for literacy instruction has been to begin by deciphering someone else's individual letters and words and only later learning to produce letters (and words) yourself. Throughout modern European and American history, many "literate" people knew only how to read—not how to write. Parchment (or paper) was very expensive, and the average person had no need to produce written documents. Being able to read the Bible and to sign your name (on a will, a deed, or a marriage certificate) usually sufficed.

In modern pedagogy, the tradition of "read first, write later" has continued to be followed, although the two skills are usually introduced in tandem. First-grade classes have long focused on "deciphering" (reading) stories written by others—be they from McGuffey's Reader, the Dick and Jane series, or other artificially constructed text. First graders have also learned to form individual letters and words and even short sentences but have not been expected to produce extended written discourse.

The problem with this educational approach is how to motivate a child to read someone else's prose, especially prose far less sophisticated than the average 6-year-old's spoken language. The standard printed fare offered to contemporary American elementary school children is **basal readers**, books specially designed to introduce a controlled vocabulary and grammar, each year becoming progressively more sophisticated. Critics such as Bruno Bettelheim have lambasted basal readers for stifling young readers. Since the spoken vocabulary of the average first grader includes many thousands of words, how can you expect him to be interested in a book containing no more than 200 or 300 different words?

And beyond the issue of constrained vocabulary and syntax, how do you motivate a child to decode someone else's story?

For at least twenty years, a growing number of educators, vexed by these dilemmas, have argued for reversing the order in literacy training. They suggest first recording a child's own stories and inviting her to read her own text. Leading the child to decode the stories of others comes later. Instead of beginning with reading and then turning to writing, children "write first, read later."

Since the average 5- or 6-year-old lacks sufficient manual facility to pen much continuous prose, how do we handle the initial transcription problem? One obvious technique is to let an adult (or an older child) serve as scribe while the younger child tells her tale. In many classrooms (from first grade reaching down through kindergarten and even into preschool), teachers transcribe children's sentences and stories and then, especially with older groups, teach children to decode their own compositions.

With the proliferation of electric typewriters and computers, children now come to "write first, read later" by recording their own stories themselves. Given the ease with which a 4-, 5-, or 6-year-old can strike letters at a keyboard, young learners can record their personal tales up to two or three years earlier than their parents did when they learned to write. Commercial programs such as IBM's "Writing to Read" (developed from a typewriter-based reading curriculum created in Florida) have enabled tens of thousands of kindergarten and first-grade children across the country to narrow the gap between speech and writing.

Do "write first, read later" programs work? Do they motivate children to write more and to read earlier than traditional approaches to literacy? "Writing to Read" has generally received excellent reviews, and teachers who use similar (often homegrown) programs have reported good results as well.

A curriculum that encourages children to write early—whether on a computer, on a typewriter, or by hand—must assume a laissez-faire posture toward spelling. Learning to spell words correctly takes many years and constrains the amount of writing young children can turn out. (Just as many toddlers will not attempt to pronounce a word if they cannot say it correctly, normative spelling is one of the biggest impediments to young writers.) Although debates still range over the benefits or dangers of not stressing correct orthography from the start, the jury is leaning towards the verdict that stimulating early interest in producing and decoding written words is far more critical than inculcating early spelling habits. Once they are hooked on print, children make the transition to correct spelling fairly easily.

The last twenty years have revolutionized possibilities for introducing children to literacy. Television has brought "Sesame Street" to millions of children, fundamentally altering their relationship with letters, numbers, and sounds. Typewriters and computers have provided children with simple alternatives to laborious letter production, and in the process, many 5- and 6-year-olds have written extended text they then learn to decipher.

But utensils never guarantee use. Assessments of the reading abilities of our nation's children continue to report that while early reading skills are at reasonable levels, the older children become, the more problematic their reading and analytic abilities.

What goes wrong?

The Sunday School Syndrome

In the neighborhood where I grew up, a curious ritual was enacted every Sunday morning. At about 9:45, cars began leaving their driveways, with Mom or Dad still in bathrobe and slippers and the children properly dressed in Sunday best. Off they went to church or synagogue, where the kids hopped out in time for 10:00 A.M. Sunday school, while their parents returned home to sleep or to read the Sunday paper. The meaning of "Do as I say, not as I do" was quickly absorbed from the inequities of Sunday morning religion.

As a parent, I have puzzled over the mixed messages children receive about reading from their parents. Given the years of schooling today's average middle-class parent has been through, coupled with the plethora of books and games, television and computer programs designed to teach children to read, I cannot help wondering why so many children fail to be drawn to or eventually turn off from reading.

Has reading has fallen victim to the Sunday School Syndrome?

Like baby ducklings imprinted in the first hours of life, young children are naturally influenced by behaviors modeled around them. The vocal cadence, bodily postures, eating habits, and even styles of laughter they encounter are likely to surface in their own behavior in years to come.

The same is true for attitudes towards literacy.

Although parental modeling hardly ensures lockstep compliance, the feelings children develop about reading and writing typically reflect parental attitudes. Common sense dictates that parents who read to their children and who read themselves are likely to engender a love of literacy in their offspring. But experience suggests the equation is not quite so simple. Two stories illustrate the point.

The first stems from an incident a number of years ago when microcomputer technology was first exploding. I had enrolled in an extension school evening course on microprocessors. The course was intended for computer professionals and was taught by a front-line researcher from a major computer manufacturing company. One evening during the break, I began chatting with the instructor and happened to inquire what kind of computer he used at home. Matter-of-factly, he replied,

> "A computer in my home? Are you kidding? I work with those things all day!"

The second story comes from my life as a university faculty member. As an inveterate reader and bookstore junkie, for many years I was fortunate that my university bookstore offered faculty members a discount on book purchases. One day I was stunned to learn that the discount had been cancelled.

> "Why?"

I inquired of the store manager. His answer:

> "Because so few faculty members purchase books here."

As practically the only bookstore in town, the campus store's problem was not competition from another vendor. The faculty simply were not buying books.

Much as the lay public naturally assumes computer professionals will have machines in their own homes, the general public understandably believes that people whose professions center on books (such as university professors) are avid readers.

Not so. Literary critic George Steiner, analyzing how attitudes towards reading have altered since the eighteenth and nineteenth centuries, observes that reading has shifted from a private activity done at leisure to a public venture engaged in for profit. Like the Japanese leaving their shoes at the door (shedding the mantle of the outside world before resuming their private lives), college-educated professionals living in the information age (be they researchers, journalists, or middle-level managers) are far less prone to relax with Charles Dickens than with the Monday Night Movie.

Children have an uncanny ability to psych out adults. Parents who take their children to the public library but check out no books for themselves, parents who read to their children each night but are rarely seen reading their own books, parents who bring their children to bookstores to buy a present for someone else but who then refuse to let their sons and daughters select books of their own: all send clear messages to their progeny that reading is not to be taken seriously.

How do our three families approach the written word—and what effects do these approaches have upon their children's attitudes towards reading?

Sara's family typifies contemporary college-educated America. Her parents collectively own 400 or 500 books (including volumes saved from college, cookbooks, and a few dozen coffee-table items collected over the years). They belong to two book clubs, subscribe to a sheaf of magazines (including one children's magazine for Sara), and visit a bookstore about a dozen times a year. By the time she was 5, Sara owned over 50 books of her own, and the family went to the local library every three weeks when Sara's books were due.

Bedtime for Sara invariably included reading one book aloud (of Sara's choice). Sara was allowed to bang on the old family typewriter but was not permitted access to her father's computer, which belonged to the accounting firm. Most newspaper, magazine, or book reading by her parents took place after Sara had gone to bed. In short, Sara's home offered a welcoming approach to literacy but did nothing beyond the obvious to encourage reading or writing.

In Ryan's household, the status of print was more tenuous. Ryan's mother had never finished college, and the hundred or so books in the household reflected pragmatic need more than literary taste: some how-to books on household repair and finances, a small cookbook collection, popular contemporary fiction for relaxation, and a few volumes on child rearing. The family subscribed to half a dozen magazines (including one for Ryan and another for Cathy). Visits to bookstores took place a couple of times a year. Ryan's own library (largely hand-me-downs from his sister) included about 20 volumes, mostly acquired as presents. Partially through habit, partially through financial necessity, any other books came from sporadic trips to the public library.

Ryan's mother strongly favored developing good early literacy habits in her children but assumed that their teachers bore primary responsibility. For her part, Ryan's mother questioned her son about what stories they were reading in school and sometimes checked out books for him from the public library on her way home from work. (To have brought Ryan with her on Saturdays would have meant fighting the crowds and noise.) Beyond his nightly book at bedtime or watching Cathy do her homework, Ryan encountered little active engagement with print at home. As a single parent, Ryan's mother almost never found time to read even the newspaper while her children were awake.

Alex's print milieu lay at the other end of the spectrum. The walls of his house were covered with books—medical books, law books, nature books, travel books, literature. New materials arrived weekly from book clubs, special orders, or frequent trips to bookstores. Many of the mailings arrived in Alex's name, including magazines and books being saved until he was old enough to read them himself. By age 5, Alex's own active library consisted of well over a hundred volumes, with another several hundred waiting in the wings (but viewable in special bookcases) until he got older.

The family nurtured an attitude toward books akin to the mind-set many children develop toward candy. From the time Alex was 2, his parents began tempting him with,

"If you're very good today, I'll give you a new book."

GROWING UP WITH LANGUAGE

By the time Alex was 4, books and reading had become the ultimate bribe and ultimate benefit. Although he disliked getting up in the morning, Alex could be coaxed awake by reading to him. For the second book of the morning, a page was read for each article of clothing donned or each quadrant of teeth brushed. On one trip to the local bookstore, Alex announced to his father,

"If you are very good, I will get you a book."

When they arrived at the store, Alex dashed off to the children's corner to make his selection.

The family typewriter and computer were open for Alex to explore, and Alex was encouraged to type out scribbles, then words, and eventually sentences. Like most other contemporary parents, Alex's mother and father had limited time to model solitary reading to their child. (Occasionally his parents managed to read a newspaper or a magazine while Alex was up, but serious reading and writing were still largely done in offices, libraries, or at home after their son had gone to bed.) However, their attitude toward print made it clear that literacy occupied a central place in their lives.

How did Sara, Ryan, and Alex respond to their print environments? None became an early reader, and none had pronounced difficulty upon encountering formal reading instruction in the first grade. However, each clearly imbibed his or her family's attitude toward reading. Sara grew up a good reader but turned to books only when there was nothing more interesting to do. Ryan became an average reader, who looked upon books as benevolent educational evils. And Alex blossomed into an avid reader, rapidly advancing past his classmates in reading level.

Sara read "when there was nothing more interesting to do." What is the major competition? Television. In the average American household, a television is on more than forty hours a week—more hours than most full-time employees work, nearly as many hours as most of us sleep.

In households with preschoolers, children typically spend a substantial portion of those forty hours planted before the set. We have already seen the potential benefits of targeted programming such as

"Sesame Street" in nurturing reading fundamentals. But what about other effects of television on early literacy?

During the mid-1980s, I offered a course on linguistics and language arts for college students preparing to teach in elementary school. One of the readings I selected was entitled "Television as Talking Picture Book: A Prop for Language Acquisition." The authors argue that just as we use picture books to expand children's knowledge of the world (and of the language used to describe it), parents can make shared television viewing a context for enhancing linguistic knowledge. Like a self-contained storybook with limited events and characters upon which parents can comment, television series intended for children offer a microworld for educational conversation.

The day the reading assignment was due, my students stormed angrily into class. Why had I assigned such nonsense? The basic premise of the article (so they told me) was ridiculous. Didn't I know that the whole point of watching television is to *escape* conversation—parents to park their kids and children to get out from under their parents' thumb?

Are television viewing habits a factor in early reading? Reading, like speaking, begins as a shared activity. By actively talking with their infants and toddlers, parents help nurture early spoken language. And the more that parents talk *about* language, the greater facility children develop with language variance and with the written word. To the extent television is a solitary—or even merely silent—activity, time spent before the set is time stolen from conversation, reading, or writing.

Studies correlating hours of television children view with reading performance reveal interesting patterns. The National Assessment of Educational Progress reports a *positive* correlation between reading performance and television watching in 9-year-olds but a *negative* correlation among 13- and 17-year-olds. Other studies have shown that while reading comprehension scores rise slightly among children who watch up to about ten hours of television a week, as the number of viewing hours rises, the level of reading comprehension rapidly falls off. While these studies do not specify whether the viewing was solitary or in groups, American viewing habits suggest that regardless of who else

213

might have been present, any conversation was not likely to enhance language development.

Were my students right? Is it unreasonable to view television as a potential source of language and literacy development through adult-child conversation? We turn to our three families as barometers of American viewing practices.

Sara's parents, like most other conscientious middle-class families, were careful to monitor the programs their daughter watched. Children's programming on Public Broadcasting was "in," as were nature programs, Disney movies, and Saturday morning cartoons; adult "dramas" were "out."

From the time she was 2, Sara had been trained to play by herself—whether building Duplo constructions in her playroom or watching television in the living room. Her parents prided themselves on Sara's growing ability to structure her own time and relished the free moments to attend to household chores or simply rest. My students were right on the mark if Sara were their prototype.

Ryan's home television situation represents the American norm. In part because of his older sister, the television in Ryan's home was on far more hours of the day than in Sara's. Programming was less monitored, and when Ryan's mother joined her children to watch, it was to relax, not to capitalize upon the program as a medium of instruction. Again, my students were right.

Alex's family television viewing fell at the other extreme. As in Sara's household, Alex's viewing was limited to age-appropriate educational programs. The difference was that Alex never watched television by himself. By default, television viewing was a joint activity.

Alex's family had not intended it that way. Because of Alex's initial speech delay, his parents had intently focused on conversing with their toddler. As a result, Alex came to expect that his parents (or some duly appointed representative) would always be available to keep him company. The adults had looked forward to the time (they figured by age 3) that Alex would begin playing by himself and watching television alone.

But the couple had trained their son too well in communal values. Left alone in his room with a mound of toys, he would plaintively bleat,

"I'm all alone in here!"

Deposited before a favorite videotape, Alex would refuse to stay put until joined by a fellow viewer. As long as they were held captive, Alex's mother and father naturally fell into talking with Alex about what was happening on the screen. This shared activity—like explaining new words in books or reading numbers on the backs of buses—directly contributed to Alex's wealth of linguistically coded experiences. The growing common arsenal provided material for subsequent conversation and eventually for the stories Alex would begin to write on the computer.

In cases such as Alex's, my students turned out wrong.

■ IDEAS AND ALERTS

How Can I Help?

Make reading to your child a dialogue, not a monologue.

Reading aloud to a child is as much an opportunity for conversation and exploration as for storytelling and exposure to the written word. Research suggests that when parents who are reading to their children pause to ask open-ended questions, to respond to children's questions, and to comment on the story, children become more advanced in their own spoken language.

Prepare to sacrifice some books to toddlers and young preschoolers.

When children initially get involved with books, torn pages and broken spines are commonplace. To chastise a 2- or 3-year-old for damage risks undermining the positive bond you are attempting to build between your child and books.

Play language games that facilitate reading and writing.

The possibilities for games that encourage word and letter decipherment are endless. Hundreds of ideas appear in "reading-readiness" workbooks and "better baby books" (see references in the "General

Reading" section at the beginning of the Notes), not to mention the techniques you concoct yourself. The best games are the ones your child likes to play.

Provide materials enabling children to form letters and words. Some children like paint or crayons on paper. Others initially prefer pre-formed letters (magnetic letters placed on a board, letter stencils, letters produced with a typewriter or a computer). Dictation games (either your child dictating words or letters to you or you dictating letters to your child) work well with many children.

Encourage but don't press your child to decipher and to write letters and words.

Just because children know the letters of the alphabet (and what sounds they make) hardly ensures they will decode letters in words on command. Similarly, though children may know how to write all 26 letters, they may not want to do so. Your child will be reading and writing for decades to come. Waiting another six to twelve months will do no harm.

Let preschoolers select at least some of their own books, at both the bookstore and the library.

The more involvement children have in selecting reading materials, the more likely they will become involved in the text, often memorizing the story and then decoding memorized words.

Model the reading and writing habits you want your child to develop.

Adults who genuinely enjoy reading (which is not the same as parents who read for a living or as an escape) cannot help but transmit their enthusiasm to their children. Many preschoolers have taught them-selves to read upside down as they sit across from their mothers or older siblings who are reading.

Few parents do as much writing as they do reading. However, the same principles of adult modeling and of children wanting to be included still hold. When I was completing this book (after spending many evenings and weekends in my office), my 4-year-old son undertook to "write" a series of "books" himself. What's more, he concluded that anyone who was working at night must be engaged in a literary endeavor. When his Aunt Laura, a dentist, called one evening from her office, the little boy took the telephone and naturally inquired, "Are you writing a book?"

Should I Be Concerned?

My child seems to have difficulty learning to read. Is he dyslexic?

Dyslexia is a catch-all label for difficulties in learning to read and in reading fluency. As with specific language impairment (see the end of Chapter 3), dyslexia is often the diagnosis given when other possible causes for reading disability have been eliminated. And again, as with specific language impairment, the occurrence of dyslexia is unrelated to intelligence. Prominent figures commonly cited as being dyslexic include Thomas Edison, Albert Einstein, Winston Churchill, and Woodrow Wilson.

It is estimated that between 5 and 15 percent of the population has some degree of dyslexia. Although particular symptoms (and their severity) may differ from one person to the next, dyslexics have general difficulty deciphering letters and words. Dyslexics report that letters seem to move across the page and transpose themselves. Other symptoms can include "mirror writing" (that is, writing backwards), the inability to break words into their component sounds or to pronounce unfamiliar words, omission of syllables, or difficulty keeping track of your place when reading. Not surprisingly, dyslexics rarely become good spellers. Dyslexia is sometimes associated with delayed or disordered speech development, problems in motor development, and deficits in visual perception or temporal sequencing.

Dyslexia is a dysfunction of the central nervous system, probably caused by abnormal prenatal brain development. In normal language users, the left hemisphere of the brain becomes specialized for language, and the language area on the left side becomes larger than its counterpart on the right. In dyslexia, the language area in the right hemisphere grows as large as the one in the left and contains a greater number of brain cells than normal. Among the theories of how this abnormality arises are that an excess of testosterone is present during prenatal development or that the fetus suffers some kind of brain injury. Evidence of these brain abnormalities can now be seen using PET (positron emission tomography) scans, which reveal different patterns of electrical activity when dyslexics (versus nondyslexics) are performing mental tasks.

Dyslexia may have a genetic root as well. Dyslexia often runs in families and has a higher occurrence in monozygotic (identical) than in dizygotic (fraternal) twins. For many years, dyslexia has been reported far more frequently in males than in females (a ratio of at least three-to-one), although recent studies suggest that reading difficulties in girls are actually equally prevalent.

Early signs of dyslexia typically surface when children are beginning to learn to read. The sooner the problem is diagnosed, the earlier intervention can be initiated and the better are the chances for overall success in school. By tracking eye movement, we can now identify dyslexia in children as young as age 6. Such diagnostics can predict reading problems two years later with 90 percent accuracy.

For more information on dyslexia and what to do if you suspect your child is dyslexic, contact the Orton Dyslexia Society (the address is given in the Notes under "Organizations.")

One caveat: Do not be overly hasty in labeling a child dyslexic. Many of the traits typically associated with dyslexia—including letter reversals (e.g., confusing *p* for *b*), difficulty pronouncing unfamiliar words, and even mirror writing—are common in children learning to read or write, and some (such as letter reversal) frequently occur among normal adults. Before seeking outside help, consider whether the "problems" you notice are simply normal stages in becoming literate.

If a child has been delayed or has had difficulties in learning to speak, is he likely to have problems learning to read?

Between 5 and 10 percent of children suffer from some kind of developmental spoken language problem, and between 5 and 15 percent of children have difficulty learning to read. Many of these are the same children.

A variety of studies have reported that young children with speech and language problems are more prone to have trouble learning to read than their normal counterparts—up to six times more trouble. Several researchers have specifically linked problems with phonological development or with metalinguistic awareness regarding sound (e.g., being aware of rhymes, being able to break words down into syllables) to slow progress in reading. Other studies have found significant correlations between reading delays and slower attainment of such lexical and grammatical milestones as the age at which a child uses 4 to 6 words, uses 50 words, and combines two words together.

Since delays in spoken language development can arise from an abundance of sources (from prematurity to twinning, retardation, or specific language impairment), delayed speech does not necessarily portend difficulty in learning to read. However, if by age 4 or 5 a child's spoken language is not developing well, the possibility of a potential reading deficit is obviously greater.

■ Epilogue

ABRAHAM LINCOLN was riding one day in a stagecoach with two fellow lawyers. As it happened, the three travelers possessed vastly differing physiques. The first had a very long trunk with equally short legs. The second had a short body and longish legs. The third—Mr. Lincoln—had the longest legs of all.

The lawyers fell into conversation about each other's build, and one inquired of Lincoln,

"How long should a man's legs be in proportion to his body?"

With typical humor and wisdom, Lincoln replied,

"I have not given the matter much consideration, but on first blush I should judge they ought to be long enough to reach from the body to the ground."

How much language must children acquire to become members of a language community? And how soon do learners achieve linguistic saturation?

By the time they turn age 5 or 6, children have made their way from incomprehensible, uncomprehending neophytes into articulate, reflective language users. They have cracked much of the language code and can largely negotiate through what was once a sea of linguistic babel. Talk for a few minutes with an average kindergartner, and you will be hard pressed to detect linguistic gaps. Likely as not, she will sound like a saturated speaker and show comprehension of what you say.

But linger a while longer, press the conversation a little further, and you will discover that our 5- or 6-year-old is not yet linguistically mature.

Approaching Saturation

Six-year-old Ryan and his mother were on their way to pick up a pizza for dinner. As the car approached the eatery, Ryan reflected,

> "I *didn't be* at the *shub shop* [= submarine shop] for a long time."

Ryan still had not sorted out the correct past tense combinations for *do*, *have*, and *be*, and like many other speakers, he was prone to mix up his *s*'s and *sh*'s when they came side by side in a word or phrase. (Recall the tongue twister, "She sells seashells down by the seashore.")

As children move into the school-age years and then into adulthood, they persist in revising and refining their knowledge of language: sounds, meaning, grammar, conversation, language awareness, and, of course, literacy. This continuing linguistic journey is marked by many common landmarks (e.g., all children learn more vocabulary words, children master the essential points of pronunciation and grammar), but the individual paths taken also reveal the richness of variation we saw in the early years of language development.

What is left to learn? Examples from Ryan, Sara, and Alex (along with vignettes from other children I have known) hint at the linguistic gaps that still remain.

One of Ryan's prime holdouts in learning the English sound system was his pronunciation of the words *the* and *a*. Saturated speakers say

> "*the* [rhymes with *duh*] man"

but

> "*the* [rhymes with *knee*] orange."

We speak of

> "*a* [again, rhymes with *duh*] man"

but

222

"*an* [rhymes with *can*] orange."

The principle at work in both sets of examples is the same: Use *thuh* and *uh* before a word beginning with a consonant (e.g., *man*) but *thee* and *an* before a word beginning with a vowel (such as *orange*).

Yet simple rules are not always simple to learn, especially when you need to know which noun you are going to say (and what sound it starts with) *before* you choose the appropriate modifier. Until he was nearly 8 years old, Ryan took potshots at pronunciations of *a* and *the*, sometimes saying

"*thee* ball"

and sometimes

"*thuh* ball,"

even within the same conversation.

While most children master the sound system by the time they are 8 or 9, the acquisition of words takes much longer. Webster's *Third New International Dictionary (Unabridged)* contains nearly half a million entries, and new candidates arise each year. It has been estimated that the average high school graduate's reading vocabulary consists of around 40,000 words (plus another 40,000 for names, places, and idiomatic expressions).

As children grow and their education becomes increasingly formal, new words or additional word meanings are frequently learned from school lessons or by asking more saturated speakers, "What does such-and-such mean?" At the same time, children continue to use their orienteering skills to puzzle out meanings for themselves. Paul, the 10-year-old son of a colleague, once treated me to a marvelous case of such lexical orienteering.

I had been taking care of the boy and his sisters for a week while their mother was out of town. I was in graduate school at the time, in the thick of dissertation research, and was eagerly awaiting the print-out of an extensive corpus of language acquisition data being compiled by another researcher. Paul had heard me speak of the corpus that would soon arrive, and he shared my anticipation.

GROWING UP WITH LANGUAGE

On Friday afternoon, I triumphantly entered the house. Arms laden with reams of computer printout, I proclaimed,

"The corpus is finally here!"

Paul excitedly galloped down the stairs, gazed at what I was carrying, and was suddenly crestfallen:

"But where's the *porpoise?*"

he demanded. Paul's orienteering strategy had led him to expect something far more exciting than a stack of paper.

Children sometimes reveal their interpretations of word meanings by volunteering definitions. When Sara was 7½, she offered her mother an insightful, though incorrect, explanation of the difference between a tunnel and a bridge.

The definitions were sparked by a drive through downtown Washington, D.C., a city designed in 1791 by Pierre Charles L'Enfant. The French engineer had inventively crisscrossed the traditional grid of horizontal and vertical streets with prominent diagonals (echoing the gardens in Versailles). To facilitate traffic flow where several roads met, L'Enfant added a number of traffic circles, most of which were gradually adorned with statues of generals or statesmen. Much later, underpasses were dug under several of the circles to speed along through traffic.

For Sara's family, a common route was under one of these traffic circles and then across the Memorial Bridge, which extends from the Lincoln Memorial (on the Washington side of the Potomac) to the Custis-Lee Mansion and Arlington National Cemetery (on the Virginia side). That morning, as they began to descend the underpass at Thomas Circle, Sara knowingly informed her mother:

"You can always tell a tunnel because it has a statue on top. Bridges are different; they have lions in front."

And right she was—sort of, since the bridge she knew best, Memorial Bridge, is flanked by two imposing lions on the Washington side.

To master the remaining grammatical components of language, children need to relinquish any remaining stakes in reasonable (but incorrect) grammatical constructions devised through analogy or scissors and paste strategies. As a preschooler, Alex had regularly formed interrogatives by pasting a question word in front of a declarative—

3;2 "Why you aren't sad?"

The boy continued the practice, at least intermittently, for several more years—

5;5 "Why the violin is screeching?"

The most obvious grammatical growth comes in mastering the intricacies of English morphology. Preschoolers frequently create analogies such as *hims* (for *his*), *downer* (for *farther down*) or *leaveded* (for *left*). Such morphological orienteering continues apace for a number of years. Six-year-old Sara, being driven to a birthday party for which she was a little late, urged her father,

"Let's go fastly!"

(*slow* : *slowly* = *fast* : *fastly*)

Ryan continued to form logical (but incorrect) past-tense verbs up through the fourth grade:

Ryan (9;11): "Cathy hitted me!"

Even adults sometimes waffle on verbs. Ask ten educated speakers for the past tense of the verb "*to dive*," and you are certain to get a split opinion between *dove* and *dived*. Other times adults simply misspeak themselves, coining plausible but inappropriate analogies. Several years back, a neighbor who had been showing me her garden apologized that we could not enter her house through the back door. She explained that while watering the roses the day before,

"Accidentally the door got wet, and it swolled [= swelled] shut."

Conversationally, the potential challenges remaining for school-aged children (and adults) are vast. One obvious domain in need of refinement is rules of conversational appropriateness: when is it your turn to talk, what is all right to say to whom, how much do you need to express to make yourself understood.

225

GROWING UP WITH LANGUAGE

Ironically, after years of coaxing language from toddlers and preschoolers, adults spend the next dozen years admonishing children *not* to speak ("No talking once the concert begins," "Please don't interrupt," "Don't breathe a word of this to your mother"). A generation ago, television host Art Linkletter built his reputation listening to "the darndest things" that children said on his afternoon talk show. Most of the humor came from what the young guests innocently revealed about their families—information never meant to be divulged in public.

In Chapter 5, we talked about the difficulties young children have in mastering basic rules for conversing with a person whom they cannot see (behind a screen, on a telephone). New technologies continually add to the conversational conventions today's speakers need to learn: telephone conference calls, electronic mail, television interviews. But the technology affecting the largest number of speakers is telephone answering machines.

Leaving a message on an answering machine seems so easy: listen to a recording, wait for the beep, then talk. Yet even adults struggle to get the protocols right. Many simply freeze (like Ryan in his first telephone conversation with William) and then hang up. Those who persevere learn to cool their heels until the beep comes (sometimes a long wait), keep their message brief (lest the tape run out), and use language appropriate for addressing someone who isn't there.

The importance of appropriateness was hammered home to me one evening when I checked my telephone messages upon returning from several days out of town. People with answering machines typically begin their greetings with their names or telephone numbers, helping legitimate callers confirm they have reached the correct party and alerting misdialers to hang up and try again. My own recorded greeting followed this basic format, and I was often treated to the message

> "Sorry!"

or just the sound of a receiver being hung up, as the caller realized he had dialed the wrong number.

This call was different. It began innocently enough:

> "Hi, Mark. It's Bud. I've got the part you want and can bring it by tomorrow morning."

Suddenly Bud realized he wasn't talking to Mark's surrogate:

"Oh, this isn't Hillis Contracting. Sorry."

A reasonable response. But his tag line wasn't:

"Talk to ya later."

As with conversational skills, development in language awareness is intensely individual. Some speakers remain content with rudimentary linguistic control, while others learn to play language like virtuosos. The awareness and humor of which children are capable is epitomized by the play on words made by the 12-year-old daughter of a neighbor. After watching a cooking show on television, Julia wryly proclaimed,

"She may be Julia Child, but I'm Julia Grown-Up!"

The linguistic awareness children eventually attain emerges from the unique chemistry of the language environment that parents (and later playmates and teachers) create, along with children's individual personalities, which often change with time. Sara, despite her early linguistic head start, never particularly developed an ear for language. While her pronunciation and grammar were fluent, she took no special interest in rhymes, metaphors, or commenting on the language around her. Ryan, thanks to a ninth-grade teacher, blossomed into an avid punner. And Alex, who continued to stumble over his words occasionally, learned to think out what he wanted to say before he began speaking.

The most obvious language growth area for children over 5 or 6 is literacy. Most children do not begin deciphering text until they are in the first grade. From then on, the prospects are open-ended. Although neither Sara, Ryan, nor Alex began as an early reader, all went on to emulate their family's attitudes toward reading.

Learning to write is also an individual process, shaped by both children's interests and personalities and the standards modeled and set by adults who see the written work. These standards are typically raised over time. One of my colleagues was delighted when Matthew, her 6½-year-old son, typed this song on a computer:

"WAN UU UISH   APAN A STR, MAKS NO DIFRTS HOO YOU R.   ANETHENG YOUR HART DZIRZ WILL CM TO YOU."

227

A year later, the mother's standards (and those of Matthew's teacher) were strongly ratcheted up.

Who Was George Lincoln? Saturation as Adequacy

The week before Presidents' Day, 6-year-old Alex was talking with his mother about the impending school holiday:

Alex:	"Who was George Washington?"
Mother:	"He was the first president of the United States."
Alex:	"Who is president now?"
Mother:	"George Bush."
Alex:	"Then who was George Lincoln?"

Alex reasonably deduced that to be president of the United States, your first name had to be George—a clever piece of logic but not one supported by the facts. Like school-aged children everywhere, Alex still had a ways to go in both empirical and linguistic saturation.

HOW much language do people need to learn? That depends on the linguistic company they keep. Speakers and listeners, readers and writers are deemed saturated if the surrounding community does not find fault with their linguistic performance and understanding. The level of expertise expected of, say, a literary colleague of Charles Dickens was light years away from the acceptable standard for the average factory worker when Dickens was writing.

But our linguistic abilities must eventually be judged against our own internal yardstick. Language users are not forever bound by the communities into which they were born. (Dickens himself grew up a factory hand.) Through access to print, electronic media, teachers, and accomplished speakers, children and adults alike set their own linguistic sights by selecting the language community they wish to have as peers.

Language growth, begun at birth, is complete only when we declare ourselves done.

■ Notes

Resources on language acquisition are rich and varied. The Notes are designed to assist readers who want more information on how children grow up with language. Four types of references are included: "General Reading," "Research Forums," "Organizations," and "Chapter Notes."

■ GENERAL READING ■

BOOKS

Books by Linguists

For the general reader, an especially well-written parent-oriented book on language acquisition is

> D. Crystal (1986). *Listen to Your Child*. New York: Penguin.

For the reader who wants more depth, an excellent collection of essays on individual language acquisition topics is

> J. B. Gleason, ed. (1989). *The Development of Language*. 2d ed. Columbus, Ohio: Charles Merrill Publishing Company.

A thorough language acquisition text is

> D. Ingram (1989). *First Language Acquisition: Method, Description, and Explanation*. Cambridge: Cambridge University Press.

"Better Baby" Books

Representatives of the "better baby" genre explicitly geared to language development include

> W. Fowler (1990). *Talking from Infancy: How to Nurture and Cultivate Early Language Development*. Cambridge, Mass.: Brookline Books.
>
> H. Weiner (1988). *Talk with Your Child*. New York: Viking Penguin.
>
> A. McCabe (1987). *Language Games to Play with Your Child*. New York: Fawcett Columbine.
>
> M. W. Hill (1989). *Home: Where Reading and Writing Begin*. Portsmouth, N.H.: Heinemann.

J. Trelease (1989). *The New Read-Aloud Handbook*. New York: Viking Penguin.
In addition, some general "better baby" books have sections on fostering language development. A good example is
J. Beck (1986). *How to Raise a Brighter Child: The Case for Early Learning*. New York: Pocket Books.

Disabilities

Three useful books reviewing a spectrum of language disabilities are
D. Bishop and K. Mogford, eds. (1988). *Language Development in Exceptional Circumstances*. Edinburgh: Churchill Livingstone.
M. Lahey (1988). *Language Disorders and Language Development*. New York: Macmillan.
W. Yule and M. Rutter, eds. (1987). *Language Development and Disorders*. London: MacKeith Press.
An excellent shorter summary of disorders in language development is
N. B. Ratner (1989). "Atypical Language Development." In J. B. Gleason, ed., *The Development of Language*, pp. 369–406, 2d ed. Columbus, Ohio: Charles Merrill Publishing Company.
For more detailed information on current research, see
J. Miller, ed. (1991). *Research on Child Language Disorders: A Decade of Progress*. Austin, Texas: Pro-Ed.

PERIODICALS

Language Acquisition

Three scholarly journals are devoted exclusively to language acquisition in children; the first is the oldest and best established:
Journal of Child Language
First Language
Language Acquisition.

Psychology

While many psychology journals include contributions on language acquisition, among those that regularly contain useful acquisition studies are
Child Development
Developmental Psychology.

Speech and Hearing

The American Speech-Language Hearing Association publishes several periodicals dealing with normal and deviant language acquisition, including
Journal of Speech and Hearing Research
Journal of Speech and Hearing Disorders.

■ RESEARCH FORUMS ■

STANFORD CHILD LANGUAGE RESEARCH FORUM

Since 1969, the Stanford University Department of Linguistics (formerly the Committee on Linguistics) has held an annual child language research conference each spring. The meetings, which are open to all for a nominal fee, provide a forum for empirical and theoretical work by language acquisition experts from around the world. The proceedings are published as the Stanford *Papers and Reports on Child Language Development*.

BOSTON UNIVERSITY CONFERENCE ON LANGUAGE DEVELOPMENT

Complementing Stanford's annual spring conference on the West Coast is Boston University's annual fall conference on language development. Begun in 1976, the meetings are also open.

■ ORGANIZATIONS ■

TWINS

The **National Organization of Mothers of Twins Clubs** assists families with twins in better understanding and fostering their children's growth and development. The group is headquartered at

    12404 Princess Jeanne, N.E.
    Albuquerque, N.M. 87112
    (505) 275-0955.

DYSLEXIA

The **Orton Dyslexia Society**, named after Dr. Samuel Orton (a pioneer in the field), is a focal point for research and therapy in dyslexia. The society holds workshops and lectures and disseminates information. The Orton Society is located at

    724 York Road
    Baltimore, Md. 21204
    (301) 296-0232.

SPEECH/LANGUAGE/HEARING PROBLEMS

The **American Speech-Language Hearing Association** is the professional organization of speech-language pathologists and audiologists. The association issues a number of research publications; certifies graduate programs, clinics, and hospital programs; and assesses community needs. ASHA is located at

    10801 Rockville Pike
    Rockville, Md. 20852
    (301) 897-5700.

DEAFNESS

The **Alexander Graham Bell Association for the Deaf** is an organization for teachers of the hearing impaired, speech-language specialists, and other professionals and laymen interested in problems of the hearing impaired. The association, which publishes both the *Volta Review* (a professional journal) and a newsletter for parents of hearing impaired children, is located at

> 3417 Volta Place, N.W.
> Washington, D.C. 20007
> (202) 337-5220

The **National Association of the Deaf** is dedicated to promoting legislation and programs to benefit the deaf. Composed of adult deaf people, parents of deaf children, and interested professionals and students in the field of deafness, the NAD publishes a quarterly journal, *Deaf American*, and fosters training in American Sign Language. (The Alexander Graham Bell Association, following the educational philosophy of its namesake, advocates that the deaf develop oral language skills.) The National Association of the Deaf is located at

> 814 Thayer Avenue
> Silver Spring, Md. 20910
> (301) 587-1788

■ CHAPTER NOTES ■

PREFACE

Noam Chomsky's early classics in transformational grammar are

> N. Chomsky (1957). *Syntactic Structures*. The Hague: Mouton.
> N. Chomsky (1965). *Aspects of the Theory of Syntax*. Cambridge, Mass.: MIT Press.

The Suzuki method and the principles behind it are described in

> S. Suzuki et al. (1973). *The Suzuki Concept: An Introduction to a Successful Method for Early Music Education*. Berkeley, Calif.: Diablo Press.

For an overview of the creation of "Sesame Street" and its educational agenda, see

> G. S. Lesser (1974). *Children and Television: Lessons from Sesame Street*. New York: Random House.

CHAPTER 1. CRACKING THE CODE
Tall Tales and Reality Checks: Beyond Boast and Concern

The comparative statistics on the number of working mothers of children under age 6 come from

> U.S. Department of Labor (August 1989). *Handbook of Labor Statistics*. Bureau of Labor Statistics. Bulletin 2349. Washington, D.C.: Government Printing Office.

Variations on a Theme: Sara, Ryan, and Alex

Linguists have increasingly acknowledged the importance of variation in children's early language learning. Two good overviews are

G. Wells (1986). "Variation in Child Language." In P. Fletcher and M. Garman, eds., *Language Acquisition*. 2d ed. Cambridge, England: Cambridge University Press.

B. A. Goldfield and C. E. Snow (1989). "Individual Differences in Language Acquisition." In J. B. Gleason, ed., *The Development of Language*. 2d ed., pp. 303–325. Columbus, Ohio: Charles Merrill Publishing Company.

Brazelton's "average," "quiet," and "active" babies are described in

T. B. Brazelton (1983). *Infants and Mothers*. Rev. ed. New York: Delta/Seymour Lawrence.

For a detailed analysis of the effects of socioeconomic status and parental education on rates of language acquisition, see

D. K. Vetter, W. H. Fay, and H. Winitz (1980). "Language." In P. J. La Benz and E. S. La Benz, eds., *Early Correlates of Speech, Language, and Hearing*. Littleton, Mass.: PSG Publishing.

The study (based on nearly 20,000 children) includes extensive correlations between language understanding and language production of 3- and 8-year-old children with such variables as sex, race, parental education, and parental socioeconomic status. A case study tracing the early language development of three young children growing up in an urban working-class neighborhood is

P. J. Miller (1982). *Amy, Wendy, and Beth: Learning Language in South Baltimore*. Austin: University of Texas Press.

Language Components

Sound

Gordon Wells's observations about parental judgments on preschoolers' language learning appear in

G. Wells (1985). *Language Development in the Pre-School Years*. Cambridge, England: Cambridge University Press.

Forms of Language

Sign and Script

The exact number of deaf and hard-of-hearing children in the United States is unknown. According to the 1985–1986 Annual Survey of Hearing Impaired Children and Youth (compiled by the Center for Assessment and Demographic Studies at Gallaudet University's Research Institute), nearly 50,000 young people (between birth and age 25) were reported by the individual states to be in special education programs because of hearing loss. The actual number of children and young adults with severe hearing problems is probably at least double or triple that number, given that according to the National Center for Health Statistics, in 1987 over 1 million children below age 18 had some degree of hearing impairment.

For a concise introduction to the acquisition of sign as a native language, see

> R. P. Meier (1991). "Language Acquisition by Deaf Children." *American Scientist* 79 (January–February):60–70.

> D. Perlmutter (1991). "The Language of the Deaf." *New York Review of Books* 38 (March 28):65–72.

More detailed accounts of signing issues can be found in

> E. Klima and U. Bellugi (1979). *The Signs of Language.* Cambridge, Mass.: Harvard University Press.

> R. B. Wilbur (1987). *American Sign Language: Linguistic and Applied Dimensions.* San Diego: College-Hill.

> C. Lucas, ed. (1990). *Sign Language Research: Theoretical Issues.* Washington, D.C.: Gallaudet University Press.

Case studies of several children of hearing parents who created their own complex gesture systems are reported in

> H. Feldman, S. Goldin-Meadow, and L. R. Gleitman (1978). "Beyond Herodotus: The Creation of Language by Linguistically Deprived Deaf Children." In A. Lock, ed., *Action, Gesture, and Symbol.* London: Academic Press.

CHAPTER 2. THE ROOTS OF LANGUAGE: FROM BIRTH TO FIRST WORDS

Imperatives and Duets

Discussions of who leads and who follows in early conversations between infants, toddlers, and parents can be found in

> L. Smolak and M. Weinraub (1983). "Maternal Speech: Strategy or Response?" *Journal of Child Language* 10:369–380.

> L. Murray and C. Trevarthen (1986). "The Infant's Role in Mother-Infant Communication." *Journal of Child Language* 13:15–29.

> L. Smolak (1987). "Child Characteristics and Maternal Speech." *Journal of Child Language* 14:481–492.

For analyses of difficulties that arise when parental conversational styles are not matched with the styles of their children, see

> K. Nelson (1973). *Structure and Strategy in Learning to Talk.* Monographs of the Society for Research in Child Development, 38 (1-2, Serial No. 149).

> L. Olsen-Fulero (1982). "Style and Stability in Mother Conversational Behavior: A Study of Individual Differences." *Journal of Child Language* 9:543–564.

> P. J. Yoder and A. P. Kaiser (1989). "Alternative Explanations for the Relationship between Maternal Verbal Interaction Style and Child Language Development." *Journal of Child Language* 16:141–160.

Baby Talk

The original survey of baby talk in a variety of cultures is

> C. A. Ferguson (1964). "Baby Talk in Six Languages." *American Anthropologist* 66 (6, pt. 2):103–114.

Choices and Consequences

For a fuller discussion of the potential effects of baby talk on language acquisition, see

N. S. Baron (1990). *Pigeon-Birds and Rhyming Words: The Role of Parents in Language Learning.* Englewood Cliffs, N.J.: Prentice-Hall Regents.

Biological Gateways

For more information on how neurological developments underlie early vocalization, see

E. Milner (1976). "CNS Maturation and Language Acquisition." In H. Whitaker and H. A. Whitaker, eds., *Studies in Neurolinguistics,* vol. 1. New York: Academic Press.

S. F. Witelson (1987). "Neurological Aspects of Language in Children." *Child Development* 58:653–688.

The brain is not literally divided, nor are cognitive functions entirely dichotomized, since the left and right hemispheres are joined by the corpus collosum, across which neural messages pass. For more information on general issues of brain laterality and language, see

M. P. Bryden (1982). *Laterality: Functional Asymmetry in the Intact Brain.* New York: Academic Press.

N. Geschwindt and A. Galaburda (1986). *Cerebral Lateralization: Biological Mechanisms, Associations, and Pathology.* Cambridge, Mass.: MIT Press.

G. A. Ojemann (1991). "Cortical Organization of Language." *Journal of Neuroscience* 11:2281–2287.

Additional discussions of the development of lateralization, along with possible sex differences between children, can be found in

D. L. Molfese and S. Segalowitz, eds. (1988). *Brain Lateralization in Children: Developmental Implications.* New York: Guilford.

One of the articles in Molfese and Segalowitz's volume (D. Molfese and J. Betz, "Electrophysiological Indices of the Early Development of Lateralization for Language and Cognition, and Their Implications for Predicting Later Development," pp. 171–190) reports on attempts to use infant lateralization tests to predict subsequent language development.

A more dated but landmark study is

E. Lenneberg (1967). *Biological Foundations of Language.* New York: John Wiley and Sons.

Excellent summaries of the developmental issues in vocal tract physiology appear in

R. D. Kent (1984). "Psychobiology of Speech Development: Coemergence of Language and a Movement System." *American Journal of Physiology* 246:R888–R894.

E. S. Crelin (1973). *Functional Anatomy of the Newborn.* New Haven: Yale University Press.

An excellent review of early attempts to teach chimpanzees to speak appears in

R. Brown (1958). *Words and Things.* New York: Free Press.

For recent information on some of the projects teaching sign language or other nonverbal communication systems to nonhuman primates, see

R. A. Gardner, B. T. Gardner, and T. E. Van Cantford, eds. (1989). *Teaching Sign Language to Chimpanzees*. Albany: State University of New York Press.

E. S. Savage-Rumbaugh (1986). *Ape Language: From Conditioned Response to Symbol*. New York: Columbia University Press.

A more journalistic account can be found in

E. Linden (1986). *Silent Partners: The Legacy of Ape Language Experiments*. New York: Times Books.

Curiously, the vocal tract configuration in chimpanzees is very similar to that of Neanderthal man and of human infants. For an analysis of the comparative anatomy and its ramifications for developing spoken language, see

P. Lieberman (1984). *The Biology and Evolution of Language*. Cambridge, Mass.: Harvard University Press.

The source of the data cited on children's pronunciation of *s* and *sh* is

R. S. McGowan and S. Nittrouer (1988). "Differences in Fricative Production between Children and Adults: Evidence from an Acoustic Analysis of /ʃ/ and /s/." *Journal of the Acoustical Society of America* 83:229–236.

The study on the effects of tracheostomies (inserting breathing tubes) in young children is described in

B. P. Hill and L. T. Singer (1990). "Speech and Language Development after Infant Tracheostomy." *Journal of Speech and Hearing Disorders* 55:15–20.

Also see

J. L. Locke and D. M. Pearson (1990). "Linguistic Significance of Babbling: Evidence from a Tracheostomized Infant." *Journal of Child Language* 17:1–16.

The case for linking vocal development with gross motor development more generally is made in

E. Thelen (1981). "Rhythmical Behavior in Infancy: An Ethological Perspective." *Developmental Psychology* 17:237–257.

J. M. Van der Stelt and F.J. Koopmans-van Beinum (1986). "The Onset of Babbling Related to Gross Motor Development." In B. Lindblom and R. Zetterström, eds., *Precursors of Early Speech*. New York: Stockton Press.

Some of the early arguments for a correlation between early gross motor development and high intellectual abilities can be found in

I. Abt, H. Adler, and B. Bartelme (1929). "The Relationship between the Onset of Speech and Intelligence." *Journal of the American Medical Association* 93:1351–1354.

L. M. Terman (1926). *Genetic Studies of Genius*. London: Harrap.

More recent studies of possible correlations include

C. T. Ramey, F. A. Campbell, and J. E. Nicholson (1973). "The Predictive Power of the Bayley Scales of Infant Development and the Stanford-Binet Intelligence Test in a Relatively Constant Environment." *Child Development* 44:790–795.

L. Siegel (1981). "Infant Tests as Predictors of Cognitive and Language Development in Two Years." *Child Development* 52:545–557.

P. A. Silva, R. McGee, and S. Williams (1982). "The Predictive Significance of Slow Walking and Slow Talking." *British Journal of Disorders of Communication* 17:133–139.

For a comprehensive study, along with data calling into question the entire relationship between motor development and intelligence, see

A. J. Capute et al. (1985). "Cognitive-Motor Interactions." *Clinical Pediatrics* 24:671–675.

Christy Brown, author of the autobiographical *Down All the Days* (and subject of the Academy Award–winning film *My Left Foot*), is a celebrated example of a person afflicted with cerebral palsy who developed sophisticated linguistic skills.

Studies of the relative maturation of the visual cortex and the auditory cortex can be found in

A. R. Lecours (1975). "Myelogenetic Correlates of the Development of Speech and Language." In E. H. Lenneberg, ed., *Foundations of Language Development*, vol. 1, pp. 121–135. New York: Academic Press.

C. B. Trevarthan (1986). "Neuroembryology and the Development of Perceptual Mechanisms." In F. Falkner and J. M. Turner, eds., *Human Growth*, 2d ed., pp. 301–383. New York: Plenum.

Data on relative emergence of first "words" in speech and sign appear in

J. D. Bonvillian, M. D. Orlansky, and L. L. Novack (1983). "Developmental Milestones: Sign Language Acquisition and Motor Development." *Child Development* 54:1435–1445.

R. P. Meier and E. L. Newport (1990). "Out of the Hands of Babes: On a Possible Sign Advantage in Language Acquisition." *Language* 66:1–23.

Genetic bases for such subtle traits as a propensity for being overweight or towards being shy are discussed in

A. J. Stunkard et al. (1990). "The Body-Mass Index of Twins Who Have Been Reared Apart." *New England Journal of Medicine* 322:1483–1487.

R. Plomin (1990). "The Role of Inheritance in Behavior." *Science* 248 (April):183–188.

J. Kagan, J. S. Reznick, and N. Snidman (1988). "Biological Bases of Childhood Shyness." *Science* 240 (April):167–171.

The longitudinal Louisville Twin Study is a major source of information on correlations between cognitive abilities in identical and fraternal twins. For more information, see

R. S. Wilson (1975). "Twins: Patterns of Cognitive Development as Measured on the WPPSI." *Developmental Psychology* 11:126–139.

R. S. Wilson (1983). "The Louisville Twin Study: Developmental Synchronies in Behavior." *Child Development* 54:298–316.

For an overview of the Colorado Adoption Project, see

R. Plomin and J. C. DeFries (1985). *Origins of Individual Differences in Infancy: The Colorado Adoption Project.* Orlando: Academic Press.

Another useful book by members of the adoption project is

R. Plomin, J. C. DeFries, and D. W. Fulker (1988). *Nature and Nurture in Infancy and Early Childhood.* New York: Cambridge University Press.

The two studies referred to dealing with language disorders and family background are

J. B. Tomblin (1989). "Familial Concentration of Developmental Language Impairment." *Journal of Speech and Hearing Disorders* 54:287–295.

B. A. Lewis (1990). "Familial Phonological Disorders: Four Pedigrees." *Journal of Speech and Hearing Disorders* 55:160–170.

Studies of twins indicating a genetic basis for phonological problems include

J. L. Locke and P. L. Mather (1988). "Genetic Factors in the Ontogeny of Spoken Language: Evidence from Monozygotic and Dizygotic Twins." Boston: Neurolinguistics Laboratory at Massachusetts General Hospital.

P. M. Howis (1981). "Concordance for Stuttering in Monozygotic and Dizygotic Twin Pairs." *Journal of Speech and Hearing Research* 24:317–321.

Getting to *Dada*

For more information on the work of Van de Carr and others attempting to communicate with the unborn, see

S. Ludington-Hoe with S. K. Golant (1985). *How to Have a Smarter Baby.* New York: Rawson Associates.

For a general review of the ability of fetuses to hear, see

T. Verny with J. Kelly (1981). *The Secret Life of the Unborn Child.* New York: Summit Books.

A more specific study of the development of hearing between 24 and 28 weeks can be found in

J. C. Birnholz and B. R. Benacerraf (1983). "The Development of Human Fetal Hearing." *Science* 222 (November 4):516–518.

Research on differential music preferences is reported in

M. Clements (1977). "Observations on Certain Aspects of Neonatal Behavior in Response to Auditory Stimuli." Paper presented at the 5th International Congress of Psychosomatic Obstetrics and Gynecology, Rome.

The studies done on the reception of sound within the womb are summarized in

D. Querleu, X. Renard, F. Versyp, L. Paris-Delrue, P. Verboort, and G. Crepin (1986). "Correspondence." *British Journal of Obstetrics and Gynaecology* 93:411–412.

A review of the studies on infant sucking preferences can be found in

G. Kolata (1984). "Studying Learning in the Womb." *Science* 225 (July 20):302–303.

The original studies of early infant sound discrimination were done by Peter Eimas and his colleagues; see

P. Eimas, E. Siqueland, P. Jusczyk, and J. Vigorito (1971). "Speech Perception in Infants." *Science* 171:303–318.

For more recent discussion, along with evidence that older infants lose their initial abilities to discriminate between certain sound contrasts, see

P. Eimas, J. L. Miller, and P. W. Jusczyk (1987). "On Infant Speech Perception and the Acquisition of Language." In S. Harnad, ed., *Categorical Perception*, pp. 161–195. Cambridge, England: Cambridge University Press.

J. F. Werker (1989). "Becoming a Native Listener." *American Scientist* (January–February) 77:54–59.

Early Sounds

Studies of infants' early cries include

C. Darwin (1977). "A Biographical Sketch of an Infant." *Mind* 2:285–294.

C. A. Aldrich, C. Sung, and C. Knop (1945). "The Crying of Newly Born Babies: I. The Community Phase." *Journal of Paediatrics* 26:313–326.

E. Müller, H. Hollien, and T. Murry (1974). "Perceptual Responses to Infant Crying: Identification of Cry Types." *Journal of Child Language* 1:89–95.

R. E. Stark, S. N. Rose, and M. McLagen (1975). "Features of Infant Sounds." *Journal of Child Language* 2:205–221.

The study questioning which variables of crying are most appropriate to analyze is reported in

P. A. Reich (1986). *Language Development.* Englewood Cliffs, N.J.: Prentice-Hall.

For more information on how intonational cues in babbling come to match those in the target adult language, see

B. de Boysson-Bardies, L. Sagart, and C. Durand (1984). "Discernible Differences in the Babbling of Infants According to Target Language." *Journal of Child Language* 11:1–15.

More general information on the evolution of babbling appears in

D. K. Oller (1980). "The Emergence of the Sounds of Speech in Infancy." In G. H. Yeni-Komshian, J. F. Kavanagh, and C. A. Ferguson, eds., *Child Phonology*, vol. 1: *Production.* New York: Academic Press.

R. E. Stark (1980). "Stages of Speech Development in the First Year of Life." In G. H. Yeni-Komshian, J. F. Kavanagh, and C. A. Ferguson, eds., *Child Phonology*, vol. 1: *Production.* New York: Academic Press.

Recent work by Laura Petitto and her colleagues at McGill University indicates that deaf children of deaf parents "babble" with their hands in much the same way that hearing children do with their voices during the months of transition to meaningful language. See

L. A. Petitto and P. F. Marentette (1991). "Babbling in the Manual Mode: Evidence for the Ontogeny of Language." *Science* 251 (March 22):1493–1496.

GROWING UP WITH LANGUAGE

First Words

The quotation from Helen Keller is taken from Joseph Lash's book on Helen and her teacher, Annie Sullivan:

> J. P. Lash (1980). *Helen and Teacher.* New York: Delacorte Press/Seymour Lawrence.

Susan Schaller describes this same kind of "aha" experience in her book on Ildefonso, an uneducated deaf man she began teaching to sign when he was 27 years old:

> S. Schaller (1991). *A Man Without Words.* New York: Summit Books.

Several studies, including one of children in Dutch-speaking environments and others of children on the verge of learning English, report on the similarity across children of sounds in late babbling and early speech:

> L. Elbers and J. Ton (1985). "Play Pen Monologues: The Interplay of Words and Babbles in the First Words Period." *Journal of Child Language* 12:551–565.

> M. M. Vihman, M. A. Macken, R. Miller, H. Simmons, and J. Miller (1985). "From Babbling to Speech: A Re-Assessment of the Continuity Issue." *Language* 61:397–445.

There is some evidence that these transition sounds seem to be the same, regardless of the target language:

> B. de Boysson-Bardies, L. Sagart, and N. Bacri (1981). "Phonetic Analysis of Late Babbling: A Case Study of a French Child." *Journal of Child Language* 8:511–524.

> D. K. Oller and R. E. Eilers (1982). "Similarity of Babbling in Spanish- and English-Learning Babies." *Journal of Child Language* 9:565–577.

Some new work suggests that the target language (e.g., English, Japanese, Swedish) may further differentiate among the specific consonants infants are most likely to babble:

> B. de Boysson-Bardies and M. M. Vihman (1991). "Adaptation to Language: Evidence from Babbling and First Words in Four Languages." *Language* 67:297–319.

Ideas and Alerts

Should I Be Concerned?

An excellent study of linguistic development in premature children is

> P. Holmqvist, C. Regefalk, and N. W. Svenningsen (1987). "Low Risk Vaginally Born Preterm Infants: A Four Year Psychological and Neurodevelopmental Follow-Up Study." *Journal of Perinatal Medicine* 15:61–72.

For a discussion of how adults respond to infants they believe are premature, see

> M. Stern and K. A. Hildebrandt (1984). "Prematurity Stereotype: Effects of Labeling on Adults' Perception of Infants." *Developmental Psychology* 20:360–362.

Until recently, researchers believed that the babbling of deaf babies was indistinguishable from that of hearing babies. We now know that while the earliest vocaliza-

240

tions and cooing of seriously hearing-impaired children sound "normal" (because these vocalizations are not shaped by auditory input), the babbling of deaf babies is quite distinct:

J. H. V. Gilbert (1982). "Babbling and the Deaf Child: A Commentary on Lenneberg et al. (1965) and Lenneberg (1967)." *Journal of Child Language* 9:511–515.

D. K. Oller and R. E. Eilers (1988). "The Role of Audition in Infant Babbling." *Child Development* 59:411–449.

For an overview of linguistic development in deaf children, see

S. Quigley and P. Paul (1987). "Deafness and Language Development." In S. Rosenberg, ed., *Advances in Applied Psycholinguistics*, vol. 1, pp. 180–219. Cambridge, England: Cambridge University Press.

The demographics of otitis media in young children are reported in

D. W. Teele, J. O. Klein, and B. A. Rosner (1980). "Epidemiology of Otitis Media in Children." *Annals of Otology, Rhinology, and Laryngology* 89 (Supplement 68):5–6.

Studies of the effects of early otitis media on toddlers' language are described in

D. W. Teele et al. (1984). "Otitis Media with Effusion during the First Three Years of Life and Development of Speech and Language." *Pediatrics* 74:282–287.

E. P. Paden, M. A. Novak, and A. L. Beiter (1987). "Predictors of Phonologic Inadequacy in Young Children Prone to Otitis Media." *Journal of Speech and Hearing Disorders* 52:232–242.

For information on possible continuing effects of early otitis media on later language development, see

J. E. Roberts et al. (1988). "Otitis Media in Early Childhood and Its Relationship to Later Phonological Development." *Journal of Speech and Hearing Disorders* 53:424–432.

An overview of language development in mentally retarded children can be found in

S. Rosenberg (1982). "The Language of the Mentally Retarded." In S. Rosenberg, ed., *Handbook of Applied Psycholinguistics: Major Thrusts of Theory and Research*. Hillsdale, N.J.: Lawrence Erlbaum Associates.

CHAPTER 3. LANGUAGE ON A SHOESTRING: FROM FIRST WORDS TO GRAMMAR

The Phantom Norm

The search for an average age at which children can be expected to reach particular language milestones may be misguided, since the range of "normal" for each milestone is broad indeed. To illustrate the problems inherent in identifying chronological norms, I have selected several language milestones and surveyed the work of a variety of specialists, nearly all of whom report different "average" ages at which children achieve these milestones.

GROWING UP WITH LANGUAGE

Three of the early language milestones most commonly charted are the first meaningful word uttered, the appearance of 50 words, and the first syntactic combination. In comparing ages identified for these milestones by diverse sources, we need to recognize that not all researchers gather information in the same way. Parental reports (often a source of pediatricians' timelines) can either overestimate or underestimate a child's abilities. (As we saw at the end of Chapter 2, parents often read meaning into children's babbles or fail to recognize intensional speech.) Formal tests of the sort commonly used by psychologists and linguists tend to underestimate children's language skills, since below the age of at least 3 or 4, children often prove fickle test subjects. The most reliable source of measurement is direct observation over a period of weeks or months (the method favored by many linguists), but the result is still usually an average, with all its attendant dangers.

For our sample of language milestones, we turn to four representative sources: a widely used early infant development test, a sampling of reports from pediatricians, longitudinal studies of children's early vocabulary, and a series of popular books on early child development.

The best-known test of overall early infant development is the Bayley Scales of Infant Development (frequently called "the Bayley"), created by Nancy Bayley at the University of California at Berkeley to measure mental, motor, and behavioral skills in children between the ages of 1 and 30 months. The Mental Scale in the test is designed to assess, among other skills, "vocalizations and the beginning of verbal communication."

After years of refining and norming the test, Bayley reports the following average age placements and age ranges for some of the basic language skills we are looking at:

- says two words: average age, 14 months; age range, 10–23 months
- combines two words together signifying two distinct concepts (e.g., "cup fall," not "bye-bye"): average age, 20.6 months; age range, 16–30 months.

Given the test battery's design, the Bayley does not report an average age for producing 50 words.

Pediatricians are the only group of professionals likely to evaluate young children's development on a regular basis. The potential role of pediatricians in language assessment is therefore critical, since they are often the first to spot problems with children's speech or hearing. Pediatricians rarely receive formal training in normal or abnormal language learning. Traditionally, they derive most of their expectations about developmental language norms from their own experience and general pediatric texts.

Recently several groups of physicians have created language inventories designed to give pediatricians a fast yet accurate read on their young patients' linguistic progress. The two tests most widely used are the CLAMS (Clinical Linguistic and Auditory Milestone Scale), developed by Arnold J. Capute and his colleagues, and the ELMS (Early Language Milestone Scale), created by James Coplan.

The CLAMS, which combines information from parents with actual observation, indicates the following average ages for early language development:

- uses *dada* and *mama*: 10 months
- uses first word (other than *dada* and *mama*): 11 months
- uses 50 words: 24 months
- combines two words together (noun plus noun): 24 months.

This separation of *mama* and *dada* from other vocabulary is common in many works on language acquisition. It reflects the popular assumption that since mothers and fathers are such constant presences in the lives of infants, names for parents will naturally be the first words from a child's lips. As we saw at the end of Chapter 2, this assumption is not always correct. Ryan's first word was *muh* (for "mine"), and Alex's first recognizable word, *duh*, referred to ducks, not daddy, despite Alex's father playing a very active role in his son's early nurturing.

The ELMS, which also relies on both parental information and direct observation, organizes its norms somewhat differently. Instead of reporting the average age at which a specific milestone is reached, the test indicates the age at which (on average) 25 percent, 50 percent, and 90 percent of children pass that linguistic milestone. Here are the reported averages:

- uses *mama* and *dada* correctly: 25 percent, 7–9 months; 50 percent, 9–11 months; 90 percent, 11–14 months
- uses first word other than *mama* or *dada*: 25 percent, 8–11 months; 50 percent, 11–14 months; 90 percent, 14–18 months
- uses 50 or more single words: 25 percent, 18–20 months; 50 percent, 20–23 months; 90 percent, 23–26 months
- combines two words together: 25 percent, 17–19 months; 50 percent, 19–21 months; 90 percent, 21–23 months.

The most accurate way of measuring children's linguistic milestones is to observe youngsters carefully over a period of time. Linguists and psychologists have a long-standing tradition of compiling observational diary studies on individual children's language development or, more recently, of assessing the progress of a larger group of children by observing them at regular time intervals (e.g., every few weeks).

For observational data on children's early linguistic milestones, we look not to a single source but a composite. Good information on the appearance of first words comes from the reigning classic in observational language studies, Werner Leopold's multivolume account of his daughter Hildegarde's language development. In surveying the existing literature at the time (Leopold was writing in the late 1930s), the author notes that most children studied were found to utter their first word at age 10 months, with a normal range of between 8 months and 17 months. On a social note, he adds that

if children in cultured families are segregated from children in lower social strata

. . . , the former group used words with meaning much earlier than the latter: 65% of . . . "cultured" children used such words between 0;8 [that is, at 8 months] and 0;11 (the remainder at 1;0–5), while 40% of . . . "uncultured" children did not reach the same stage until 1;0–2, and 31% were delayed until 1;3–1;5 (the remainder until 1;6–2;0).

Hildegard's first word, *pretty*, was recorded at 9 months of age. She did not articulate a name for her father (*papa*) until age 1;1 and a name for her mother (*mama*) until age 1;3.

For information on when children, on average, can express 50 words, we go to a vocabulary study by Katherine Nelson. Once a month for about a year, Nelson and her colleagues observed eighteen children in their homes. The researchers both gathered their own information and collected vocabulary lists from the children's mothers as well. On average, the children Nelson studied were able to express 50 words by slightly younger than 20 months, with the range extending from 14 months to 24 months.

Linguists have shown comparatively little interest in noting the first grammatical combination used by children. Their hesitancy reflects an awareness that very early combinations may be more significant in the mind of the hearer than of the child. Children on the verge of grammar are often prone to imitate the word combinations of others, and among children's own early utterances are items such as *thank you* and *all gone*, which are more accurately analyzed as single words than as productive grammar. Katherine Nelson notes that her subjects averaged ten different word combinations by just slightly under 20 months (with a range from 16 to 24 months), nearly precisely the age at which they averaged 50 words.

Among popular authors writing on young children's overall growth, two of the most enduring are early childhood educators Frank and Theresa Caplan (*The First Twelve Months of Life, The Second Twelve Months of Life, The Early Childhood Years: The 2 to 6 Year Old*). Each chapter in these chronologically organized books ends with a summary of milestones in such areas as motor development, language development, mental development, and social development, along with an indication of the age at which these milestones are, on average, achieved. Prominently featured at the bottom of each summary is a warning reminiscent of the surgeon-general's message on cigarette packs:

> Dear Parents:
>   Do not regard this chart as a rigid timetable.
>   Young children are unpredictable individuals. Some perform an activity earlier or later than this chart indicates.
>   Just use this information to anticipate and appreciate normal child development and behavior. No norms are absolute.

The Caplans' warning has as much effect on parents as packaging labels do on confirmed smokers. Parents understandably gloat when their children reach a milestone before other age-mates and worry inordinately when their offspring seem to lag behind the norm.

When, according to the Caplans, do children utter their first words? *The First Twelve Months of Life* indicates that *mama* and/or *dada* may appear as early as the seventh month, with one or two other words sometimes being added by the tenth month. By age 12 months, children may have between 2 and 8 words besides *mama* and *dada*.

Many popular works on language acquisition identify specific words that children may be expected to learn by particular ages. Caplan and Caplan, for example, tell us to expect *ta-ta* (for "thank you") at age 13 months. Yet since specific word use is highly determined by pragmatic need, parental modeling, and difficulty in pronunciation (like the *th-* in *thank you*), the practice of identifying a precise age when a given word will appear is risky. Neither Sara nor Alex attempted any version of "thank you" until after age 2, and Ryan didn't come up with *tanku* until age 18 months.

What about the 50-word landmark? In their final month's entry in *The Second Twelve Months of Life*, the Caplans indicate that upon entering their third year, average children have an "expressive vocabulary of 50 or more words." In their sequel to this book (*The Early Childhood Years: The 2 to 6 Year Old*), the authors' judgment is more tempered. Describing children between the ages of 25 and 30 months, the Caplans note: "Vocabulary of more than 3 but less than 50 words; some have vocabulary of 200 to 300 words."

When, according to the Caplans, do children create their first combinations? At age 16 months, when, the Caplans note, children's active vocabulary consists of "6 or 7 clear words." Compared with findings reported by our earlier experts, the Caplan age-stamping for this grammar milestone is fairly early, while their concomitant vocabulary estimate seems quite low.

NOTES TO THE ABOVE COMPARATIVE ANALYSIS OF LANGUAGE MILESTONES

The Bayley Scales of Infant Development are described in detail in

> N. Bayley (1969). *Manual of the Bayley Scales of Infant Development*. New York: The Psychological Corporation.

Descriptions of the CLAMS (Clinical Linguistic and Auditory Milestone Scale) can be found in

> A. J. Capute and P. J. Accardo (1978). "Linguistic and Auditory Milestones During the First Two Years of Life." *Clinical Pediatrics* 17:847–853.

> A. J. Capute et al. (1986). "Clinical Linguistic and Auditory Milestone Scale: Prediction of Cognition in Infancy." *Developmental Medicine and Child Neurology* 28:762–771.

For information on the ELMS (Early Language Milestone Scale), see

> J. Coplan (1983). *ELM Scale. The Early Language Milestone Scale*. Tulsa: Modern Education Corporation.

J. Coplan (1985). "Evaluation of the Child with Delayed Speech or Language." *Pediatric Annals* 14:203–208.

J. Coplan et al. (1982). "Validation of an Early Language Milestone Scale in a High-Risk Population." *Pediatrics* 70:667–683.

D. Walker et al. (1989). "Early Language Milestone Scale and Language Screening of Young Children." *Pediatrics* 83:284–288.

Alongside these language scales developed by pediatricians are an array of assessment tools created by linguists or speech-language therapists, often with the goal of screening toddlers and preschoolers for possible language delays or disorders. Among the more recent scales based on vocabulary development are the Early Language Inventory by Elizabeth Bates and her colleagues and the Language Development Survey of Leslie Rescorla:

E. Bates, I. Bretherton, and L. Snyder (1988). *From First Words to Grammar: Individual Differences and Dissociable Mechanisms.* New York: Cambridge University Press.

L. Rescorla (1989). "The Language Development Survey: A Screening Tool for Delayed Language in Toddlers." *Journal of Speech and Hearing Disorders* 54:587–599.

Werner Leopold's meticulous analysis of his daughter's language acquisition is chronicled in

W. Leopold (1939–1949). *Speech Development of a Bilingual Child: A Linguist's Record.* 4 vols. Evanston, Ill.: Northwestern University Press.

Katherine Nelson's analysis of the first 50 vocabulary words appears in

K. Nelson (1973). *Structure and Strategy in Learning to Talk.* Monographs of the Society for Research in Child Development, 38 (1-2, Serial No. 149).

The Caplans' three books surveying development from birth through age 6 are

F. Caplan (1973). *The First Twelve Months of Life.* New York: Bantam.

F. Caplan and T. Caplan (1977). *The Second Twelve Months of Life.* New York: Bantam.

F. Caplan and T. Caplan (1983). *The Early Childhood Years: The 2 to 6 Year Old.* New York: Bantam.

Sources of Variation

Gender and Self-Fulfilling Prophecies

The issue of sex differences in fetuses and infants is reviewed in

D. G. Freedman (1974). *Human Infancy: An Evolutionary Perspective.* Hillsdale, N.J.: Lawrence Erlbaum Associates.

Evidence that infant boys tend to vocalize less than infant girls is offered in

M. Lewis (1969). "Infants' Responses to Facial Stimuli During the First Year of Life." *Developmental Psychology* 1:75–86.

M. Lewis and R. O. Freedle (1973). "Mother-Infant Dyad: The Cradle of Meaning." In P. Pilner, L. Kramer, and T. Alloway, eds., *Communication and Affect: Language and Thought.* New York: Academic Press.

For the classical account of sex differences in early language acquisition, see

D. McCarthy (1954). "Language Development in Children." In L. Carmichael, ed. *Manual of Child Psychology.* 2d ed. New York: John Wiley and Sons.

In Katherine Nelson's study (*Structure and Strategy in Learning to Talk*), the girls on average knew 50 words by age 18 months, while the boys' average age for reaching this milestone was 22.1 months (p. 60).

One large-scale epidemiological study of developmental language problems in boys versus girls is

P. A. Silva (1980). "The Prevalence, Stability, and Significance of Developmental Language Delay in Preschool Children." *Developmental Medicine and Child Neurology* 22:768–777.

For information on color differentiation in neonates, see

J. G. Bremner (1988). *Infancy.* Oxford: Basil Blackwell.

Research on the ways adults address little boys versus little girls is described in

H. Moss (1967). "Sex, Age, and State as Determinants of Mother-Infant Interaction." *Merrill-Palmer Quarterly* 13:19–36.

S. Goldberg and M. Lewis (1969). "Play Behaviors in the Year Old Infant: Early Sex Differences." *Child Development* 40:21–31.

L. Cherry and M. Lewis (1976). "Mothers and Two-Year-Olds: A Story of Sex-Differentiated Aspects of Verbal Interaction." *Developmental Psychology* 12:278–282.

J. B. Gleason (1987). "Sex Differences in Parent-Child Interaction." In S. Stede and C. Tanz, eds., *Language, Gender, and Sex in Contemporary Perspective.* Cambridge, England: Cambridge University Press.

K. Roe, A. Drivas, A. Karagellis, and A. Roe (1985). "Sex Differences in Vocal Interaction with Mother and Stranger in Greek Infants: Some Cognitive Implications." *Developmental Psychology* 21:372–377.

A good popular account of some of these issues appeared in *Newsweek*:

L. Shapiro (1990). "Guns and Dolls." *Newsweek* (May 28): 56–65.

Data on correlations between the amount parents converse with children more generally and their rate of early acquisition appear in

G. Wells (1985). *Language Development in the Pre-School Years.* Cambridge, England: Cambridge University Press.

Acquisition in Context

The terms **referential** and **expressive** were introduced by Katherine Nelson in

K. Nelson (1973). *Structure and Strategy in Learning to Talk.* Monographs of the Society for Research in Child Development, 38 (1-2, Serial No. 149).

(In the intervening years, the meanings of the terms have evolved from Nelson's original usage.) Nelson points out that parental education level (especially when paired with the child's birth order) is a critical variable in determining whether an American child is likely to adopt a referential or an expressive style of early language acquisition:

> More children of highly educated parents (those above the median) fell in the R[eferential] group (seven out of nine), while more children from families below the median on education fell in the E[xpressive] group (six out of nine). . . . [A]ll of the firstborn children of the most highly educated families (those with college educations and better) were found in the R[eferential] group. (p. 61)

When children outside the United States are added to the mix, parental education and even children's birth order become less important factors. In analyzing the early acquisition strategies of Brazilian and Korean children born into middle-class households, several of my graduate students have found the expressive strategy to be more generally pervasive than in comparable family groups in the United States. Interestingly, in more traditional Korean households, the expressive strategy was especially dominant, while in Korean households that were more Westernized, the referential strategy was more prevalent.

A more recent study of comparative rates of vocabulary development in referential and expressive children appears in

> B. Goldfield and J. S. Reznick (1990). "Early Lexical Acquisition: Rate, Context, and the Vocabulary Spurt." *Journal of Child Language* 17:171–183.

For information on language acquisition among twins, see

> E. Day (1932). "The Development of Language in Twins: A Comparison of Twins and Single Children." *Child Development* 3:179–199.
>
> P. Mittler (1970). "Biological and Social Aspects of Language Development in Twins." *Developmental Medicine and Child Neurology* 12:741–757.
>
> H. Lytton, D. Conway, and R. Sauvé (1977). "The Impact of Twinship on Parent-Child Interaction." *Journal of Personality and Social Psychology* 35:97–107.
>
> D. Conway, H. Lytton, and F. Pysh (1980). "Twin-Singleton Language Differences." *Canadian Journal of Behavioral Science* 12:264–271.
>
> S. Savić (1980). *How Twins Learn to Talk*. New York: Academic Press.
>
> M. Tomasello, S. Mannle, and A.C. Kruger (1986). "Linguistic Evidence of 1- and 2-Year-Old Twins." *Developmental Psychology* 22:169–176.
>
> D. A. Hay, M. Prior, S. Collett, and M. Williams (1987). "Speech and Language Development in Preschool Twins." *Acta Geneticae Medicae et Gemellologiae* 36:213–223.

Studies of the effects of older siblings on the language development of younger children are reported in

> C. J. Wellen (1985). "Effects of Older Siblings on the Language Young Children Hear and Produce." *Journal of Speech and Hearing Disorders* 50:84–99.
>
> A. Woollett (1986). "The Influence of Older Siblings on the Language Environment of Young Children." *British Journal of Developmental Psychology* 4:235–245.

C. P. Jones and L. B. Adamson (1987). "Language Use in Mother-Child and Mother-Child-Sibling Interactions." *Child Development* 58:356–366.

A case study of the effects of staff ratios on preschoolers' language acquisition appears in

K. McCartney (1984). "Effects of Quality Day Care Environment on Children's Language Development." *Developmental Psychology* 20:244–260.

Findings on how middle-class parents compensate in their speech to children enrolled in full-time preschool programs are reported by

S. A. Ackerman-Ross and P. Khanna (1989). "The Relationship of High Quality Day Care to Middle-Class 3-Year-Olds' Language Performance." *Early Childhood Research Quarterly* 4:97–116.

An analysis of the ways in which day care providers alter their own speech depending upon the child's age and the number of children in the group is presented in

M. L. M. Pellegrino and A. Scopesi (1990). "Structure and Function in Baby Talk in a Day-Care Centre." *Journal of Child Language* 17:101–114.

Personality and Presupposition

For information on early personality differences in infants and toddlers, see

A. Thomas and Stella Chess (1977). *Temperament and Development.* New York: Bruner/Mazel.

A. H. Buss and R. Plomin (1984). *Temperament: Early Developing Personality Traits.* Hillsdale, N.J.: Lawrence Erlbaum Associates.

Do Bright Kids Talk Early?

Studies arguing for a relationship between early language development and intelligence include

I. A. Abt, H. M. Adler, and P. Bartelme (1929). "The Relationship between the Onset of Speech and Intelligence." *Journal of the American Medical Association* 93:1351.

A. J. Capute and P. J. Accardo (1978). "Linguistic and Auditory Milestones During the First Two Years of Life." *Clinical Pediatrics* 17:847–853.

A. J. Capute et al. (1986). "Clinical Linguistic and Auditory Milestone Scale: Prediction of Cognition in Infancy." *Developmental Medicine and Child Neurology* 28:762–771.

F. B. Palmer et al. (1983). "Infant Vocabulary Acquisition as a Predictor of Three-Year Cognitive Level." *Pediatric Research*, Supplement, 101A.

Research indicating that correlations of gross motor, language, and IQ scores seem to hold for groups but not for individual scores is reported in

B. K. Shapiro et al. (1989). "Giftedness: Can It Be Predicted in Infancy?" *Clinical Pediatrics* 28:205–209.

Sex differences in the power of the Bayley to predict adult intelligence are reported in

J. Cameron, N. Livson, and N. Bayley (1967). "Infant Vocalizations and Their Relationship to Mature Intelligence." *Science* 157:331–333.

GROWING UP WITH LANGUAGE

Use of early IQ scores to predict later language development at age 2 is discussed in

> L. S. Siegel (1981). "Infant Tests as Predictor of Cognitive and Language Development at Two Years." *Child Development* 52:545–557.

In recent years, the entire question of IQ testing has come under serious attack, and earlier models assuming a single "general intelligence" have been challenged. Two of the most interesting challenges have come from psychologists Howard Gardner and Robert Sternberg, who both argue that human intelligence is actually a multidimensional concept. For more on these theories, see

> H. Gardner (1985). *Frames of Mind: The Theory of Multiple Intelligences.* New York: Basic Books.

> R.J. Sternberg (1985). *Beyond IQ: A Triarchic Theory of Human Intelligence.* New York: Cambridge University Press.

The Einstein reference is taken from

> B. Hoffmann (1972). *Albert Einstein: Creator and Rebel.* New York: Viking.

A recent book reviewing the literature on early indicators of intelligence and/or precosity (including language) is

> M. Storfer (1990). *Intelligence and Giftedness: The Contributions of Heredity and Early Environment.* San Francisco: Jossey-Bass.

Storfer argues that parents can substantially increase their children's intellectual abilities through appropriate patterns of interaction and training. In his discussion of language, Storfer draws heavily upon the work of William Fowler (e.g., *Talking from Infancy*, 1990; see the section on "better baby" books at the beginning of the **Notes**).

Juice Crayons: Language on a Shoestring

Strategies with Sounds: Substitutions, Silence, and End Runs

For discussions of the role of homonyms in children's early language, see

> T. M. S. Priestly (1980). "Homonymy in Child Phonology." *Journal of Child Language* 7:413–427.

> L. B. Leonard et al. (1989). "Unusual Phonological Behavior and the Avoidance of Homonymy in Children." *Journal of Speech and Hearing Research* 32:583–590.

Worlds of Meaning: Topics and Boundaries

Children who do not know the correct name for an object often create ingenious substitutes. For a discussion of how these naming strategies evolve as children become more linguistically sophisticated, see

> N. S. Baron (1977). "The Acquisition of Indirect Reference: Functional Motivations for Continued Language Learning in Children." *Lingua* 42:349–364.

Ideas and Alerts

How Can I Help?

For studies of differences in the ways fathers versus mothers tend to speak to toddlers and preschoolers, see

R. M. Golinkoff and G. J. Ames (1979). "A Comparison of Fathers' and Mothers' Speech with Their Young Children." *Child Development* 50:28–32.

E. G. Hladik and H. T. Edwards (1984). "A Comparative Analysis of Mother-Father Speech in the Naturalistic Home Environment." *Journal of Psycholinguistic Research* 13:321–332.

E. Masur and J. B. Gleason (1980). "Parent-Child Interaction and the Acquisition of Lexical Information During Play." *Developmental Psychology* 16:404–409.

N. B. Ratner (1988). "Patterns of Parental Vocabulary Selections in Speech to Very Young Children." *Journal of Child Language* 15:481–492.

Should I Be Concerned?

For an overview of language disorders (including specific language impairment), see the references in the "**Disabilities**" section at the beginning of the **Notes**.

An analysis of comprehension, production, and gestures in late talkers appears in

D. Thal and E. Bates (1988). "Language and Gesture in Late Talkers," *Journal of Speech and Hearing Research* 31:115–123.

Prognoses for outgrowing language impairment are discussed in

L. Rescorla (1989). "The Language Development Survey: A Screening Test for Delayed Language in Toddlers." *Journal of Speech and Hearing Disorders* 54:587–599.

D. M. Aram and J. E. Nation (1980). "Preschool Language Disorders and Subsequent Language and Academic Difficulties." *Journal of Communicative Disorders* 13:159–170.

D. V. M. Bishop and A. Edmundson (1987). "Language-Impaired 4-Year-Olds: Distinguishing Transient from Persistent Impairment." *Journal of Speech and Hearing Disorders* 52:156–173.

For a description of vocabulary problems (comprehension and production) in children with specific language impairment, see

L. B. Leonard and R. G. Schwartz (1985). "Early Linguistic Development of Children with Specific Language Impairment." In K. E. Nelson, ed., *Children's Language*, vol. 5, pp. 291–318. Hillsdale, N.J.: Lawrence Erlbaum Associates.

CHAPTER 4. WHY YOU DON'T LIKE MY CHOOSES? GRAMMATICAL ORIENTEERING

Language Orienteering

Grammatical Orienteering: Rules or Playdough?

The original research arguing that preschool children have rules underlying their grammatical neologisms is reported in

J. Berko (1958). "The Child's Learning of English Morphology." *Word* 14:150–177.

Why Because? Adult Corrections

The example of "Nobody don't like me" is discussed, among other places, in
> D. McNeil (1966). "Developmental Psycholinguistics." In F. Smith and G. A. Miller, eds., *The Genesis of Language*. Cambridge, Mass.: MIT Press.

Ideas and Alerts

Should I Be Concerned?

For comparative findings on language delay in 2- and 3-year-olds (based on vocabulary size), see
> L. Rescorla (1989). "The Language Development Survey: A Screening Tool for Delayed Language in Toddlers." *Journal of Speech and Hearing Disorders* 54:587–599.

The case study of a child whose sentence length did not increase from age 15 through 22 months (and then tripled between 22 and 25 months) is reported in
> L. Feagans and J. M. Miyamoto (1985/86). "Non-Word Speech in Discourse: A Strategy for Language Development." *First Language* 6:187–201.

Roger Brown's landmark longitudinal study of three children's early language development is presented in
> R. Brown (1970). *A First Language*. Cambridge, Mass.: Harvard University Press.

CHAPTER 5. BAGS ON THE BANKS: ORIENTEERING IN MEANING, SOUND, AND CONVERSATION

The Aunt from Ami: Mastering the Sounds of Language

Sara and Ryan's attempts to puzzle out the relationship between modifiers and nouns is reminiscent of a phenomenon hundreds of years ago in the history of English, when our linguistic forebears struggled to make sense of the connection between indefinite articles (*a, an*) and following nouns. Modern words like *apron* and *newt* came about through a misunderstanding similar to Sara and Ryan's. In Old English, the words were actually *napron* and *ewt*. But because the relationships between the preceding article ("a napron" and "an ewt") got confused somewhere along the way, the new phrases turned out to be "an apron" and "a newt."

No Thank You! Becoming a Conversational Partner

Jean Piaget's views on egocentrism in children are presented in
> J. Piaget (1959). *The Language and Thought of the Child*. New York: Humanities Press.

The Princeton study of children's communication across a visual barrier was reported in
> S. Glucksberg, R. M. Krauss, and R. Weisberg (1966). "Referential Communication in Nursery School Children." *Journal of Experimental Child Psychology* 3:333–342.

Ideas and Alerts

Should I Be Concerned?

Two overviews of the stuttering research (including stuttering in children) are

> G. Andrews et al. (1983). "Stuttering: A Review of Research Findings and Theories Circa 1982." *Journal of Speech and Hearing Disorders* 48:226–246.
>
> W. Perkins (1990). "What Is Stuttering?" *Journal of Speech and Hearing Disorders* 55:370–382.

A recent review of the relationship between children's stuttering and other language disorders can be found in

> M. Nippold (1990). "Concomitant Speech and Language Disorders in Stuttering Children: A Critique of the Literature." *Journal of Speech and Hearing Disorders* 55:51–60.

Two other useful references on stuttering are

> D. Prins and R. S. Ingham, eds. (1983). *Treatment of Stuttering in Early Childhood*. San Diego: College-Hill Press.
>
> O. Bloodstein (1987). *A Handbook on Stuttering*. Chicago: National Easter Seal Society.

The book growing out of the work on stuttering prevention at the Temple University Stuttering Prevention Clinic is

> C. W. Starkweather, S. R. Gottwald, and M. M. Halfond (1990). *Stuttering Prevention: A Clinical Method*. Englewood Cliffs, N.J.: Prentice-Hall.

CHAPTER 6. ZUCKERMAN'S FAMOUS AIRPLANE: LANGUAGE AWARENESS

Why Are There No Lady Holes? Language about Language

Reflecting on Language: "What Did I Call 'Popcorn'?"

The classic study of children's play and practice monologues is

> R. Weir (1962). *Language in the Crib*. The Hague: Mouton.

More recent analyses appear in

> K. Nelson, ed. (1989). *Narratives from the Crib*. Cambridge, Mass.: Harvard University Press.

Word decomposition is a favorite theme in children's books. A delightful recent example is

> B. Most (1991). *Pets in Trumpets and Other Word-Play Riddles*. New York: Harcourt Brace Jovanovich.

Look at the Chien: Functioning in Two Languages

Growing Up Bilingual: Do Children Benefit?

Three comprehensive overviews of bilingualism are

> K. Hakuta (1986). *The Mirror of Language*. New York: Basic Books.
>
> S. Romaine (1989). *Bilingualism*. Oxford: Basil Blackwell.

F. Grosjean (1982). *Life with Two Languages*. Cambridge, Mass.: Harvard University Press.

For a collection of essays on more theoretical issues, see

E. Bialystok, ed. (1991). *Language Processing in Bilingual Children*. Cambridge, England: Cambridge University Press.

Hayakawa's argument for making English the official language of the United States has appeared in many places, including

S. I. Hayakawa (1987). "Make English Official: One Common Language Makes Our Nation Work." *Executive Educator* 9:36.

The March 1988 issue of *English Journal* presents a balanced summary of the issues.

The 1890 tract counseling against raising children bilingual was

S. S. Laurie (1890). *Lectures on Language and Linguistic Method in the School*. Cambridge, England: Cambridge University Press.

Saer's research was reported in

D. J. Saer (1923). "The Effect of Bilingualism on Intelligence." *British Journal of Psychology* 14:25–38.

For a review of studies in the first half of the century claiming that bilingualism has deleterious effects on children's developing intelligence, see

R. Diaz (1983). "Thought and Two Languages: The Impact of Bilingualism on Cognitive Development." In E. Norbeck, D. Price-Williams, and W. McCord, eds., *Review of Research in Education*, vol. 10, pp. 23–54. Washington, D.C.: American Educational Research Association.

The report from the Arizona educator on the outcomes of administering IQ tests in both English and Spanish comes from

A. J. Mitchell (1937). "The Effect of Bilingualism in the Measurement of Intelligence." *Elementary School Journal* 38:29–37.

The story of Olivia Martinez and Elena appeared in the *New York Times* on September 16, 1979.

The landmark Canadian study reporting higher cognitive skills in bilinguals than in monolinguals is

E. Peel and W. E. Lambert (1962). "The Relation of Bilingualism to Intelligence." *Psychological Monographs* 76 (546):1–23.

An overview of more recent research and current thinking on the issues can be found in

K. Hakuta and R. Diaz (1985). "The Relationship between Bilingualism and Cognitive Ability: A Critical Discussion and Some New Longitudinal Data." In K. E. Nelson, ed., *Children's Language*, vol. 5. Hillsdale, N.J.: Lawrence Erlbaum Associates.

Some linguists have argued that children growing up bilingual initially confuse the two language systems, while other scholars suggest that these children actually begin by learning a single language, which eventually bifurcates. For a discussion of both positions, see

254

M. Vihman (1985). "Language Differentiation by the Bilingual Infant," *Journal of Child Language* 12:297–324.

F. Genesee (1989). "Early Bilingual Development: One Language or Two?" *Journal of Child Language* 15:161–179.

An excellent guide on how to raise a child bilingual is

E. Harding and P. Riley (1986). *The Bilingual Family: A Handbook for Parents.* New York: Cambridge University Press.

The explicit conversational strategy of "one person, one language" (e.g., the father only speaks Spanish and the mother addresses the child exclusively in English) was first described in 1913:

J. Ronjat (1913). *Le Développement du langage observé chez un enfant bilingue.* Paris: Champion.

Throughout the twentieth century, many observers of bilingual development have reported the technique to be highly effective.

Growing Up with Two Dialects: "Watch Out for the Be-ad Guys"

For an overview of dialects—what they are, where they come from, and how speakers use them—see

W. N. Francis (1983). *Dialectology.* New York: Longman.

The status of black English has been a subject of intense debate over the past twenty years. While black English was traditionally assumed to be a degraded form of standard English, contemporary research traces its origins to Africa. For more on the subject, see

J. F. Dillard (1973). *Black English: Its History and Usage in the United States.* New York: Vintage Books.

H. U. Taylor (1989). *Standard English, Black English, and Bidialectalism.* New York: P. Lang.

Ideas and Alerts

How Can I Help?

Studies of positive effects of rhyming on early reading readiness skills and subsequent reading abilities are discussed in

M. Maclean, P. Bryant, and L. Bradley (1987). "Rhymes, Nursery Rhymes, and Reading in Early Childhood." *Merrill-Palmer Quarterly* 33:255–281.

P. E. Bryant et al. (1989). "Nursery Rhymes, Phonological Skills, and Reading." *Journal of Child Language* 16:407–428.

CHAPTER 7. BEYOND ELEMENO: EMERGING LITERACY

Finding *S*'s in Spaghetti: Recognizing Letters and Numbers

The hunt for Waldo was first launched in

M. Handford (1987). *Where's Waldo?* Boston: Little, Brown.

The account of the deaf adult who learned to add before he could use words is in

S. Schaller (1991). *A Man Without Words*. New York: Summit Books. (See especially Chapter 2.)

Television and Modern Literacy: The "Sesame Street" Generation

An excellent history of the development of "Sesame Street" is

G. S. Lesser (1974). *Children and Television: Lessons from Sesame Street*. New York: Random House.

For observations on the effects on early reading of watching "Sesame Street," see

R. T. Salzer (1984). "Early Reading and Giftedness: Some Observations and Questions." *Gifted Child Quarterly* 28:95–96.

Decoding the Written Word

Flesch's book is

R. Flesch (1955). *Why Johnny Can't Read and What You Can Do About It*. New York: Harper & Row.

Over the years, Jeanne Chall of the Harvard School of Education has chronicled the controversy between the "whole word" and the "phonics" approach to early reading:

J. Chall (1967). *Learning to Read: The Great Debate*. New York: McGraw-Hill;

along with the updated 1983 edition of the book. A more recent synoptic review of the literature is

M. J. Adams (1990). *Beginning to Read*. Cambridge, Mass.: MIT Press.

The Doman Legacy: Does Age Matter?

Glenn Doman's original book arguing that preschoolers can be taught to read is

G. Doman (1964). *How to Teach Your Baby to Read: The Gentle Revolution*. New York: Random House.

First Strokes

Type First, Read Later: Pragmatic Routes to Literacy

For an excellent analysis of basal readers, see

K. Goodman et al. (1988). *Report Card on Basal Readers*. New York: R. C. Owen.

Bettelheim's critique of basal readers appears in

B. Bettelheim and K. Zelan (1982). *On Learning to Read: The Child's Fascination with Meaning*. New York: Vintage Books.

One of the best-known arguments for using writing as a stepping-stone to reading is

C. Chomsky (1971). "Write First, Read Later." *Childhood Education* 41:296–299.

For an introduction to IBM's "Writing to Read," written by the founder of the program, see

J. H. Martin and A. Friedberg (1986). *Writing to Read*. New York: Warner Books.

A review of "Writing to Read," conducted by the Educational Testing Service in the early 1980s, suggests that children in the program showed higher levels of reading and writing skills than a control sample. However, the two groups may not have been evenly matched, since children in the Writing to Read group spent more time overall in reading instruction; see

> R. T. Murphy and L. R. Appel (1984). *Evaluation of the Writing to Read Instructional System, 1982–1984* (ETS Report). Princeton, N.J.: Educational Testing Service.

For discussion of the use of computers in teaching reading, see

> D. Reinking, ed. (1987). *Reading and Computers.* New York: Teachers College Press.

> D. S. Strickland, J. T. Feeley, and S. B. Wepner (1987). *Using Computers in the Teaching of Reading.* New York: Teachers College Press.

A review of current literature on invented spelling appears in

> M. J. Adams (1990). *Beginning to Read.* Cambridge, Mass.: MIT Press.

The Sunday School Syndrome

For George Steiner's analysis of the changing function of reading in contemporary times, see

> G. Steiner (1972). "After the Book?" *Visible Language* 6:197–210.

The article on using television as a "talking book" is

> D. Lemish and M. Rice (1986). "Television as a Talking Picture Book: A Prop for Language Acquisition." *Journal of Child Language* 13:251–274.

The data correlating reading performance with television viewing are reported in

> National Assessment of Educational Progress (1981). *Procedural Handbook: 1979–80. Reading and Literature Assessment.* Denver: Education Commission of the States.

> R. C. Anderson, P. T. Wilson, and L. G. Fielding (1988). "Growth in Reading and How Children Spend Their Time Outside of School." *Reading Research Quarterly* 23:285–303.

For other in-depth analyses of the relationship between reading skills and television viewing, see

> J. W. J. Beentjes and T. H. A. Van der Voort (1988). "Television's Impact on Children's Reading Skills: A Review of Research." *Reading Research Quarterly* 23:389–413.

> S. B. Neuman (1988). "The Displacement Effect: Assessing the Relation between Television Viewing and Reading Performance." *Reading Research Quarterly* 23:414–440.

Ideas and Alerts

How Can I Help?

A group of researchers at the State University of New York at Stony Brook is responsible for the research showing that parents' reading styles can affect 2-year-olds' spoken language development. The findings are reported in

G. J. Whitehurst et al. (1988). "Accelerating Language Development through Picture Books." *Developmental Psychology* 24:552–559.

Should I Be Concerned?

For an overview of dyslexia, see
F. R. Vellutino (1987). "Dyslexia." *Scientific American* (March) 256:34–41.
An analysis of dyslexia focusing on cognitive issues is
M. Snowling (1987). *Dyslexia: A Cognitive Developmental Perspective.* Oxford: Basil Blackwell.
For a detailed presentation of some of the neurological research, see
N. Geschwind and A. M. Galaburda (1986). *Cerebral Lateralization: Biological Mechanisms, Associations, and Pathology.* Cambridge, Mass.: MIT Press.
A representative study of the use of PET scans to track dyslexia is
K. Gross-Glenn et al. (1990). "PET Scan Reading Studies: Familial Dyslexics." In G. Th. Pavlidis, ed., *Perspectives on Dyslexia*, vol. 1, pp. 110–118. New York: John Wiley and Sons.
Research indicating that both girls and boys are equally likely to suffer from dyslexia is reported in
S. E. Shaywitz et al. (1990). "Prevalence of Reading Disability in Boys and Girls." *Journal of the American Medical Association* 264 (August 22–29):998–1002.
A discussion of diagnostic tests for dyslexia using eye movements can be found in
G. Th. Pavlidis (1990). "Detecting Dyslexia through Ophthalmo-Kinesis: A Promise of Early Diagnosis." In G. Th. Pavlidis, ed., *Perspectives on Dyslexia*, vol. 1, pp. 199–220. New York: John Wiley and Sons.
For a review of studies showing correlations between developmental language disorders and difficulty in learning to read, see
V. A. Mann and S. Brady (1988). "Reading Disability: The Role of Language Deficiencies." *Journal of Consulting and Clinical Psychology* 56:811–816.
Discussion of the specific relationship between problems in phonological development and in learning to read can be found in
M. de Montford Supple (1986). "Reading and Articulation." *British Journal of Audiology* 20:209–214.
An analysis of the relationship between metalinguistic awareness of sounds and reading development is in the review by Mann and Brady noted above. Data correlating difficulties in reading with slow attainment of vocabulary and grammar milestones are reported in
B. K. Shapiro et al. (1990). "Precursors of Reading Delay: Neurodevelopmental Milestones." *Pediatrics* 85:416–420.

EPILOGUE

The story about Abraham Lincoln, cited in
P. M. Zalle, ed. (1982). *Abe Lincoln Laughing.* Berkeley: University of California Press, pp. 141–142

is taken from William E. Curtis's *Life of Lincoln* (1902, 5th ed. 1905), pp. 367–368.

Approaching Saturation

Some dialects of American English have only one pronunciation of *the*—*thee*—and use *a* (rhymes with *hey*) instead of *a* (rhymes with *duh*) before a word beginning with a consonant (e.g., *ey man*). (This is the same pronunciation of *a* as the name of the letter "A.")

The estimate on how many words children learn appears in

>G. A. Miller and P. M. Gildea (1987). "How Children Learn Words." *Scientific American* 257(September):94–99.

More analysis of vocabulary acquisition in the school years can be found in

>M. G. McKeown and M. E. Curtis, eds. (1987). *The Nature of Vocabulary Acquisition*. Hillsdale, N.J.: Lawrence Erlbaum Associates.

Examples of children's conversational candor are collected in

>A. Linkletter (1957). *Kids Say the Darndest Things!* New York: Bonanza.

For a discussion of how children become skilled readers (along with an excellent chapter on spoken language development after age 5), see

>J. Oakhill and A. Garnham (1988). *Becoming a Skilled Reader*. Oxford: Basil Blackwell.

■ Index

Index

Index

Index

Index

401.93
B

Baron, Naomi S.

Growing up with
language.

$ 21.11

DATE			